PIONEERING MINDS

WORLDWIDE

Contents

On the principles of cultural entrepreneurship

This book is a collection of the latest research on cultural entrepreneurship, done by pioneers within their own field of expertise and an international oriented focus. There are many research publications and academic oriented policy reports, but a blind reviewed publication on actual research is still lacking. With this book, that holds contributions form more than 30 authors in 17 countries, this void has been resolved.

The absence of research publications might be explained in two ways. First cultural entrepreneurship is relatively a new knowledge domain, that asks for a period of exploring best practices, formulating case studies and - more praxis oriented – developing academic educational programs (Hagoort G., 2007). In such a climate researching cultural entrepreneurial issues on a more fundamental way has not received the highest priority of researchers, policymakers or educators. Moreover, the dynamics of the increasing cultural and creative industries (CCIs) seem to ask for pragmatic policy oriented studies, more than a research on the fundaments, concepts and principles of a new phenomenon. The second explanation has to deal with the academic interdisciplinary character of cultural entrepreneurship, with a strong focus on interactivity with professionals from the cultural and creative fields. Professionals do develop reflective competences, but are not initially interested in long term studies with its focus more on *Why and What* than on *How*.

With this book on the tables of research and educational institutes – the main target group of this publication – we can leave this phase behind us. However, this does not mean that the supportive infrastructure to finance more scientific research in the area of cultural entrepreneurship is thriving. Most of the writers of this book have an academic research position, but there are also researchers who own a private agency, are self-employed, or have a combination of academic and professional tasks as a financial basis to fund (partly) their research activities.

Because of the colorful background of this research community there is an inspiring story to tell behind each article of this book. For the academic committee that initiated this publication these stories were an important motive to select a broad variety of subjects, methods and approaches covering the topic of cultural entrepreneurship. In doing so, it was possible to publish research results from very different perspectives, paying honor to the multidimensional nature of the cultural and creative industries (Hagoort & Kooyman, Creative Industries, Colourful fabric in multiple dimensions, Sept 2010).

Cultural Entrepreneurship and the cultural and creative industries or sectors have many definitions and meanings. For the purpose of this first book, we were curious about the diversity more than trying to impose one single definition. Some authors refer to the interdisciplinary frameworks of the Utrecht Research Group, others prefer to take a more mono-disciplinary (economic, cultural policy) approach. More and more it became clear that social issues and innovations can no longer be ignored (Thomassen, 2009). The committee expects that with the help of this book the next step in our research community can be a contribution to a more common ground approach, with shared frames and collaborative research practices.

The structure of the book is outlined in five sections. Each section collects the main aspects of principles of cultural entrepreneurship within a particular area. A section starts with a number of extensive contributions, followed by short articles which a more specific approach or case study. The selection presented in this book embodies contributions from a global community of research and researchers. We feel very fortunate to have worked with this collection of authors and without doubt this publication will contribute to the debated research field of cultural and creative entrepreneurship. We envisage that this book will support further refinement and unpacking of the principles of CCIs, and help to articulate models of thinking and framing of the foundations and approaches. In sum the contributions are pivotal to innovation in CCIs. Therefore we have grouped the contributions per area of development; 1) key elements, 2) concepts and perspectives, 3) urban development and CCIs, 4) issues of innovation and 5) educational approaches to CCIs.

In section One *Key elements*, the articles are strongly oriented on the components of cultural entrepreneurship. Critical approaches show that it is important to have research dialogues on the assumptions and creative practices of this form of entrepreneurship. To understand the cultural and creative firms in their specific phase of their existence, but also to understand the relationship between technology, leadership, finance related to Life Cycle Modeling. Critical approaches have also been formulated on the position of the Western, postcolonial approach of the creative economy, the analysis of entrepreneurial artists in non-regulated areas, and the way researchers can approach strategic and organizational cultural processes within cultural and creative organizations.

Section Two is sturdily oriented on the internal and external environment of the creative industries, and its relevancy for the functioning of organizations. *Creativity* is a keyword in this environment as an individual value, yet at the same time as a collective potential if artistic and managerial creativity can be combined. Clusters as a supportive concept, personal ties within networks and the analysis of symbolic values behind the cultural and creative industries are in this section the dominant aspects. Within a targeted, supportive approach, one can consider general (regional) policies, and policies geared towards specific sectors. Sustainability, as discussed in this section, can be seen as a challenge for new research on cultural entrepreneurs and creatives, to contribute for a sustainable planet in our own environment and worldwide.

Section Three is discussing more specific issues between the relation of the *entrepreneurial dimension* of the cultural and creative industries and *urban development*. Cities are fast growing and more than half of the mankind does live in *urban environments*. Cultural and creative entrepreneurs are playing an important role in (re)designing these cities. In this section different models, such as the Creative Zone Innovator and Cultural Routes, highlight the relevance of the entrepreneurial approach in the (re)vitalization of urban quarters and regions. Examples from Istanbul and Berlin prove that '*culturepreneurs*' promote highly professionalized events, in order to strengthen cultural and creative sectors within the urban context.

Section Four focuses on *innovation* and in particular how innovation can enable *social improvement* in areas through cultural and creative entrepreneurial processes and models. Quite often innovation as such is discussed as an important area of the Research and Development of the creative industries. However the contributions in this section elaborate and unpack on how cultural and creative entrepreneurship can actually be seen as leading innovation in areas that have greatly benefitted from novel approaches. The case studies provide a wealth of paradigms on the application of the theoretical models described throughout the book. Central to this section is the notion of '*sense-making*'; understanding that innovation should be inclusive to society and its citizens. This understanding can only be achieved through addressing specific creative and cultural entrepreneurial skills such as problem-solving, creativity and design thinking and thereby leading *change as an agent for social transformations through design*.

Section Five is oriented on the development of the potential of cultural entrepreneurship. If we take the supposed role of the cultural and creative sectors to a sustainable development of countries and regions seriously, investigation in *education and training* is strongly needed, in combination with the creation of entrepreneurial research and educational institutes. In this section a collection of academic studies indicates that training and education is related to the transition process in the direction of a more creative knowledge and service economy. And as this section illustrates, the importance of research in the training and education area is a condition for robust results.

In their second Creative Economy Report 2010, produced by UNCTAD (Dos Santos Duisenberg, 2010) the United Nations express their responsibility for a human and sustainable development of cities, regions and nations, inspired and fed by the cultural and creative industries.
This policy document shows how important it is to have vital academic platforms on art, culture, creativity, management, technology, economics and social sciences as a base for developing strategies on a local level and worldwide. More specific, the UNCTAD report indicates creative entrepreneurship as one of the driving forces to play a vital role in the social and cultural contexts.

The Utrecht Research Group Art and Economics of Utrecht University-UU/Utrecht School of the Arts-HKU acknowledged the fact that this report processes results of its global research within the field of entrepreneurship and creativity. The UNCTAD Creative Economy Report in 2008 formed the starting point for the idea to produce a blind peer reviewed research book as a scientific challenge, and to give research on cultural entrepreneurship on a better exposure. The second inspirational source is the HKU study on the *Entrepreneurial Dimension of the Cultural and Creative Industries*, published in 2010, commissioned by the EU European Commission (HKU, 2010). The HKU study is primarily focused on SMEs in the 27 EU member states, investigating their needs on support at the local, regional, national and European level. This study has resulted in the new EU policy proposal Creative Europe for the period of 2014-2020. The EU policy is initiated in order to strengthen the cultural and creative sectors, including the specific position of the cultural and Creative SMEs (EU Commission, 2011). And last – but certainly not least - this publication on research in the CCIs is a result of the HKU, celebrating its 25th anniversary.

In line with the publications mentioned – and with the academic mission of the Utrecht University and Utrecht School of the Arts to focus on excellent research and education in mind – the principle goal of this book is to deepen the academic debate about significance and methods of cultural entrepreneurship. It is a challenge to invite and support (young) researchers to design research projects in one of the most interesting and challenging knowledge domains of the 21ste century.

**Academic Committee of the Utrecht University/
Utrecht School of the Arts
Research Group Arts and Economics**

Prof. Giep Hagoort (UU/HKU)
Assoc. prof. Aukje Thomassen (AUT)
Drs. Rene Kooyman DEA MUAD (Ed) (Ars Nova)

REFERENCES

- Dos Santos Duisenberg, E. (Ed) (2010). *Creative Economy Report 2010. E feasible Development Option.* Geneva: UNCTAD.
- EU Commission. (2011, 11 23). *Creative Europe: support programme for Europe's cultural and creative sectors from 2014.* Retrieved 02 12, 2012, from European Commission, Culture; Creative Europe: http://ec.europa.eu/culture/creative-europe
- Hagoort, G. (2007). *Cultural Entrepreneurship. On the freedom to create art and the freedom of enterprise.* (Inaugural Speech). Utrecht: Utrecht University.
- HKU. (2010). *Creative Industries, Colourful fabric in multiple dimensions.* Chicago: Chicago of University Press.
- Hagoort, G., & Kooyman, R. (Ed) (2010). *The entrepreneurial dimension of cultural an creative industries.* Utrecht/Brussel: HKU/EACEA.
- Thomassen, A. (2009). Social Innovation through employing Design Actualisation. In Hagoort, G., & Kooyman, R. (Ed). (Sept 2010). *Creative Industries, Colourful fabric in multiple dimensions.* Chicago: Chicago of University Press.

During the past decade the debates covering the Cultural and Creative Industries (CCIs) has gained speed. Different definitions have been developed and tested, supported by academic research, long-term policy development and real-life operational projects. This publication is offering a State of Affairs overview of both the academic discussions, educational progress and policy development. The book is build around five central topics. It starts off with the Key Elements of the discussions around the Cultural and Creative Economy. Section two gives an overview of actual Concepts and Perspectives. The Cultural and Creative Industries have bee embraced by urban and regional planners. Section three is dedicated to Urban Development. The fundamental principles of Creativity and Innovation are discussed in Section four. The last section is structured around Professional and Academic Education.

Section 1: Key Elements

Giep Hagoort discusses the development of Creative Life Cycle Modeling when developing sustainable cultural and creative firms. He presents an overview of different life-cycle models, and proposes a life-cycle framework for supporting the CCIs.

De Beukelaer observes the CCIs from a global, postcolonial perspective. He points at a double perspective used simultaneously. On the one hand there is an increased attention for culture in development thinking, arguing that the cultural and creative economies foster both economic and social development. At the same time there is a call for a greater rationalization of the entrepreneurial aspects of this creative economy, which echoes thinking much in line with Western modernization theory.

Maria Ptqk points in clear statements at myths, paradoxes and contradictions in the thinking regarding the talent economy. The promotion of creativity is usually identified with personal fulfillment, freedom and empowerment. Yet in reality Creative Workers operate in niche economies, with high levels of precariousness and self-management, self-regulated or non-regulated labor conditions.

Javier Hernández-Acosta puts the cultural entrepreneur at centre stage. Expanding upon the results of the research done in South America he provides a model for developing cooperation models.

Miriam van de Kamp makes an analyses of the operational principles of CCIs. Departing from an analysis of global industries, she points at the importance of cultural factors, organizational cultures and personal qualities of cultural entrepreneurs.

Johan Kolsteeg concentrates on the strategy formation in creative organizations. Using a Strategy-as-Practice approach he studies both the syntaxis and habitus of cultural organizations in making-sense of their surroundings.

Woong Jo Chang adds the concept of 'bricolage' - making do by utilizing the resources at hand. He identifies three factors that allow creative entrepreneurs to engage in the 'bricolage' process: flexibility, close-knit personal networking, and use of IT.

Fabrice Thuriot is discussing the position of the government when dealing with CCIs in a mixed economy. In analyzing the dependency on governmental support he points at the necessity to create a cooperation between both public and private actors.

Section 2: Concepts & Perspectives

Jacob Oostwoud Wijdenes starts with pointing at the system theory of creativity as a powerful instrument to understand the problems artists and entrepreneurs encounter when trying to valorize their ideas, products and services.

Roberta Comunian analyses the complexity and the role of the cluster concept within the CCIs. There has been a growing interest in the way that social and cultural dimensions are intertwined with the sites of exchange and consumption, but also with the value of production systems and supply-chains. She points at the role of networks as learning infrastructures and support.

Barbara Heebels, Oedzge Atzema, Irina van Aalst expand the debate regarding cultural networks from their research done in the book-publishing sector. Publishers govern networks not just by pecuniary incentives. Networks consisting of personal ties function as channels for the exchange of symbolic knowledge of which the cultural meaning has to be (re)created continuously.

Alain Guiette, Sofie Jacobs, Ellen Loots, Annick Schramme and Koen Vandenbempt study the Symbolic Value of the Creative Industries. They confront confronts the intrinsic value of the creative industries on the one hand, versus extrinsic value allocated by both individuals and society, on the other.

Trine Bille and Donatella De Paoli discuss –from their Northern European perspective - the insufficient public and state support mechanisms, systems and incentives towards the CCIs. They put the issue of state support mechanisms towards the cultural and creative industries on the research agenda, and discuss the experiences from both Denmark and Norway.

John Huige offers ten reasons to pursue sustainability for the CCIs. It is widely recognized that cultural and creative activities are important in modern society. At the same time there is a growing need for creating a system of long-term sustainability within our society. He pleads for a sustainable transition of the CCIs.

Section 3: Urban Area Development

Rene Kooyman states that all major cities have to cope with the never-ending cycle of attracting new entrepreneurial activities, economic growth and decay. When trying to renovate run-down quarters, city planners look at the creative industries. Evaluating the results of the CCIs is a daunting task. The Creative Zone Innovator is introduced, with accompanying measurable indicators.

Bart Kamp is pointing at cultural routes as levers for innovation and entrepreneurship. Cultural paths or routes of historical significance are often based on a common, thematic, denominator. They allow and aim for cultural 'consumption' that goes beyond place-based enjoyment of cultural goods, events or heritage. Both a network assessment and market failure are being analyzed.

Adarsha Kapoor offers us an urban design approach from the Asian' perspective. The socio-cultural setup of Asian cities and urban centers is largely shaped by the unorganized worksector of the society. This unorganized sector has redefined creativity to such an extent that it has become an important factor in the changing urban environments of urban centers.

Yigit Ecren and Zeynep Merey Enlil examine Istanbul, one of Europe's mega cites, in the light of the creative city discourse. They focus on Istanbul's creative industries tendency to clustering within the city, and discuss the challenges that these sectors face.

Esra Aysun expands the perspective from Istanbul, discussing the position and function of urban development within the background of International Contemporary Art Exhibitions, such as the Biennale. He points at the need for both the City and the State to formulize a strategy to communicate to its constituencies the relevance of these events, with a focus on the social entrepreneurship.

Bastian Lange expands this debate adding the experiences from Berlin. He highlights the use of field configuring events. He explains how Culturepreneurs use space for the purpose of professionalization in the design segment of Berlin.

Section 4: Innovation

The debate on CCIs and Innovation is started by **Aukje Thomassen**. She highlights the possibilities to use creative entrepreneurship as innovator within social contexts. The analysis is based on the experience from co-creation and entrepreneurship within the design sector.
Sofie van den Borne, Joost Heinsius and Lucie Huiskens highlight the EU 'Training Artists for Innovation' project. They collect and compare experiences from Denmark, Finland, Sweden, Spain and the Netherlands.
Frances Joseph explores the economies of interaction. An interactive screen exhibition program in Auckland, New Zealand has been initiated, in order to materialize emergent local government cultural strategies.
Burak Özgen looks at the feasibility of a 'Fair Music' business model, in order to support both music creators and consumers. He indicates various possibilities and challenges arisen from the progress of new media in music business.
Tsen-Yao Chang and Che-Ting Wen look at the overwhelming debate on authenticity in product design from a far-East perspective. The basic quest is to distinguished a cultural product from a souvenir. The quality of a design can however affect cognition of cultural authenticity by customers.

Section 5: Education

Paul Coyle looks at the role of entrepreneurial graduates and their contribution to the cultural and creative economies. From a UK perspective he introduces the concept of 'the entrepreneurial university'.
Pernille Askerud has gathered extensive experience in developing countries. From the UNESCO global drive for 'Education for all' she develops a need-based perspective on creative entrepreneurship, aiming at the development of a 'Gross National Happiness'.
Nancy de Freitas is involved in the development of entrepreneurial internships, as a bridge between educational institutions and the CCIs. She offers a bridging model as a framework for flexible introduction for artists or designers to industry conditions.
Ayse Coşkun Orlandi and Serkan Bayraktaroğlu discuss the capabilities of the jewellery design education in Turkey. There is a need for re-defining a new design language in the contemporary context of the emerging industry in Turkey.
Gerardo Neugovsen discusses the shift from industrial towards the knowledge era. He explores the relevance on the economic and productive (re)valuation of the concepts of culture, innovation, creativity and knowledge. His concepts are derived from the experience in Chili and Panama.
Julia Calver and Jeff Gold close the Educational section by discussing the University engagement with the Creative Industries. Within the context of university and sector cooperation they discuss the opportunity to develop new skills, strengthen relationships, and enhance opportunities to collaborate in a university program.

Up for discussion
We finish with a final shot, up for discussion. When looking at the CCIs we will have to deal with products, markets and distribution channels. When thinking about the entrepreneurial dimensions, we
cannot ignore the developments regarding income generation and intellectual property rights (IPR).
Joost smiers argues in his polemic essay that we should create a market without property. Food for
thought!

Rene Kooyman
Managing Editor
rkooyman@rkooyman.com

New Knowledge needed on Creative Growth & Development
Creative Life Cycle Modeling to design sustainable cultural and creative firms

Giep Hagoort

Abstract

Life Cycle models for organizational growth and development form a part of the modern management approach. These models help researchers and practitioners to understand the functioning of organizations in a more fruitful way. In general, these models have not been designated towards research on art management and cultural entrepreneurship. To fill this lack of knowledge, this article discusses some central models and presents a translation to the cultural and creative industries. There is an urgent need to create a better understanding of cultural and creative firms: the essential contribution to a sustainable world.

Introduction

In general theories and models on Life Cycles of organizations play a dominant role in understanding the functioning of organizations (Mintzberg, 1989; Keuning & Eppink, 2000; Stokes et al, 2010). Especially in the literature on organizational change, Life Cycle issues are supportive for analyzing the current position of an organization and for designing interventions to prepare the organization to realize the next phase of its development (Quinn, Cameron, 1983).
It is hard to explain why in the cultural and creative industries such an approach is lacking. In most of the books of this new knowledge domain the authors are not discussing the relevancy of the Life Cycle theories and models (Hagoort 2007). There are some exceptions: Noordman based his Dutch book Kunstmanagement (1997, in Dutch: 'Art Management') on a three phase model for cultural organizations. But the limitation of his approach is that his model is focused on subsidized cultural institutes like museums and theatres, and not on the cultural and creative firms as such, which are mostly very small SMEs (Small Medium Sized Enterprises) (Kooyman, 2009). At the other extreme, Pestrak (2008) is strongly oriented on profit making creative businesses with the help of general Life Cycle models.

Within the recent HKU study on *The Entrepreneurial Dimension of the Cultural and Creative industries* (2010), prepared for the European Commission, we re-invent the Life Cycle approach and put it on a more structural level. Firstly in order to promote a deeper *understanding* of the functioning of cultural and creative organizations, this is needed in the fast changing cultural and creative industries. But also as a model for designing a *supportive* infrastructure to stimulate the entrepreneurial spirit, related to the specific phase of growth and development.
There is a growing need to fill the gap in art management theories and practices through a systematic approach of birth and death of cultural and creative organizations. Worldwide there is a transition going on for a sustainable economic and societal development (Thomassen, 2009; Unctad, 2010; Huige, 2012).. This development asks for an awareness of the limitations of natural sources, the well-being of people from all corners of the world and the responsibility of corporate and cultural governance to develop sustainable strategies and organizations.
There is no reason to think that cultural and creative firms have no relationship with this phenomena. Research on the Life Cycle Approaches can be motivated from their suggested function to understand more on the development of sustainable organizations in the context of their growth. When the cultural and creative organizations will contribute to a more sustainable world, it is necessary that creative people themselves show how their organization can grow and develop in these new contexts.

The life cycle approach of organizations

A Life Cycle of an organization can be considered as a specific phase of its growth and development (Hagoort, 2005). Lievegoed (1984) sees three basic phases within the life cycle approach: the pioneering phase; the differentiation phase and the integration phase. The pioneering phase has a pioneer/entrepreneur as a central key figure who is strongly economically oriented. In the differentiation phase the organization will be structured with the help of standardization and specialization. The integration phase can be characterized as a merging of economic, technical and social objectives with creativity and innovations as dominant sources, and marketing as a central focus. After elaborating the different typologies of organizations, based on a set of parameters, Mintzberg (2000) puts his typologies within a life cycle scheme.

This scheme illustrates the following phases:

- Formation (entrepreneurial form)
- Development (machine form, missionary form)
- Maturity (diversified form, professional form, innovative form)
- Decline (politicized form).

Mintzberg is pessimistic about re-vitalization of organizations in their decline-phase. To keep them alive takes away space for new entrepreneurial and innovative forms that will have a better future than the old ones.

A more specific growth model – oriented on specific management crisis of growth - has been developed by Greiner and is used in most of the management books (see Griffin; Stokes et al). In this model, the growth sources have been identified and their typical crises which shows the urgent need to enter a new phase to have more growth chances (from small in the beginning to big at the maturity phase). The model has six phases:

1 Growth through creativity, type of crisis: leadership of the founder;
2 Growth through direction to new managers, type of crisis: lack on autonomy;
3 Growth through delegation to departments, type of crisis: lack of control;
4 Grow through coordination, type of crisis: bureaucracy;
5 Growth through collaboration, type of crisis: a lot of meetings;
6 Growth through deregulation.

The Life Cycle approaches do not exist without debate and critical issues (Perenyi et al , 2008, 2012). The main issues mentioned are:

- Empirical data are mostly based on limited sources (e.g. examples); longitudinal data are lacking.
- The second group of critical issues has to do with the limited results of research: results are often geared towards symptoms and less on the underlying phenomenon, and more on quantitative parameters (and numbers) and not on more sophisticated issues like innovation.
- A third criticism can be found in the assumption that each organization has to go through each stage of development of a particular Life Cycle Model, while regression has not been considered or is excluded because of the limitations of the involved research. The underlying deterministic idea of life cycles has been questioned.
- The fourth group of problematic issues has to do with the supposed linear nature of the Life Cycles. Stages do not always have a growth curve but a 'dead end', which cannot be explained within the Life Cycle Model with its growth logic.

Flamholz (2006) offers to integrate Life Cycle aspects in a wider perspective, in order to understand success and failure of organizations. In his approach he considers six key Building Blocks which have a specific expression in each phase of development ('a set of critical development tasks'), from top to bottom: Corporate Culture; Management Systems; Operational Systems; Resource Management; Product & Services; Markets.

Life cycle models within the cultural and creative industries

As we noticed, in the literature on art management and cultural entrepreneurship just a few authors have discussed Life Cycle approaches as a way to understand cultural and creative organizations in a more effective way (see Verbergt, 2011).
In discussing Cultural Entrepreneurship (Hagoort, 1992) we proposed four phases, derived from the existing models in those days:

1 Start -up (the birth of an organization)
2 Build -up (structuring of the organization)
3 Build -out (production of a variety on products and services within several departments)
4 Re-orientation on the existing strategy

As a result of the case studies by students and practitioners, over the years the model has been developed into four phases form the core of the Life Cycle (Hagoort 2000):

a *Idea phase* centered on artistic leadership and ideas (maximum of 5 years);
b *Structure phase* with the division of artistic and management tasks (maximum of 10 years);
c *Strategy phase* with new future focused initiatives from (new) artistic leadership (maximum of 15 years),
d *Festival phase* around innovative projects and teamwork.

In each phase unique positions can be found with the following components:

- Starting situation,
- Dominant development factors,
- Strategy formation,
- Main organizational characteristics,
- Duration (the length of a phase),
- Cooperation and leaderships.

As already indicated in Greiner's model, if phasing of organizations does not take place on an organic development, then crisis will cause that organization to enter the next phase.
As indicated earlier Noordman (1997) has developed its model for the subsidized cultural sector, based on the ideas of Lievegoed In short one can sketch three positions (Hagoort, 2005)

- Pioneer phase
- Investment phase
- Continuity phase

In the *Pioneer phase*, the central person is the artistic entrepreneur. A small group of assistants and board members assists him or her. The organizational structure is the project form. In this phase the artistic idea of the pioneer has to be proved viable. In the next phase – *the Investment phase* – artistic power in not sufficient. The project organization will change into a more structured one, and some people will leave the organization. Improved structuring often requires a separate business leader, apart from the artistic leader. Financial investment is needed for location, marketing, technology, transport and automation. In the third phase, *the Continuity phase*, the cultural organization becomes anchored in the environment. A general art manager with expertise in cultural marketing, is responsible for the whole organization. Consistency is an important word here, related to organizational design and strategy formation. The organization in this phase often has a subsidized monopoly position in an artistic, financial and geographic context.

Another approach for profit oriented creative businesses has been developed by Pestrak (2008). He integrates the following categories: Management Style, Organizational Structure, Formal Systems Strategy and Business and Owner relationship. These categories are components of a growth model with five stages (from Churchill and Lewis): Existence, Survival, Success-Disengagement, Success-Growth, Take-off and Resource Maturity. Pestrak indicates that applying growth models can help creative businesses to professionalize their (profit) management more effectively.
New research, conducted by Kolsteeg (2012), shows the importance of discourse analysis to understand the strategic growth practice within a cultural or creative firm. Growth strategies have been considered as an artistic process strongly connected with the artistic identity and/or creative reputation. In general business formulations about growth strategies are lacking.
One can expect that in the near future this research approach can strengthen our understanding of the way members of cultural and creative firms express themselves about their own growth and development process, and which artistic and business values they integrate in their daily practice. They are not processing Life Cycle Models but inform us in a narrative approach about the way they are dealing with problems and perspectives within a specific stage of their development.

The HKU-model

The models discussed are mainly focused on the existence and functioning of cultural and creative organizations. In 2008 the Utrecht School of the Arts (HKU) got the assignment of the European Commission to study the Entrepreneurial dimension of the cultural and creative industries (HKU, 2010). One of the aims of the study was to formulate recommendations for a supportive infrastructure (on a local, regional, national and European level). To elaborate this infrastructure with its focus on micro and small organizations, a new (simple) Life Cycle framework was developed to stimulate support in accordance with the needs of these SMEs.
In addition to the usual process of development, the so-called *pre-positioning phase* was introduced (in the model: Preparing the Ground). Here (young) creative people prepare to start their own creative firm. The introduction of this phase was based on research on how creatives during their education see their cultural and creative businesses themselves, and what is needed to develop their ideas (Horlings, 2005). Also newly introduced is the fifth phase after the build-out Phase; the phase of *connecting*. In this fifth phase the organization is dealing with mature growth within a strong networked environment; one of the characteristics of the cultural and creative industries. The origin of this phase is related to the upcoming creative network industries, in which flexibility and fast going changes are more the rule than the exception, and networked ways of working are important (Unctad, 2008). The Start-up, Build-up and Build-out phases are derived from the basic phases as mentioned earlier the *'Utrecht model'* has five phases as the scheme shows:

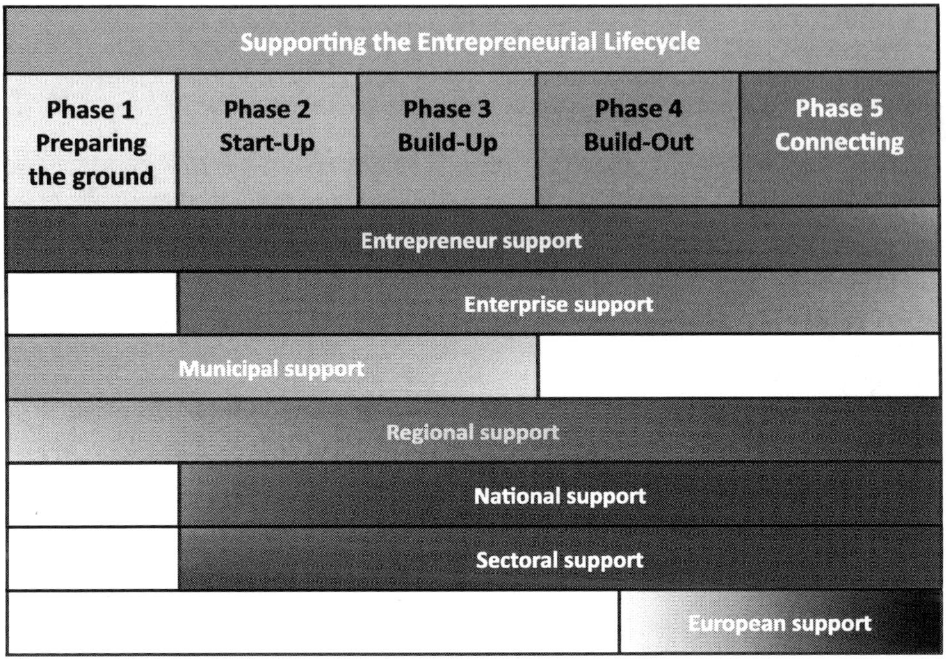

Supporting the Entrepreneurial Lifecycle				
Phase 1 **Preparing the ground**	**Phase 2** **Start-Up**	**Phase 3** **Build-Up**	**Phase 4** **Build-Out**	**Phase 5** **Connecting**
Entrepreneur support				
	Enterprise support			
Municipal support				
Regional support				
	National support			
	Sectoral support			
			European support	

Figure 1 Life-cycle framework for supporting the CCIs

The model also introduces a separation between entrepreneurial support (on personal motivation and needs, mainly in the first phases) and supporting the enterprise itself (organizational aspects, mainly in the phases 3, 4 and 5).
In an explanation, the study states the linear and the top-down approach of the model does not fully correspond to the dynamics of the cultural and creative sector. One of the problems the study mentions is the desire of growth as suggested in the model. To develop more creative ideas and project does not necessarily have the same 'management' expression as strategic growth and organizational development of entrepreneurship (HKU, 2010: 106).

Next step: towards a methodological creative life cycle modeling 2.0

In this chapter we discussed several Life Cycle models for a better understanding of (cultural and creative) firms. One can indicate that research on processing Life Cycle Models can contribute to the new knowledge domain of art management and cultural entrepreneurship. Creating additional research is needed to fill the gap in what ways, with what kind of problems, and with which perspectives cultural and creative organizations design their development and growth.
But as we have seen, Life Cycles are not just a purely rational process of development. There is a personal influence of the creative entrepreneur, the environment and innovative technology on Life Cycle phases and their corresponding parameters. But above all more research is needed to construct a robust model that suits the qualities and needs of cultural and creative firms to fulfill their mission. As the Utrecht Model' has indicated Life Cycles approaches can also be productive in developing supportive external environments.

Another observation is that according to the critics on the models of Life Cycle approaches, these models do not fully express the dynamics of the functioning of (cultural and creative) organizations. They question what really happens in the unique reality of a growing organization on their road to a sustainable world, with a permanent interactivity between creatives, managers, entrepreneurs, spectators, clients, financiers and policymakers, which asks for a more dynamic approach of the Life Cycle models. Within this approach the financing of firm activities can play a special role. As the HKU research (2010) shows, each phase has its own specific needs to realize a business model that suits the development of the organization. The current economic crisis, the fast growing ICT and the 'glocalization' of the creative economy demands for a specific tailor made business modeling. We need a method of 'Creative Life Cycle Modeling (CLCM)' that brings together (1) the growth and development options of cultural and creative firms, (2) the dynamics of creativity of artists and entrepreneurs, (3) the digital technology, and (4) the management functions according to the process of professionalization within a specific phase of its existence. This strong methodological oriented 'CLCM' can be considered as the following step to deepen our interdisciplinary knowledge on art, culture, creativity and sustainability, in combination with management and entrepreneurship. According to Flamholz, and more specifically Pestrac the results of this research can deliver key Building Blocks and an additional, targeted comprehension of the Life Cycle approach for cultural and creative organizations. These Building Blocks will not have the structure of a traditional Life Cycle model but form an open system to help the creatives to professionalize their own organization with – according to Kolsteeg - a language that is strongly connected with their daily practice as an expression of a specific stage of their existence.

References

- Dos Santos Duisenberg (Ed), (2010). *Creative Economy Report 2010*, UNCTAD, Geneva.
- Flamholz Eric G. (2006): Towards an Integrative Theory of Organizational Success and Failure: Previous Research asnd Future Issues, in: Andrew E. Burke (ed.), *Modern Perspectives on Entrepreneurship*, Senate Hall, Dublin.
- Hagoort, Giep and Rene Kooyman (2011): On the principles of Cultural Entrepreneurship: Balancing between Imagination and Financial Profit, in: Cristina Ortega Nuere (ed.), *New challenges of cultural observatories*, University of Deusto, Bilbao.
- Hagoort, Giep (2005): *Art Management Entrepreneurial Style*, Eburon Utrecht.
- Hagoort, Giep (2007): *Cultural Entrepreneurship. On the freedom to create art and the freedom of enterprise*, Inaugural Lecture, UU/HKU Utrecht.
- HKU, (2010.) *The Entrepreneurial Dimension of the Cultural and Creative Industries*, Utrecht School of the Arts HKU, Utrecht .
- Horlings, Tjaard (2008): Prospects for Creative Entrepreneurs, in: , in: *Growth and Development of Creative SMEs*, ECCE/HKU.
- Kolsteeg, Johan (2012), Strategic Practice in creative organizations, in: *Pioneering Minds Worldwide*, Eburon Utrecht.
- Huige, John (2012), Sustainability and the cultural and creative industries. In: Rene Kooyman (Ed): Pioneering Minds Worldwide, Eburon Utrecht.
- Keuning D., D.J. Eppink (2000), *Management & Organisatie. Theorie en Toepassing*, EPN, Houten.
- Kooyman, R. (2009). Minimize me. The Creative Industries: setting the research agenda. In : Kooyman (Ed), *Creative Industries; colourful fabric in multiple dimensions*. Utrecht, the Netherlands: Utrecht School of the Arts (HKU).
- Lievegoed B.C.J. (1984): *Organisaties in ontwikkeling*, Lemniscaat, Rotterdam.
- Mintzberg, Henry, (1989): *Mintzberg on Management, Inside our strange world of organizations*, Free Press, New York.
- Noordman, Th. B. J. (2005): Kunstmanagement, Vuga, Den Haag, 1997 (As mentioned in: Giep Hagoort, *Art Management Entrepreneurial Style*, Eburon.
- Perenyi Aron, Christopher Selvarajah Siva Muthaly (2008): *The Stage Model of Firm development: a conceptualization of SME growth*, AGSE Hawthorn Australia.

- Pestrak, Greg (2008): Managing The Growth Challenge in Creative Businesses, in: *Growth and Development of Creative SMEs*, ECCE/HKU.
- Quinn, Robert E. and Kim Cameron (1983): Organizational Life Cycles and Shifting Criteria of Effectiveness: Some Preliminiary Evidence, in: *Management Science*, Vol. 29, No. 1 (Jan, 1983).
- Stikes David, Nick Wilson, Martha Mador (2010): *Entrepreneurship*, South-Western, CENGAGE Australia.
- Thomassen, Aukje (2009): Social Innovation through Employing Design Actualization. How to use design entrepreneurship as the innovator in social contexts, in: *Yearbook Creative Industries*, Eburon, Delft.
- Verbergt, Bruno (2011) : Algemeen en strategisch management, in: Annick Schramme et al, *Cultuurmanagement. De regels van de kunst*, LannooCampus, Leuven.

About the author

Giep Hagoort (NL) is cultural entrepreneur, professor art and economics at the Utrecht University and the Utrecht School of the Arts, and dean of the Amsterdam School of Management. He is author of a collection of books on management, innovation, entrepreneurship and the cultural and creative industries. Giep Hagoort has been visiting lecturer at universities and academies in Antwerpen, Barcelona, Beograd, Berlin, Bordeaux, Coimbra, Cracow, Hanoi, Helsinki, Istanbul, Johannesburg, Kiev, Los Angeles, New York, Prague, Skopje, St. Petersburg, Shanghai, Tbilisi, Vienna, Warwick, Zagreb, among others.
giep.hagoort@central.hku.nl

The cosmopolitan homo economicus and the global cultural economy
Remarks from a postcolonial perspective
Christiaan De Beukelaer

Abstract

It is commonly asserted that the global creative economy has a great potential to foster economic, social and cultural development in developed and developing countries. This article is largely sympathetic to the notion of a fruitful link between social and economic advancement on the one hand, and cultural and creative practices on the other hand. There does however remain a crucial paradox in the claims that are made pertaining to developing countries.
Following the increased attention for culture in development thinking it is argued that the cultural and creative economies (CCIs) foster economic and social development. However, there is a simultaneous call for a greater rationalization of the entrepreneurial aspects of this creative economy, which echoes thinking much in line with Western modernization theory. As such, the cultural complexity of societies and communities is by and large neglected when commoditizing culture and creativity through the CCIs. The way in which the international reports on CCIs largely call for rationalization and further economization of the sector worldwide is challenged. Accordingly, an attempt is made to provide an initial theoretical framework, influenced by postcolonial studies, through which greater understanding of the complexity of 'culture' in both cultural and creative industries might be achieved.

Introduction

It is commonly asserted that the global cultural and creative industries (CCIs) have a great potential to foster economic, social and cultural development in developed and developing countries (e.g. UNCTAD 2008; 2010). While I am largely sympathetic to the notion of a fruitful link between social and economic advancement on the one hand and cultural and creative practices on the other hand, the complex interplay of culture and economy in the relationships between CCIs and development is insufficiently explored in the context of the Global South.
It would seem that the global CCIs entrepreneur should be a homo economicus, acting in a uniform, rational way, while working with culturally rich 'products' in a cosmopolitan sector. This outlook largely echoes an academically obsolete, yet practically longstanding, take on development. In early 1950s development thinking and practice, hegemonic 'economism' (Escobar, 2005: 140) provided a rigorous categorization of culture. Mass consumption was argued to be the epitome of societal order, and accordingly ranked as the highest of the five stages of development (Rostow, 1959). In this modernization theory, other forms of social and cultural organization were argued to be intrinsically backward, yet at some early stage of progress towards the model of Western civilization: modernity. At a later stage in development thinking—from the late 1980s onwards—culture has actively permeated the ways development was perceived and approached. This so-called cultural turn in development called for a thorough consideration of culture as starting point for development initiatives (Nederveen Pieterse, 2010: 72-3; UNESCO, 1982). It was not only argued that 'rational' economics—i.e. modernization thinking—is in itself culturally informed, but also that locally rooted outlooks on life can yield great benefits to the way development is conceptualized and enacted. In short, modernization and westernization were questioned.

As such, the concept of culture, initially alien to mainstream development discourse, slowly made its way into development thinking. In this context, culture signified a way-of-life. Parallel to the shift from the 'culture industry' (critique on mass media and popular culture) to the 'cultural industries' (in the plural, as a more nuanced understanding of CCIs as symbolic texts) in the 1980s (Hesmondhalgh, 2007: 16), the concept of culture shifted from a very broad definition towards a narrower one.

It should be noted that intentions, uses and outcomes of the insertion of CCIs logic in (development) policy discourse are most diverse (Garnham, 2005; Cunningham, 2009; Poettschacher, 2010) and their logic is, albeit positively put forward by many (e.g. Florida, 2003; Howkins, 2002; Singh, 2007; Barrwclough, and Kozul-Wright, 2008) not uncontested (e.g. Tremblay, 2011; McGuigan, 2009; Oakley, 2006), and neither can it be easily transferred between countries (Pratt, 2009). Yet, the idea that culture can be a whole 'way of life', but also a collection of artistic and symbolic practices which can be traded as commodities, creates an ontological divide between different conceptualizations of culture that are not mutually interchangeable. I will accordingly argue that the cultural complexity of societies and communities is by and large neglected when commoditizing culture through the CCIs.

Cultural & Creative Industries as vector of development

Through the CCIs, culture is—strongly, but not exclusively—seen as a locus of human development. This assertion is substantiated primarily through several reports, initiatives and meetings that established and upheld the central position of culture-as-product in development discourse. The most explicit, recent examples of this insertion of CCIs discourse in development thinking are arguably the creative economy reports (CERs), published by UNCTAD in 2008 and 2010. The first report specifically focuses on *The challenge of assessing the creative economy* towards informed policy-making, whereas the second one bears the subtitle *Creative Economy: A Feasible Development Option.* In short, the message these reports convey can be argued to be the following:

> *Creative products and cultural activities have real potential to generate economic and social gains. The production and distribution of creative products can yield income, employment and trade opportunities, while fostering social cohesion and community interaction.* (UNCTAD, 2010, p. 253).

Culture is no longer an obstacle to, but a rather driver of, development. Similarly, Barrowclough and Kozul-Wright (2008) provide an account of how the CCIs are firmly inserted in thinking on development. They argue that the CCIs 'are beginning to be seen as a way of regenerating local communities and catalyzing entire cities; of diversifying and re-positioning traditional or regressing economies; of boosting human capital, skills levels and innovation; and of opening a door to global knowledge economy' (UNCTAD, 2008, 4).

Hence, culture is seen as means to an end: through the cultural and creative industries, the symbolic expressions are argued to contribute to development. Yet, the CERs point at crucial 'obstacles to the expansion of the creative economy: lack of capital, [...] lack of entrepreneurial skills, [and] lack of infrastructure and institutions.' (UNCTAD, 2008, 40). These remarks do, however, echo an outdated view on development:

> *[So-called] traditional societies ... are underdeveloped because of a lack of important propellants of development, including a work ethic, morals, innovative and entrepreneurial capacity, free market mechanisms, a propensity for taking risks and organizational acumen. The absence of these factors, according to the theory, is itself a function of flaws in the culture, customs and social mores of traditional societies* (Sorenson, 2003, p. 79 in Njoh, 2006, p. 16).

It could reluctantly be concluded that 'making of the third world' (Escobar, 1995) is as such repeated in UNCTAD's call for the transformation of the existing cultural sector into an exogenous model of cultural and economic conduct. The second CER, however, proclaims the need for this transformation more elusively: '*a salient feature of the common to most developing countries is the need to establish or reinforce institutions, as well as a regulatory framework and a financing mechanism*' (UNCTAD, 2010, 257).

The questions that arise in this regard are how the CCIs relate to the cultural turn in thinking on development, and how we can understand the influence this exerts on the complex position of culture in this field.

Cultural turn and the expediency of culture

It is essential to further investigate the complex relation of different conceptualizations of culture to the thinking and practice of development. Thereby, two different notions of culture are employed:

- On the one hand, culture *'indicates a particular way of life, whether of a people, a period, a group or humanity in general'* (Williams, 1976, p. 90). This 'anthropological' perspective on the subject may however be interpreted rather easily as unchangeable and steady. In response, *'analysts have begun to combine more open definitions of culture with an understanding of racial formations, political economies and history'* (Radcliffe, 2006c, p. 232). Culture does however remain a 'way of life', or as Apthorpe (2005, p. 137) argues: *'a pattern of living.'*
- On the other hand, culture is an *'independent and abstract noun which describes the works and practices of intellectual and especially artistic activity'* (Williams 1976, p. 90). In other words, *'culture as product treats culture as a set of material objects [cultural goods] and distinctive behaviors [cultural services]. When this interpretation of culture is inserted into development thinking, it promotes the orientation of culturally distinctive products and services onto the market'* (Radcliffe 2006c, p. 242).

This temporary demarcation of culture into two (admittedly tentative) notions facilitates our further elaboration on the subject. This is most apparent when looking at the ways the CCIs are included in policy discourse relevant to development:

> *Perhaps the greatest impact of the [CCIs] is not only within the traditional [CCIs] but in the way their skills and business models are being used to create value in other areas of life* (Howkins, 2007, xvi).

This idea would support our thesis that the commoditization of culture is not a mere neutral application of an economic logic to cultural production. On the contrary; rather than merely increasing the economic viability and socio-cultural significance of the CCIs, they similarly influence the wider realm of social and economic life.

Postcolonial framing of culture and economy

In order not to render the practice of the 'other' merely exotic, it is helpful to turn to a postcolonial framing of the economic realm. As such, the cultural economy could be seen as a diverse and locally defined construct, where the cosmopolitan cultural entrepreneur acts as a hybrid agent, negotiating terms of modernity; both spatially and temporally. Looking at economic conduct, Zaoual argues that the lively, entrepreneurial praxis of the Soussis in Morocco, through their *'neo-tribal enterprise culture,'* defies the doxa of *'development packages'* (1999, p. 476). Moreover, Escobar argues that:

> *Capitalism, industrial civilization and the market economy— as well as the whole realm of cultural practices associated with them—are not immanent qualities of all societies, but rather historically contingent productions. Moreover, there has been in the Third World (and there are still today) important forms of resistance to the extension of the practices associated with the dominant Western economic rationality* (2005, p. 164).

Challenging modernization thinking and orthodox economics, we have to make a case for cultural economics influenced by postcolonial thinking. Following Zaoula's reading of the prevailing heterodox economic practices, one could say that no matter how similar cultural industries may seem in different places, they are more likely to be the timely result of ongoing dialectics between the economic and the cultural, thereby negotiating internal and external changes, based on the same influences and bases. This thought can be linked to Development as Freedom, the seminal work of Amartya Sen (1999), in which he argues for development interventions and evaluations to widen focus beyond mere income (deprivation) and to include both the intrinsic and instrumental value of *'political freedom, economic facilities, social opportunities, transparency guarantees and protective security'* (1999, p. 38). Alongside the (economic) outcome, the process and the social and cultural development are also of importance.

As such, it may be observed that the discursive promotion of the CCIs may neglect the subtleties that may prevail in postcolonial economic conduct, as the explicit call for a greater rationalization of the sector does little justice to these very idiosyncrasies. It can be argued that globalizing CCIs discourse builds on a somewhat old-fashioned notion of development, that silently ignores endogenous cultural traits, through its focus on development as a largely economic process. The argument is not that cultural production is located either in the community or in the market; but that it resides in both. Hence it is my contention that the emergent notion of postcolonial economies (Pollard, McEwan and Hughes, 2011; Charusheela and Zein-Elabdin, 2004) may provide theoretical frameworks to rethink the complex interplay of CCIs and development. While practices are often ostensibly similar, they can be thought to be divergent beneath this superficial similarity. As such, CCIs are functional to the extent that cultural goods and services are traded in some way or another. It is precisely at this stage that a heterodox—i.e. postcolonial—reading of economics is of great significance:

> *Postcolonial readings of the economy emerged first in practice rather than in theory, as economic, juridical and legal structures in various places have struggled to reconcile diverse understandings of land, kinship and use* (Larner, 2011, p. 91).

In this way, it is crucial to draw on the existing praxis in glocalized CCIs, to understand the ways in which they can develop further.

We could thus reluctantly conclude that the call for a greater professionalization of the CCIs worldwide may hold water to some extent, but mostly neglects the lack of rational management in the sector as a whole, and greatly underestimates the existing functioning of the sector in the 'South'. Yet the intrinsically cultural traits of production, trading and consumption are often equally underestimated. Economics as a whole, and CCIs in particular should thus be encouraged to develop in their own right, for the dialectics of economic praxis cannot be forcefully modernized.

Conclusions

This chapter attempts to provide an initial theoretical framework, influenced by postcolonial studies, through which greater understanding of the complexity of 'culture' in the CCIs might be achieved. It questioned the extent to which CCIs discourse may be too focused on development in a traditional—i.e. ideologically obsolete—sense. Culture is used in a rather narrow sense (CCIs), while claims are made that largely build on a broader, more encompassing notion of culture (as a way-of-life, cfr. the cultural turn).

Challenging modernization thinking and orthodox economics, this chapter attempts to make a case for cultural economics influenced by postcolonial thinking. As such, parallel to the development of idiosyncratic art-forms, endogenous accounts of economics have emerged over time. As such, even though the cosmopolitan homo economicus may seem universal, I would argue that there is a greater need to actively acknowledge cultural difference—bearing in mind both notions of culture provided here—and see this as central to the discourse of the globalizing cultural industries.

References

- Anheier, Helmut, en Yudhishthir Raj Isar (ed.). (2008). *The cultural economy.* Los Angeles CA, London: Sage.
- Apthorpe, Raymond. (2005). Its [the] Culture, Stupid! Why Adding Culture is Unlikely to Make Any Serious Difference to International Developmentalism. In: *The Asia Pacific Journal of Anthropology* , 6 (2): 130–141.
- Barrowclough, Diana, en Zeljka Kozul-Wright, red. (2008). *Creative industries and developing countries : voice, choice and economic growth.* London, New York NY: Routledge.
- Belfiore, Eleonora, en Oliver Bennett. (2008). *The social impact of the arts : an intellectual history.* New York NY: Palgrave Macmillan.
- Cunningham, Stuart. (2009). Trojan horse or Rorschach blot? Creative industries discourse around the world. In: *International Journal of Cultural Policy* 15 (4): 375–386.
- Dos Santos Duisenberg, Edna. (2008). *Creative economy report 2008 : the challenge of assessing the creative economy : towards informed policy-making.* UNCTAD United Nations, Geneva.
- Dos Santos Duisenberg, Edna. (2010). *Creative economy report: Creative Economy: A Feasible Development Option.* UNCTAD United Nations, Geneva .
- Escobar, Arturo. (1995). *Encountering development : the making and unmaking of the Third World.* Princeton NJ: Princeton University Press.
- Florida, Richard. (2002). *The Rise of the creative class : And how its transforming work, leisure, community and everyday life.* New York: Basic Books.
- García Canclini, Néstor. (1995). *Hybrid cultures : strategies for entering and leaving modernity.* Minneapolis MN: University of Minnesota Press.
- Gudeman, Stephen. (2001). *The anthropology of economy : community, market, and culture.* Malden MA: Blackwell.
- Hesmondhalgh, David. (2007). *The cultural industries.* 2nd ed. Los Angeles CA: Sage.
- Howkins, John. (2002). *The creative economy : how people make money from ideas.* London: Penguin.
- Kaul, Nitisha. (2004). Writing Economic Theory anOther Way. In: *Postcolonialism meets economics* (ed.) S. Charusheela en E. Zein-Elabdin. London, New York NY: Routledge.
- Larner, Wendy. (2011). Economic geographies as situated knowledges. In: *Postcolonial economies* (ed.) Jane Pollard, Cheryl McEwan, en Alex Hughes. London, New York NY: Zed Books Ltd.
- Njoh, Ambe. (2006). *Tradition, culture and development in Africa : historical lessons for modern development planning.* Aldershot , Burlington VT: Ashgate.
- Oakley, Kate. (2006). Include Us Out—Economic Development and Social Policy in the Creative Industries. In: *Cultural Trends* 15(4): 255-273.

- Poettschacher, Erich. (2010). The rise of the Trojan horses in the creative industries. In: *International Journal of Cultural Policy* 16: 355-366.
- Pollard, Jane, Cheryl McEwan, en Alex Hughes, red. (2011). Postcolonial economies. London, New York NY: Zed Books Ltd.
- Pratt, Andy C. (2009). Policy Transfer and the Field of the Cultural and Creative Industries: What Can Be Learned from Europe? In: *GeoJournal Library*: 98(1): 9-23.
- Radcliffe, Sarah (ed). (2006). *Culture and development in a globalizing world : geographies, actors, and paradigms.* London, New York NY: Routledge.
- Rostow, Walt Whitman. (1990). *The stages of economic growth : a non-communist manifesto.* 3rd ed. Cambridge, New York NY: Cambridge University Press.
- Singh, J. P. (2007). Culture or Commerce? A Comparative Assessment of International Interactions and Developing Countries at UNESCO, WTO and Beyond. In: *International Studies Perspectives* (8): 36–53.
- Throsby, David. (2010). *The economics of cultural policy.* Cambridge, New York NY: Cambridge University Press.
- Towse, Ruth. (2003). *A handbook of cultural economics.* Cheltenham, Northampton MA: Edward Elgar.
- Tremblay, Gaetan. (2011). Creative statistics to support creative economy politics. In: *Media, Culture & Society* 33 (2): 289–298.
- Williams, Raymond. (1988). *Keywords : a vocabulary of culture and society.* Rev. and expanded ed. London: Fontana.
- Yúdice, George. (2003). *The expediency of culture : uses of culture in the global era.* Durham: Duke University Press.
- Zaoual, Hassan. (1999). The Maghreb Experience: A Challenge to the Rational Myths of Economics. In: *Review of African Political Economy* 26 (82).
- Zein-Elabdin, Eiman and S. Charusheela. (2004). *Postcolonialism meets economics.* London, New York NY: Routledge.

About the author
Christiaan De Beukelaer (UK) is a doctoral researcher at the University of Leeds Institute of Communications Studies. He previously obtained an MSc in Cultures and Development Studies, and an MA in Cultural Studies at the University of Leuven, after completing a BA in Musicology at the University of Amsterdam.
christiaandebeukelaer@gmail.com
There is no reason to think that cultural and creative firms have no relationship with this phenomena. Research on the Life Cycle Approaches can be motivated from their suggested function to understand more on the development of sustainable organizations in the context of their growth. When the cultural and creative organizations will contribute to a more sustainable world, it is necessary that creative people themselves show how their organization can grow and develop in these new contexts.
christiaandebeukelaer@gmail.com

Be Creative Under-Class!
Myths, Paradoxes and Strategies in the Talent Economy
Maria Ptqk

Abstract

During the last few years, the apparently paradoxical expression *'creative economy'* has emerged with astonishing success. Creative work has achieved recognition in the new labor theory. Artists are identified as individuals or small groups, specialized in intense immaterial production, whose professional practice is associated with high degrees of subjectivity, informality and autonomy.
The promotion of creativity is usually identified with personal fulfillment, freedom and empowerment, and thus perceived as an improvement in the working conditions. In reality Creative Workers operate in niche economies, with high levels of precariousness and self-management, self-regulated or non-regulated labor conditions, no precise professional categories, and many concessions to the invisible economy. They combine occasional contracts with periods of inactivity and experiences of self-employment. Their actual survival depends to a large extent on informal collaboration networks - both personal and professional. Often facilitated by family-based support - and on the many ramifications of the Welfare State, such as grants, public funding or social benefits. Overall, their situation is hardly sustainable in the long term.

Introduction

During the last few years, the apparently paradoxical expression *'creative economy'* has emerged with astonishing success. It has burst into public policies, corporate agendas, higher education curricula, economic magazines and cultural events that unanimously celebrate it as the winning paradigm that will lead us out of the current crisis and into a new era of economical and social progress.

These transformations are real and profound. Yet, along with them, a parallel process has taken place, one of a narrative nature, aimed at identifying and explaining such changes in a clear and seductive manner. In order to be effective, the creative economy had to find a name - and is still at it: *talent economy, knowledge economy, cultural, semiotic* or *informational capitalism*, the terminology is wide and inviting – and produces charming and empowering stories itself. Such stories tell us about causes, cycles, opportunities and protagonists, they contribute to a feeling of cohesion around a shared and common project and provide us with a reliable road-map that can help us deal with uncertainty. Creativity and the emerging concept of creative work, in all their multiple variations, are both part of this storytelling.

One pioneer in this process was Tony Blair's New Labour Government, who coined the term 'creative industries' as part of a double maneuver of economizing culture and culturizing economy. The Cool Britannia artifact deployed two co-ordinated actions. On the one hand, it redefined what had hitherto been known as the cultural and service industries: film, TV, radio, publishing, music, art, performing arts, antiques, crafts, computer games, architecture, fashion, software development, IT services and design [1] On the other hand, it implemented *a strong public campaign to persuade the world that the country that Napoleon once depicted as a nation of shopkeepers had become a country of artists and designers* (Ross, 2007).

---

[1] Sectors included in the list of creative industries in the U.K.: Department of Culture, Media and Sport, Creative Industry Task Force: Mapping Document (London 1998).

More than a decade after the boom of the creative industries, we now witness the staging of a second narrative move. The aim is no longer only to promote the development of some economic fields, but to analyze the essence of creative work in order to qualify it as the professional model of the new economy. In current management literature, the message is simple: to achieve the paradigm shift, we need to understand and theorize this new form of intangible production, and to promote it in the frame of a wide culture of creativity that can impregnate all levels of economic activity and become socially internalized as the new culture of labor. What Ulrich Beck once called *'the brave new world of work'* (Beck, 2000).

When talent makes capital dance[2]

Creative work has achieved recognition in the new labor theory though two referential subjects: artists and hackers. Artists -together with their *ersatz*: cultural workers- are identified as individuals or small groups specialized in intense immaterial production, whose professional practice is associated with high degrees of subjectivity, informality and autonomy (McRobbie, 2004). Hackers - and free software programmers - embody the evidence that it is possible to be highly competitive by challenging the rules of traditional industrial production and that the lack of schedules, ties and verticality do not hinder efficiency, but foster it (Himanen, 2000).

The assimilation between artists and software programmers had a key role in the early genesis of the creative industries. Despite its heterogeneity, the field clearly combines two types of activity that were previously considered as different: the old and highly theorized *'cultural industries'* and the recent and promising business born from the cutting-edge technological revolution. Both are based on high doses of applied knowledge, provide a genuinely non-commercial added value that is, still, not so easy to outsource[3] and operate within the logics of agglomeration economies, radically different from the traditional economies of industrial mass production.

These fields are usually inhabited by small organizations or freelancers, working with porous boundaries and a variable geometry in which networks and information are openly exchanged. The economy of agglomeration, usually identified with arts and culture, is also the major organizational model in environments of high technological innovation such as Silicon Valley (Landa, 2008). It seems today that contemporary corporations, if they want to embrace the current economic changes, should become something like a permanent laboratory, halfway between a start-up, a hacklab, and an artist's studio, which appear to be the ideal working environments to transform knowledge and creative skills into commodities.

As a consequence, creative workers (in the broadest sense: artists, architects, software designers, etc.) are increasingly demanded for innovation agendas and tasks related to informational and knowledge-based paradigms (participatory processes, citizen media, networks, peer-to-peer organizations, etc.). The project Disonancias is an example of such interactions:

[2] The title of this section is a reference to Kjell A. Nordström and Jonas Ridderstråle, *Funky Business. Talent Makes Capital Dance* (London, 1999: Pearson Education), presented by the authors themselves as *'a manifesto for the new world of business'*.

[3] Programming tasks are being outsourced to Asian countries such as India and South Korea, but this doesn't substantially change the economic organization of the IT industry. Intellectual property rights and profits are still mainly controlled by Western countries corporations.

'Disonancias is a platform aimed at companies, research centers or public entities interested in collaborating with artists in order to promote their innovation. It is based on the premise that artists are researchers by definition. Within the framework of collaborating with organizations, they are able to propose new and different innovation paths, introducing detours and dissonance into the usual processes of thought and action, providing creativity and work methodologies and serving as a catalyst for team members. The Disonancias platform views innovation not as an end in itself, but as a tool to change ways of acting, attitudes and values, beyond that of economic benefit. In the long term, Disonancias aims to transmit to society the importance of developing creative environments and extending innovation culture in all its aspects, as well as promoting social responsibility in organizations and a commitment of artists with society' (Disonancias, 2012).

The promotion of creativity

The promotion of creativity is usually identified with personal fulfillment, freedom and empowerment, and thus perceived as an improvement in the working conditions. According to Rosalind Gill (2007), when asked about the nature of their work, freelancers and employees in new media (an emerging professional sector demanding a high degree of creative and technological skills), mention the following key elements: pleasure and fun; autonomy, entrepreneurship and lack of hierarchies; innovation and permanent learning; informal communication and exchange; the possibility to take part in projects with a social impact; the perception that these working environments are egalitarian and open to diversity; and the fascination with the novelty of the sector. Zoe Romano (2009) points out one more element: prestige and peer recognition. Both researchers emphasize the fact that creative workers are deeply convinced that what they do is beneficial to society as a whole, and that they all experience their profession as an adequate space for social action. They also both agree that, among their motivations, money and security are secondary. As one of Gill's interviewees says: *'If I wanted to have a stable job and earn money, I'd do something else'.*

One key element that is not explicitly mentioned but is embedded in their answers is that, for creative workers, the limits of the time/space of life and the time/space of work are diluted. They have transformed their hobbies into a profession, and account it as an advantage and a victory against conventional work and all it represents in terms of alienation and servitude: 'It's as if you were getting paid for your hobby' (Gill, 2007). Turning subjectivity into a productive resource, or, to put it more poetically, becoming 'an artist of one's own life': this is the successful slogan of the contemporary discourse on work which the creative workers embody, that radically sets them apart from other kinds of workers. As Marion Von Osten (2007) puts it:

'From the perspective of groups orientated around long-term employment like civil or labor parties, it becomes difficult to determine how, why and when to differentiate between 'work' and 'non-work'. The artist seems to be a key figure in comprehending this situation, operating as a touchstone for mediating this new understanding of living and working to a broader audience'.

Because when one works for his or her own personal fulfillment - when work merges with one's own subjectivity and personal life - one is willing to do it *anyway.*

The rise of the creative under-class

Ten years ago, at the beginning of the 21st century, Richard Florida announced that a new urban high-skilled professional class was born. Whatever approach one might have towards his theories, one point seems to be beyond discussion. Neither Florida's celebratory discourse nor the policies inspired have turned into a real analysis of what creative work actually is and how it operates, but have rather assumed some standardized ideas on what it should be - or more precisely: how it should *be told* - in order to meet the needs of the public and corporate agendas. As a result, the creative workers – the men and women that do work in the creative field - have been, firstly instrumentalized as a reference model, and then left out of the picture.

> *'New media employees helped to glamorize the 24/7 workweek, design, art, architecture, and custom craft were embraced as engines for boosting property values in the real estate boom, the amateur (MyCreativity) ethic became the basis for a whole new discount mode of production that exploited the cult of attention as a cheap labor supply'.*[4]

Creative workers operate in niche economies, with high levels of precariousness and self-management, self-regulated or non-regulated labor conditions, no precise professional categories, and many concessions to the invisible economy. They combine occasional contracts with periods of inactivity and experiences of self-employment. Their actual survival depends, to a large extent, on informal collaboration networks - both personal and professional, as well as family-based - and on the many ramifications of the Welfare State, such as grants, public funding or social benefits. Overall, their situation is hardly sustainable in the long term.

What transpires from the interviews realized by Gill is that the salaries in the new media (in United Kingdom and The Netherlands) are much lower than in other sectors. More than a third earn less than 20.000 € /year, half of whom less than 10.000 € / year, while only another third has an income above the national average, which is of 30.000 € / year. In contrast, 9 out of every 10 permanent employees earn over 30.000 € a year. And, while the latter work an average of 35 and 40 hours a week, new media professionals work between 55 and 80 hours a week. Job insecurity is joined here by the lack of a regular flow of work (periods of high intensity alternate with others in which projects are in short supply), the pressure of permanent training and a compulsive sociability with professional aims (in 99% of the cases, projects arise from a personal relationship). Many of the people interviewed also recognize that, for them, maternity is a very difficult option (Gill, 2009).

From the standpoint of the new management theories, these conditions of informality are praised to excess. The basic premise is that in order to survive in an increasingly competitive environment, the contemporary worker *must be free*, and that insecurity and instability are inevitable structural conditions of cognitive capitalism.

> *'Maybe the logic of dependence at work has been part of the arsenal deployed by the contracting party to dominate the contracted party. The asymmetry of the relationship burrowed into the wound: an employed, subcontracted, paid worker, dominated by a hierarchical superior. A whole language of dependencies. But this doesn't make sense anymore'* (Ormaetxea 2008).

---

[4] Andrew Ross interviewed by Geert Lovink in *My Creativity Reader. A Critique of Creative Industries,* edited by Geert Lovink and Ned Rossiter (Amsterdam 2007: Institute of Network Cultures).

According to this logic, the worker should become a nomadic and flexible labor resource, with no stable connections to any company, in a dynamic of competition/collaboration with his or her peers. That is, to become a conglomerate of skills and knowledge in a permanent state of adaptation, which can be deployed at any moment, depending on market needs. The figure that best embodies this professional attitude is that of the entrepreneur, identified with the talent economy success model. Beyond the triumph of creativity or the impact of cognitive skills as a driving force of development, the true virtue of creative work is that, by idealizing freedom, it contributes to hide the labor de-regulation, the lack of stable work and the economic instability. The consequence is that the latter lose their conflictive dimension and can be unproblematically transferred to the public opinion as an attractive, successful and desirable lifestyle choice. The cognitive worker is seen as a role-model for any worker, whose aim is to become *an ever-flexible provider of immaterial services, available on demand.* That is the dark side of the myth of entrepreneurship, promoted by innovation consultants, public policy makers, and other Floridian enthusiasts, who often elaborate their theories under the protection of big companies, universities, public administrations or personal situations which allow them to jump safely into the adventure of creativity.

Conclusion

Creative workers are trapped in a paradoxical situation that often borders on schizophrenia. Their position is, at the same time, strategic and subsidiary. They possess the most appreciated skills in the labor market, but their conditions of work are miserable. When they provide their services for policies leading to the promotion of creativity and the transformation of the current economic model, they often don't appreciate the context, or the use that is made of their contribution. Facing their own contradictions, they oscillate between, on the one hand, the fascinating figure of the cognitive elite *à la* Florida, and, on the other hand, the stereotype of the net-slave or the techno-cultural precariat suggested by Gill. Both referents appear close to them, but none captures the complexity and ambivalence of their position. Moreover, from the point of view of classic socio-economic theory, these are opposed figures. How can one be part of an elite and proletarian at the same time? And, above all, how can a mass of freelance and disorganized workers, who perceive themselves as independent, articulate an efficient language of collective professional claims?

> *'Knowledge and cultural workers are accustomed to think of themselves as in the vanguard, and it will probably take a generation of 'proletarianization' and another big recession to persuade them that collective organizing is in their long-term interest.'[5]*

On a daily basis, creative workers like to think of themselves as resistance agents. They know that the decisions that affect them are taken at political and corporate levels, at which they never participate. But they tend to protect themselves with short- and mid-term tactics. They avoid collaborating in projects whose aims they don't share or tell themselves that this is just for immediate economic necessity. They resort to their full informal repertoire of survival techniques in order to keep on *doing what they like.* The problem is that the niche economy, the logics of the subsidy, the personal networks and the daytime job that sustains the creative one are not sustainable in the long-term. And they will become less sustainable as the immaterial productive model continues to develop. It is

[5] Andrew Ross interviewed by Geert Lovink in *My Creativity Reader. A Critique of Creative Industries.*

then urgent to implement parallel counter-narratives that question profoundly the current public discourse around the talent economy and explain it from the inside, with its highlights and its shadows. And, using that same creativity, imagine new possibilities of political action that can transform the key position of creative workers into a professional, collective and sustainable strategy.

References

- Beck, Ulrich (2000): *The Brave New World of Work*. Oxford 2000, Polity Press.
- *Disonancias* website: retrieved from: http://www.disonancias.com/en/articulo/249-what-is-disonancias/ , as consulted 04 Jan 2012.
- Gill, Rosalind (2007): *Technobohemians or the new Cybertariat?* New media work in Amsterdam a decade after the web, (Amsterdam : Network Notebooks 01, Institute of Network Cultures).
- Himanen, Pekka (2001): *The Hacker Ethic* (New York , Random House).
- Iturbe Ormaetxea, (Julen November 29, 2008): 'Trabajo (in)dependiente' in: *Consultoria Artesana en Red weblog*. retrieved from: http://blog.consultorartesano.com/2008/11/trabajo-independiente.html.
- Landa, Manuel de (2008): 'Economics, Computers and the War Machine' in: *Public Netbase: Non-Stop Future. New Practices in Art and Media*, (Graz: Revolver - Archiv für aktuelle Kunst).
- Lovink, Geert and Ned Rossiter (Ed) (2007): *My Creativity Reader. A Critique of Creative Industries*. Amsterdam: Institute of Network Cultures.
- McRobbie, Angela, Everyone is Creative (2004): *Artists as Pioneers of the New Economy* . London Department for Media and Communication, Goldsmith College.
- Nordström, Kjell A. and Jonas Ridderstråle (1999): *Funky Business. Talent Makes Capital Dance* . London: Pearson Education.
- Osten, Marion van (2007) : 'Unpredictable Outcomes: A Reflection After Some Years of Debates on Creativity and Creative Industries' in: *My Creativity Reader. A Critique of Creative Industries*, edited by Geert Lovink and Ned Rossiter. Amsterdam: Institute of Network Cultures.
- Romano, Zoe (2009): *Creative Labour* , presented at Network Cultures Winter Camp, Amsterdam, March 3-7 , 2009.
- Ross, Andrew (2007): 'Nice Work If You Can Get It. The Mercurial Career of Creative Industries Policy', in *My Creativity Reader. A Critique of Creative Industries*, edited by Geert Lovink and Ned Rossiter (Amsterdam: Institute of Network Cultures).

About the author
Maria Ptqk (ES) is a freelance curator, consultant and researcher working at the confluence of cultural policies, new media, and gender studies. Member of GenderArtNet, and moderator/initiator of the Blog:
http://ptqkblogzine.blogspot.com
mariaptqk@gmail.com

Cultural Entrepreneurship: building from the artists' experiences
Javier Hernández-Acosta

Abstract

Thinking of a creative industry with growth and sustainability requires focusing on the cultural entrepreneur as the center of its development. Research has suggested that the study of entrepreneurship transcends the economic analysis and requires a multidisciplinary approach. Here the expressed concerns from three different research methodologies are presented: in-depth interviews with artists regarding their experiences as entrepreneurs, a survey of 165 artist-entrepreneurs on educational needs and views of the creative sector, and a case study of an artists' cooperative, as an alternative for the development of medium-sized enterprises in the cultural sector. The aim is to provide a basis for developing indicators and practical recommendations for the development of the sector.

Cultural entrepreneurship: Building from the artists' experiences

There are great opportunities in the creative economy. In recent years, countries have made significant efforts to explore the capabilities of cultural industries as an alternative for economic development (Quartesan c.s., 2007). While analyzing the impact of the cultural sector on macro-economic variables is necessary, it is also important to understand the determinant factors for that development. Besides analyzing the scope of the creative sector, and its cultural and economic value, it is imperative to give attention to the center of the sector: the artist. If the sector is analyzed in its broadest conception, and compared with an organic system, then the artist could be the atom of the creative economy. For this reason, understanding artists' experiences and processes can help strengthen cultural and creative enterprises.

Although it has been argued that there is a difficulty in linking artists to business management, the concept of creative entrepreneurship could be redundant (Ministerio de Cultura de Colombia, 2005). Some research has suggested that the mindset of entrepreneurs is closer to artists than to managers (Groves c.s., 2008). How important can cultural entrepreneurs be in economic development? Research suggests that innovation is the main source of economic growth (Wong, 2005). If creativity is the main ingredient of innovation, and the arts are the maximum expression of creativity, then we have a clear connection that should be employed by public policy. Also, there is research to be done in terms of the interactions of cultural entrepreneurs and management practices in other sectors. Research on artists' approaches to business practices such as planning, strategy, teamwork, project management and human resources, could result in the proposition of a new perspective of the artist as a creative mentor for the traditional manager.

Considering the case of Puerto Rico could be of great significance for the discussion. Puerto Rico is a Caribbean country with a Latin American culture. Like many countries in the region, this culture has been enriched by historical and cultural processes that include Indigenous people, African descended people and people of European descent. However, since 1898 Puerto Rico has been a U.S. territory, so it is subject to its legal, political and commercial framework. This framework poses major difficulties within the local culture, and artists face great challenges launching their ventures. With a cultural policy model of minimum government intervention, artists have to rely on their entrepreneurial spirit.

Often research on entrepreneurship requires a multidisciplinary approach (Ripsas, 1998). For that reason, it is important not to limit the research to a single theoretical framework or empirical research methodology. Here we first describe a qualitative methodology through in-depth semi-structured interviews with a group of six cultural entrepreneurs. Then, a quantitative approach is applied through a sample of 165 artists. Finally, a case study is used to propose cooperative entrepreneurship as an alternative for the development of medium-sized cultural enterprises (Dos Santos, 2010).

The artist-entrepreneur: motivations, experiences and evaluation

Our theoretical model has been formed on the basis of in-depth interviews with six cultural entrepreneurs in different disciplines. Several aspects related to the entrepreneurial process are examined, including the management of a cultural project and evaluation of their venture. As a result of the analysis, a model for studying the experiences of these entrepreneurs has been constructed. Without attempting to address the dilemma of whether the entrepreneur is born or made, leadership experiences were found in early stages, such as creating musical groups, producing plays or publications at school. Certainly, these efforts can be coordinated to promote cultural entrepreneurship. Also, the answers provided in the interview demonstrate that creating and sharing arts is the artists' main factor motivating their ventures. This interest goes beyond the economic outcome, although they understand it is also necessary for the project. However, dissatisfaction with the traditional industry, caused by bad experiences with companies and intermediaries, is expressed as the main external factor that exerts influence in becoming an entrepreneur. Although artists had diverse work experiences, none of the respondents had formal education in business administration.

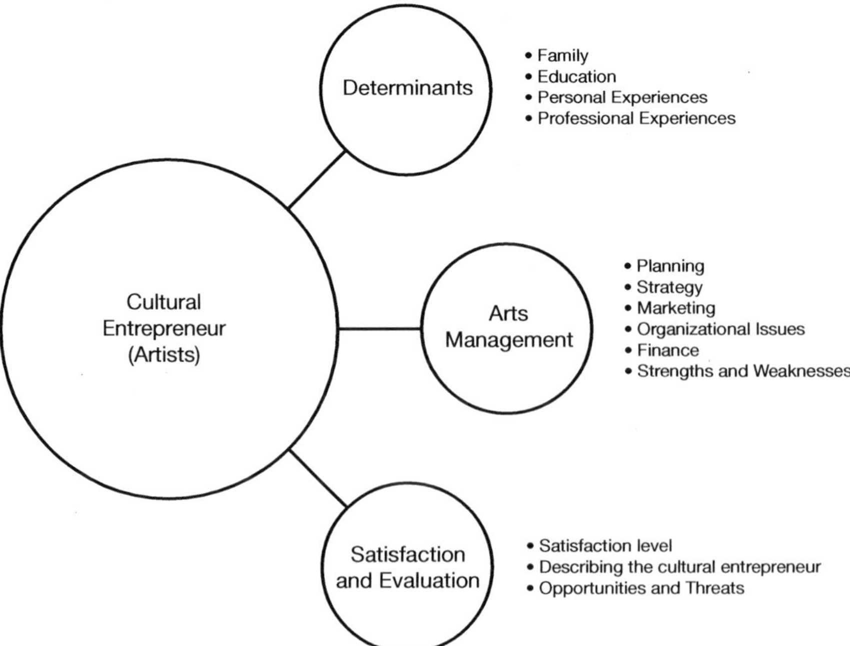

Figure 1. The artist-entrepreneur: motivations, experiences and evaluation.

Probably, the most important finding of this research is the presence of a tacit knowledge in art management practices. Our findings suggest a different vision from the traditional manager, sometimes referred to as a 'cultural mission', which relates to the cultural offering and is expressed as a social change or through collective and community welfare.

Planning is the first approach that shows some differences. The artists bring to the discussion the concept of improvisation, not as an act of lack of preparation and analysis, but through an application from the arts as the act of 'composing in front of the audience'. This happens through a process of learning and practice that enables them to adapt to changes in the external environment. Certainly, this is very consistent with the findings of academic research in business (Galbraith, 2002). Despite not using a business language, some artists seem to be clear about the concept of strategy. Similarly, some artists in the performing arts and music have developed a diversification strategy by offering creative services to private companies, understanding that this helps to improve their financial situation, expanding recognition and gaining access to resources that allow more freedom to create. Also, eliminating the middleman seems to be a strategy to promote loyalty and stimulate demand. The entrepreneurs also expressed the importance of 'competition through cooperation' between artists, understanding that it is a strategic resource that helps to cultivate demand or strengthen a niche market.

Innovation could be a natural input for artists, not only in terms of artistic creation, but through marketing variables such as distribution and promotion, tools that are essential for implementing their branding strategy. For artists, the brand is a matter of reputation, and transcending the artist-fan relationship is necessary for positioning in a very competitive market. In this regard, social networks have become an additional tool, even with the creativity required to transcend in the middle of too much information.

Regarding human resources, a flexible organizational structure and distribution of tasks was identified. Although it can be exhausting, all artists included in our research assume the role of entrepreneurs, amidst multiple roles in order to ensure the continuity and success of the project. However, within that informality and decentralization, the figure of a leader is recognized, *not as the one who has the last word, but the one who gives security to the crew*. Finally, artists use voluntary cooperation from colleagues as an alternative to finance their projects.

As research has suggested, artists demonstrate a high level of satisfaction by having greater control over their career (Menger, 1999). However, they resent the time it takes away from creative activity, and how tiring it is to *'swim against the tide'*, in clear reference to the lack of public support. Similarly, alternative mechanisms must be designed to measure the performance of these projects, understanding that economic value does not measure the total return produced by the cultural entrepreneur.[1]

Entrepreneurship education for the artist-entrepreneur

Through a survey of 165 artists, some trends were identified around their needs and interests relating to business education. Artists were interviewed in all major disciplines, including visual arts, performing arts, music and publishing. The main objectives of the research were to determine how important it is for artists to develop business skills, in which areas of management and through which means they want to access the information. Finally, their views on the development of the cultural sector were explored.

---

[1] For personal quotes, see: Javier Hernández, *El artista como emprendedor: un estudio exploratorio*, (Master Thesis, University of Puerto Rico, 2010), 37-64.

Analyzing the findings, it appears that artists recognize the importance of business education and are very interested in receiving this type of training, regardless of whether at the time of the survey they were leading cultural projects. This may suggest an interest in becoming entrepreneurs and/or expectations of engaging in arts as a full time job. An interesting aspect is that Marketing is the area that gathers the greatest interest, which contradicts the myth of the 'bohemian entrepreneur' who refuses the commercialization of his artistic creation (Ministerio de Cultura de Colombia, 2005; p 16-18). Also, a Also, a strong interest was identified in areas such as accounting and project management, which is of great importance given the way cultural enterprises are organized (Hagoort, 2003).

It is necessary to evaluate through which means they want to receive the required training. The complexity and mobility that characterizes employment in the arts, seems to influence this aspect, since seminars and the Internet are the main alternatives of interest. It is important to design proposals on specific issues and use technological tools.

In addition, it is important to consider artists' opinions when analyzing the performance of the sector and the design of public policy. In our research, artists identified four key factors in the development of cultural industries: cultural policy, financing, business education and organizational issues. In general terms, artists acknowledge the importance of developing interdisciplinary projects, financing alternatives based on the reality of the sector, more and better infrastructure for local exhibition and export, and government support promoting the importance of the arts and the role of artists in society. However, an interesting aspect is the need to create cultural cooperatives as a tool to facilitate marketing and financing. This leads to the analysis of the development of an artists' cooperative as an example of medium-sized enterprises in the cultural sector.

	Inernal	**External**
Positive	- Strengths - Cultural Mission - Improvisation - Personal Branding - Cooperation - Flexibility - Satisfaction and motivation	- Opportunities - Social Networks - Artists' cooperatives - Access to new markets - International Cooperation
Negative	- Weaknesses - Business Skills - Balance between cultural mission and economic sustainability	- Threats - Macroeconomic environment - Legal framework for cultural entrepreneurship - Access to financing - Access to distribution - Public Support

Table 1. SWOT cultural cooperatives.

Cooperative entrepreneurship: a case study

In 2001, a group of singers-songwriters decided to meet and discuss alternatives for the development of their careers. They began offering their services to entertainment businesses, rotating or raffling the performances. The revenues from those presentations were used to record their first musical production. In 2003, the group decided to become a formal cooperative, the first in more than 30 years in the arts sector.

In Puerto Rico, the cultural cooperative was formed, named *Taller Cé*, which means a workshop and the pronunciation of the letter C, because in Spanish the words culture, cooperatives and singer-songwriters, all begin with that letter. The mission of the Cooperative was to provide stable jobs and income for their members, although its philosophical approach was to change the working conditions of the music industry. Under the slogan of being *'on the artists' side'* and *'authors with authority'*, the Cooperative offered an alternative model to the earning distribution in the music industry and the extent of phonographic licenses, which in this case remained under the ownership of the artist (Ramírez , 2011). Under this model, 7 compilation albums were produced. In 2005, the Cooperative opened a theater with a capacity for 200 people, a stage that throughout three years produced over 1,000 events of artists in all disciplines, both locally and internationally. Similarly, the Cooperative diversified its operations, establishing a school of arts, rehearsal rooms, a recording studio, a division offering educational workshops for different populations, and creative services to companies.

Under the cooperative model, member-owners, which in this case came to be 54 singer-songwriters, made monthly contributions of $10, equivalent to a stock. The surplus, after separating 20% for educational and social reserves, were distributed on the basis of patronage to the Cooperative, in this case hours worked. In this model, all partners have the same right to vote, regardless of the total shares held.

One of the great benefits of this cooperative model was to provide access to promotion and distribution, something traditionally reserved for large companies. The theater became an incubator for artistic projects that allowed access to an interested audience and good quality feedback. The democratic and inclusive nature triggered an avalanche of projects that strengthened networks between industry actors, especially multidisciplinary collaboration. On the other hand, despite being a self-managed and self-financed project, it provided a platform for the efficient use of labor subsidies. While the cooperative held its administrative structure, production costs for artistic performances were minimal. In this way, the artists benefited indirectly from subsidies that normally are not within their reach.

However, the experience of Taller Cé as an artists' cooperative was not all positive. In 2010 the company became inactive after a long internal conflict and conflict with government agencies, caused mainly by a legal framework that did not recognize the particular characteristics of the cultural sector. Similarly, it is difficult for cultural organizations to achieve economies of scale and standardize processes when their main input is based on an artistic nature. In that sense, it is important that the organizational design responds to the cultural mission, having the flexibility to manage projects and still benefit from specialization. Another important challenge is to properly balance economic and cultural indicators in the internal assessment of performance.

Conclusions

Research related to cultural entrepreneurship requires a lot of emphasis on the artists' experiences. It is essential to use multiple methodologies and build an applicable body of knowledge. Similarly, it is necessary to use technology to develop educational tools, appropriate to the needs of each segment. It should be a priority for the cultural sector to strengthen supporting networks, both formal and informal, and adapt the legal framework for the development of medium-sized cultural enterprises.

However, adequate research depends largely on a system of indicators, collecting all the dimensions of value that are generated in the cultural sector. We propose developing the concept of 'Cultural Return' as a system collecting the total surplus generated by cultural entrepreneurs, including the financial statements. This may incorporate their impact on the cultural sector, community welfare and on the implementation of cultural policy.

References

- Bhide, Amar (1994). 'How Entrepreneurs Craft Strategies that Work.' *Harvard Business Review* (March-April 1994): 150-161.
- Caves, Ricard (2000). *Creative Industries: Contracts between arts and commerce.* Cambridge: Harvard Press, 2000.
- Colbert, Francois (2003). 'Entrepreneurship and Leadership in Marketing the Arts.' *International Journal of Arts Management* 6, no. 1 (2003): 30-39.
- Dos Santos Duisenberg, Edna (2010): *Creative Economy: 2010 Report.* UNCTAD United Nations, Geneva.
- Elmeier, Andrea (2003). 'Cultural Entrepreneurialism: On the Changing Relationship Between the Arts, Culture and Employment.' *The International Journal of Cultural Policy* 9, no. 1 (2003): 3-16.
- Galbraith, Jay (2002). *Designing Organizations: An Executive Guide to Strategy, Structure, and Process.* California: John Wiley & Sons, 2002.
- Groves, Kevin c.s. (2008). 'An Examination of the Nonlinear Thinking Style Profile Stereotype of Successful Entrepreneurs.' *Journal of Enterprising Culture* 16, no. 2 (2008): 133-159.
- Hagoort, Giep (2003). *Art Management: Entrepreneurial Style.* The Netherlands: Eburon Academic Publishers, Utrecht.
- Hernández, Javier (2010). *'El artista como emprendedor: un estudio exploratorio.'* Master Thesis. University of Puerto Rico.
- Menger, Pierre-Michael (1999). 'Artistic Labor Markets and Careers.' *Annual Review Sociology* 25 (1999): 541-574
- Ministerio de Cultura de Colombia (2005). *Arte y Aparte: Manual para el emprendimiento en artes e industrias creativas.* (Colombia: Ministry of Culture, 2005).
- Mintzberg, Henry (1998). 'Covert Leadership: Notes on Managing Professionals.' *Harvard Business Review* (November-December, 1998): 140-147.
- Quartesan, Alessandra c.s. (2007). *Las Industrias Culturales en América Latina y el Caribe: Desafíos y Oportunidades.* Banco Interamericano de Desarrollo, 2007.
- Ramirez, José J (2011). *'Cooperativa Taller de Cantautores: Vicisitudes de una cooperativa cultural de trabajadores.'* Paper presented at the 1st Biennial Conference on Cooperatives and Solidarity Economy, Fajardo, Puerto Rico, February 26, 2011.
- Ripsas, Sven (1998). 'Towards an Interdisciplinary Theory of Entrepreneurship.' *Small Business Economics* 10 (1998): 103-115.
- Wong, Poh c.s. (2005): 'Entrepreneurship, Innovation and Economic Growth: Evidence from GEM Data.' *Small Business Economics* 24, (2005): 335-350.

About the author
Javier J. Hernández-Acosta (PR) is a PhD student in Entrepreneurial Development at the Interamerican University of Puerto Rico. He received an MBA from the University of Puerto Rico, and is a part-time lecturer at the University of the Sacred Heart. He is also a musician and founder of Inversión Cultural, a project for cultural entrepreneurs.
javihernandez@yahoo.com

Miriam van de Kamp

Abstract

Traditionally, research on international cultural industries mainly addresses the global operation of companies, and focuses on their overall operation and structure. An analysis of the operation of Sony, Universal and Warner's music and film divisions in the Dutch market between 1990 and 2005 showed that the local operation of a major actor is not only based on international principles of the global economy. This chapter departs from these findings and discusses another way to look at the operation of (international) cultural industries. The findings imply that research into the entrepreneurial principles of these industries should not only examine which principles are used and why, but that one should also explore how culture, values and the networks and career paths of managers affect the use of these principles.

The role of organization culture

Strategy and structure are not isolated elements of a company, as they are often viewed in business theories, but are developed based on the company's organization culture and implementation by the company's managers (Hofstede, 2005). Changes in structure or strategy do not become apparent as long as employees that apply them remain the same and do not change their activities. Furthermore, issues such as a company's market perception, its management and its reaction to market opportunities are defined by the company's origins and the ways it developed to deal with the dynamic market of the cultural industries; its organization culture (Küng-Shanklemann, 2000). The important role of organization culture for the operation of companies in the cultural industries becomes especially apparent in three aspects of organization culture: the company's country of origin, its adaptability and the way the company deals with uncertainty and risks.

With regard to the main players in the cultural industries, there is an important distinction between those with American origins and those with non-American origins. The central position of the United States in most of the cultural industries, in combination with its large home market, results in some American majors, primarily focusing on American artists or products and having a less adaptive approach to smaller foreign markets such as the Dutch one. Other American majors do show some interest for domestic products in smaller foreign markets but solely during periods when the market shares for these products are on the rise, and demand in their home market saturated. This highlights that not only the country of origin but also the adaptability of a company, another element of the organization culture, influences its operation.

Amongst the non-American majors are European majors such as EMI, the former BMG (later SonyBMG, now Sony) and former Polygram (now Vivendi Universal). Not benefiting from a (very) large home market, they rather try to achieve competitive advantages of scope, by offering their international audience a broad portfolio of national and international products.

In general, there are two opposite kinds of organization culture: adaptive and unadaptive ones, which determine how a company deals with the dilemma of creativity & innovation versus control (Küng-Shankleman, p 217). A media firm with an adaptive organization culture is open to external opportunities to develop the company. When the organization's orientation is unadaptive, a company is isolating itself from its environment and might therefore miss out on new market opportunities. A company in the cultural industries with an adaptive organization culture is likely to offer its product managers a large degree of creative autonomy to explore new products. This may result in a more diverse and innovative product portfolio than that of companies which organization's culture is unadaptive.

Consumer's taste for cultural products is subject to trends and differs from person to person (DiMaggio, 1977). It is therefore difficult to predict and anticipate demand. 'Nobody knows' which new song, film or book will be successful (Caves, 2000). Companies in the cultural industries have, therefore, developed institutional principles to reduce uncertainty and to deal with high risks, such as to produce goods within a particular school, genre or style that have proven to be successful in the past (Rya, 1999). Besides, some firms have designed a hierarchical and streamlined organization that acquires, promotes and distributes a small number of cultural products that have a high chance of becoming successful. Other companies adopt adaptive processes to ensure access to different resources that enable them to pick up successful products. It offers them the flexibility to join new trends but also contains the risk of having no successful products. They, however, perceive taking risks as an essential way to explore new business and product opportunities. The preference for control or flexibility is reflected in the organization culture and the related centralized or decentralized structure for the creative and business activities within the company (DiMaggio, 1977).

In the cultural industries, companies continuously have some form of product innovation as every film, book or CD is a new product. Process innovation or new ways for distribution, however, rarely occur because internal institutional structures have developed over time and have become common standards. They usually ease the process and decisions within the company, but offer less flexibility to tap into newly emerging market opportunities. It partly explains why computer company Apple, an outsider in the music industry, was the one that successfully opened an online music store and designed a digital media player, iTunes. However, a (new) manager within the company can perceive the market differently and operate as an entrepreneur, a cultural broker. The company may focus on the threats such as barriers and risks, whereas entrepreneurs may centre on the opportunities and discover new (niche) markets (Van de Kamp, 2009).

Need to include organization culture and cultural entrepreneurs in analysis

Processes that have mostly been perceived as primarily guided by economic logic are heavily influenced by the discussed cultural factors, organization culture and cultural entrepreneurs. This may actually result in different and unexpected outcomes such as involvement in domestic music or film products in a small local market. Future research on the cultural industries should, therefore, also address how staff at different levels of the company perceive a market, how they assess innovations and dynamics in the cultural industries (e.g. disruptive technologies and multiple platforms) and how they interpret and adapt the companies' strategies and products. Besides, it is important to take into account where the company was founded (Europe, the United States, Asia or for example Latin America), if it adapts its operation to the dynamics in the market environment or that it rather has an unadaptive orientation and if it prefers control above exploration and taking risks or the other way round.

Given the social and cultural processes, but also the economic logic and (international) strategies within the cultural industries, the use of only one research discipline is in many cases not appropriate. Organizational structures and corporate strategies, such as studied by business theories and media economics, serve and can explain the efficient operation of a company guiding it in dynamic and uncertain markets. Individuals, however, develop these organizational and economic tools and alter them through their application and interpretation (Hofstede, 2005). It is, therefore, important to take this human factor, such as studied by cultural sociologists, into account when analyzing the business behavior of companies in the cultural industries. Further research has shown that the combination of insights from various disciplines can result in a more comprehensive view and new insights (Van de Kamp, 2009).

A new analytical framework

Based on the need to include organization culture and cultural entrepreneurs in analyses of the operation of companies in the cultural industries and to apply a multidisciplinary approach, an analytical framework has been developed (figure 1). The framework takes economic logic as well as cultural factors into account. The elements strategy, structure and market perception relate to the industrial organization model. This model is used in media economics to analyze the operation of different media industries. It assumes a causal relation between the structure of the market, a firm's behavior and its success (Hoskins, 2004). The elements in combination with organization culture refer to the way Küng-Shankleman (2000) describes the relation between an organization's culture, its (changing) environment and its strategy. Based on our research findings, cultural entrepreneurs were included as an element in the framework.

The elements each can take various shapes (see figure 2) that affect how a media and entertainment company in theory deals with the issues of creativity versus commerce and autonomy versus control. The unique interplay between strategy, organization culture, cultural entrepreneurs, and structure defines how a company perceives the market in which it operates and how that shapes its activities. This interplay is dynamic and can change over time because the elements may change.

Figure 2 is an application of the framework that is developed to enable its use in empirical analyses of the operation of companies in the cultural industries. Every element consists of a number of components, which each can have different forms as well. The components together delineate how the company operates, and help to explain its product portfolio and business behavior.

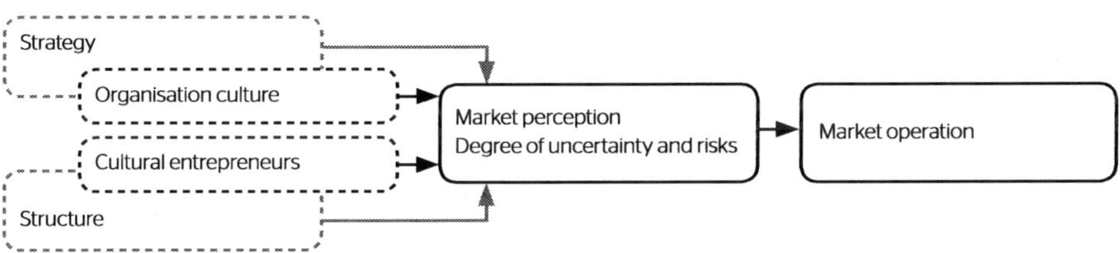

Figure 1 Another way to look at the operation of (international) cultural industries.

Element	Components	Possible forms
Strategy	Product strategy	Production in and for home market -> international network of production and distribution Small number of products -> broad and extensive portfolio
	Investment strategy	Mix of 'cash cows' and 'stars' -> mix with 'question marks' and 'dogs'
Organization culture	Country of origin	USA, Europe, Asia, Central and Latin America, Africa, Australia
	Adaptability	Adaptive-> unadaptive
	Way of dealing with uncertainty and risks	Control -> flexible access
Cultural entrepreneurs	Presence	Present or absent
	Position within the company	Managing director or manager in creative department
	Role within the company	Prominent -> not prominent
	Personal style	Explorer but conservative -> risk taker
Structure	Ownership structure	Part of entertainment corporation or not Owner = employee -> owner is not involved in daily operations
	Organization structure	Hierarchical -> open Centralized -> decentralized
	Relationship headquarters and subsidiaries	Directive -> interactive
Market perception	Company's impression of the market	Risky -> stable and profitable Pure distribution function -> good resource
	Reaction to developments in the market	Laggards -> innovators

Table 1. Indicators for the analytical framework.

In order to deepen and improve our understanding of the dynamics of the cultural industries, we have to adopt another way to look at their operations. For a start, research into the current entrepreneurial principles of the cultural and creative industries should not only examine which principles are used and why, but should also explore how (organization) culture, values and the networks and the career paths of managers affect the use of these.

References

- Caves, Richard (2000). *Creative industries. Contracts between Art and Commerce.* Cambridge, Massachusetts: Harvard University Press.
- 'Cultural Industries' (2006) In: *The Business of Culture. Strategic Perspectives on Entertainment and Media.* Edited by J. Lampel, J. Shamsie and T.K. Lant,), 275-286. Mahwah, NJ: Lawrence Erlbaum Associates, 2006.
- DiMaggio, Paul (1977). 'Market structure, the creative process and popular culture' *Journal of Popular Culture* 11(2) (1977): 436-452.
- Hofstede, Gert, and Gert Jan Hofstede (2005). *Cultures and Organizations. Software of the Mind. Intercultural Cooperation and Its Importance for Survival.* Revised and expanded 2nd edition. New York: McGraw-Hill.
- Hoskins, C., S. McFayden and A. Finn (2004). *Media Economics: Applying Economics to New and Traditional Media.* Thousand Oaks: Sage.
- Küng-Shanklemann, Lucy (2000). *Inside the BBC and CNN. Managing Media Organizations.* London: Routledge.
- Lampel J., and J. Shamsie (1999). 'Uncertain Globalization: Evolutionary Scenarios for the Future Development of Cultural Industries' In: *The Business of Culture. Strategic Perspectives on Entertainment and Media.* Edited by J. Lampel, J. Shamsie and T.K. Lant,), 275-286.
- Negus, Keith (1999). *Music Genres and Corporate Cultures.* London: Routledge.
- Picard, Robert (2002). *The Economics and Financing of Media Companies.* New York: Fordham University Press.
- Ryan, J., and W.M. Wentworth (1999). *Media and Society. The Production of Culture in the Mass Media.* Boston: Allyn and Bacon.
- Schein, E (2004). *Organizational Culture and Leadership.* 3rd Edition. San Francisco: Jossey-Bass.
- Van de Kamp, Miriam (2009). 'Where Corporate Culture and Local Markets Meet. Music and Film Majors in the Netherlands, 1990-2005'. PhD dissertation, Erasmus University.

About the author

Miriam van de Kamp (BE) is a postdoctoral research fellow at the Centre for Modern Urban Studies at Leiden University. She obtained her PhD at Erasmus University in 2009. Her dissertation addressed how music and film majors in the Netherlands dealt with the Dutch market and domestic products between 1990 and 2005.

m.c.van.de.kamp@cdh.leidenuniv.nl

Strategic practice in creative organizations

Johan Kolsteeg

Abstract

This research project (2009 – 2013) looks at strategy formation in creative organizations in the Dutch city of Utrecht. A Strategy-as-Practice approach is taken on the subject: discourse analysis and longitudinal observation are expected to lead to a better understanding of the strategic and operational thinking in these organizations. In this chapter, preliminary observations and reflections are presented. They pertain to the themes of power, growth, maintaining artistic visibility and identity, networking and the relationship between creativity and business in daily practice.

Introduction

Looking at how growth and development models apply to arts organizations, Hagoort (1998) describes a model of discrete phases in an organization's life. In this view, such phases are separated by strategic turning points, critical events that force an organization to reconsider its strategy. Strategy is understood here as planning ahead, within an objectively knowable reality. Several authors (a.o. Weick 1979, Mintzberg 1998) observe that strategy has evolved, from planning beforehand into reflecting upon recent events, and that the phenomenon of strategy formulation is more influenced by the fast pace of change in society than traditional strategic models can accommodate. Also, phase-theory can be criticized *in view of the circumstance that one of the defining features of the so-called new economy [in which creative organizations operate] is its persistent postponement of anything like the stage of maturity' (Scott, 2006: 2).*

The idea that a strategic decision and a subsequent change have a causal relationship may seem logical at first sight, but research (quoted in Hendry, 2000) shows it is not always easy to pin down how one leads to the other. This realization has consequences for how we think about strategy. Mintzberg (1998) broadens the concept of strategy by observing that it can have an emergent character or can even be understood as rationalization in hindsight. Weick (1979) and Hendry (2000) conceptualize an organization as a social system, in which actors continually *'make sense'* and influence their environment, proposing that strategic decisions can be understood as a 'discourse' in this practice. This position opens a perspective on the matter that does justice to the complexity of practice, human interaction and motivations.

A research project on strategic practices

Strategy is a core area of attention for creative organizations. Since we contend that management in a cultural and creative context encounters different challenges from management in non-creative sectors, it is assumed that strategy formation in creative organizations has specific important characteristics of which we should be aware.

We recently initiated a research project relating directly to the proposed workfield of arts management alumni. The theoretical framework of our study is based on Hendry's (2000) conceptualization of strategic decisions as part of an organizational discourse inside a complex practice (Tsoukas, 2005) in which organizational actors continuously 'make sense' of their situation (Weick 1979). Following this line of reasoning, the strand in organizational science known as *Strategy-as-Practice* builds on the insight that people continually influence, and are influenced by, their 'organizational and institutional context' (Johnson et.al. 2007, 7). Bourdieu's concepts of cultural capital and habitus offer us instruments to understand how organizational actors make sense of their situation. Whittington (2010) and Gomez (2010) invoke Giddens' constructionist perspective to arrive at a position that is attentive to *'the subtle relation between agents and the field embedded in practice'* (Gomez 2010: 150), and to how agency and structure define an actor's autonomy. Tsoukas (2005, 2010) informs our theoretical framework with insights from complexity theory (also Stacey 2007), while showing how a narrative (Tsoukas and Hatch 2001) analysis can lead to understanding complex practice.

This leads to an understanding of strategy as part of routine and daily practice; as an interaction of organizational agents who exist in a complex context and may experience this context as hindering or conducive to their strategy. We attempt to understand this interaction from a narrative point of view.

Strategy-as-Practice allows for a diversity of methodological approaches. Discourse analysis (Heracleous 2006, Rouleau 2010), ethnography (Samra-Fredericks 2003) and other forms of grounded research are found (Johnson et.al. 2007). For this research we have used discourse analysis and longitudinal observation.

Cultural and creative field

For the present research we look at cultural and creative organizations in Utrecht. The geographical limitation of Utrecht is a purposeful one, because of the shared geographical and economic-political and cultural-political context, which enhances the comparability of the cases in the observation, following Mommaas (2009). Scott (2006, page 3) offers us the option to delineate the field of observation. For Scott, a creative field is *'any system of social relationships that shapes or influences human ingenuity and inventiveness...'* (thus defining creativity) *'... and that is the site of concomitant innovations',* where *'the innovations it triggers will also act back upon it'.* In this view, *'such a field might correspond with any number of different organizational arrangements'.*

Ten creative for-profit and not-for-profit organizations in Utrecht are sampled, covering a range of creative fields and business types, such as a youth music theater group, a game design company, an *'imagineering'* company, a jazz concert hall and a graphic design company. The sample contains subsidized foundations and for-profit firms; experienced teams and start-ups; traditional organizational forms and virtual networks.

The units for analysis in the first empirical round are texts written over a period of two years; subsidy applications, internal reports, public relations material and personal blogs. This constitutes a selection ranging from carefully deliberated texts in which strategic aims are consciously embedded (Heracleous 2006, Daigle and Rouleau 2010) to spontaneous texts. The aim of the first observation is to disclose underlying themes in organizational discourses. The distance between the static material of texts to the organizational practice, as well as the absence of spoken input from the writers/organizational actors themselves during the process of coding, reduces the risk of influencing organizational practice during observation. As a conclusion of the analysis, the organizational actors are interviewed and confronted with the observations. The second empirical round consists of observations of live interaction.

The observations show how creativity and artistry and business are confronted, and how for-profit and not-for-profit creative organizations show different approaches to this theme.

Initial findings

Organizational actors tend to distinguish several relevant networks. First there is a horizontal network of similar organizations in which they aim to obtain or improve their position, driven by their creative identity. The word network is understood as *'a group of people sharing our philosophy'.* The second network is a vertical network of institutional or business partners, chosen for a particular role they can play, actively or passively, in strengthening the organization's position. A word count of the surveyed documents shows that *'cooperation'* was the most frequently used expression. The city administration is considered an important part of the vertical network.

Subsidized organizations and the city administration are caught in a discourse pertaining to the question of artistic growth, understood as the expansion of activities that have previously had artistic and popular success. In this discourse, artistic considerations are paramount, while the need for a business underwriting of this growth is downplayed. So, growth is related to expansion and agency inside artistic identity. Indeed, for-profit firms concur with subsidized organizations on how they prioritize artistic identity. They too tend to define growth in terms of creative reputation, but are more explicit about organizational growth: they try to avoid it, in order to protect creative identity.

Observed commercial organizations differ from subsidized ones in balancing creativity and business. They are observed to dismiss the potentially unmanageable *'out of the box'* paradigm of creative problem solving, and develop structures in order to manage the creative process. By comparison, subsidized organizations - despite showing agency for the middle-long term, which is required in the growth discourse mentioned above - can experience the individual creative process as intrinsically unmanageable, and project management is seen as a rude interference in creative processes. In order to solve this tension, profit organizations are seen to develop client management- and conceptualization processes, in which artistic freedom, identity and process are balanced, and where the client is involved *('co-creation')* to avoid cognitive dissonance. What triggers this choice?

Building mode

Originating from an arts-background themselves, members of the start-ups are also seen to experience a growing distance between themselves, existing in a commercial, independent and risky context, and the representatives of the subsidy-driven *'old world'*, represented by people whom they know and understand well, but who are seen to belong to an older and relatively protected generation.
We encountered a cultural organization dealing with an acute threat, reverting to a top-down strategy formation, which is in contrast with the organization's regular open and democratic organizational culture. The regular coping strategy (Heidegger's *'dwelling mode'*) is temporally suspended to determine how the exogenous turbulence is (to be) understood, and how the organization will react strategically (now the organization is in Heidegger's *'building mode'*). The strategy is formulated in artistic terms, but simultaneously a business strategy is developed separately.

What does this mean? The strategic episode, in which the organizations communicate their organizational strategy, brings Mintzbergs' definitions of strategic *'schools'* to mind. In these schools, strategy formation can be understood as an analytical and formal process. In contrast, however, the general practice in these organizations would much more indicate that we're looking at organizations with a collective consciousness for routine and gradual strategy formation, reminding us of Mintzbergs *'cultural school'*. The temporary suspension of dwelling mode and its corresponding organizational paradigm seems to reveal how the organization understands *'strategy-making'*: as a top down management matter, instantiating the power of the institutional context. Both subsidized and independent organizations experience crises as a trigger to develop a sound business structure. Actors' expectations about the efficiency of their choices after experiencing a crisis depend on whether they perceive the institutional context to either conduce or hinder their options, and whether they consider themselves to be *'in charge'* of developments.

References

- Alasuutari, Pertti. (1995). Researching Culture: Qualitative Method and Cultural Studies. London: Sage.
- Daigle, Pascale. and Linda Rouleau. 2010. 'Strategic Plans in Arts organizations: a Tool of Compromise between Artistic and Manegerial Values.' International Journal of Arts Management 12 (3): 13-30.
- Hagoort, Giep. (1998). Strategische dialoog in de kunstensector. Eburon.
- Hendry, John. (2000). 'Strategic Decision Making, Discourse, and Strategy as Social Practice'. Journal of Management Studies 40 (1): 955-978.
- Heracleous, Loizos. (2006). Discourse, Interpretation, organization. Cambridge: Cambridge University Press.
- Heracleous, Loizos and John Hendry. (2000). 'Discourse and the Study of organization: Toward a Structurational Perspective.' Human Relations 53 (10): 1251-1286.
- Johnson, Gerry, Ann Langley, Leif Melin and Richard Whittington. (2007). Strategy as Practice: Research Directions and Resources. Cambridge: Cambridge University Press.
- Mintzberg, Henry. (1998) . Strategy Safari. New York: Free Press.
- Mommaas, Hans. (2009). 'Spaces of Culture and Economy: Mapping the Cultural-Creative Cluster Landscape'. In Creative Economies, Kong, L. and J. O'Connor. Springer.
- Samra-Fredericks, Dalvir. (2003). 'Strategizing as Lived Experience and Strategists' Everyday Efforts to Shape Strategic Direction.' Journal of Management Studies 40 (1): 40-57.
- Scott, Alan. (2006). 'Entrepreneurship, innovation and industrial development: geography and the creative field revisited.' Small Business Economics 26 (1): 1-24.
- Stacey, Ralph D. (2007). Strategic Management and organizational Dynamics. The Challenge of Complexity. Edinburgh: Pearson Education Limited.
- Tsoukas, Haridimos and Mary Jo Hatch. (2001). 'Complex Thinking, Complex Practice: The Case for a Narrative Approach to organizational Complexity.' Human Relations 54: 979-1013.
- Tsoukas, Haridimos. (2005). Complex Knowledge. Studies in organizational Epistemology. Oxford: Oxford University Press.
- Tsoukas, Haridimos. (2010). 'Practice, Strategy Making and Intentionality.' In Cambridge Handbook of Strategy as Practice, edited by D. Golkorskhi, L. Rouleau. D. Seidl and E. Vaara, 47-62. Cambridge: Cambridge University Press.
- Weick, Karl. (1979) . The Social Psychology of Organizing. Randomhouse, New York.
- Whittington, Richard. (2010) . 'Giddens, Structuration Theory and Strategy as Practice.' In Cambridge Handbook of Strategy as Practice, edited by D. Golkorskhi, L. Rouleau. D. Seidl and E. Vaara, 109-126. Cambridge: Cambridge University Press.

About the author

Johan Kolsteeg (NL) held positions in contemporary and classical music as a musicologist, programmer, journalist, policy maker, advisor for funding bodies. At present he is Professor of Arts and Economics at the Utrecht School for the Arts, and conducts PhD research into strategy in creative organizations.
jkolst@xs4all.nl

Abstract

As small arts organizations (SAOs) navigate institutional and economic constraints, they use creative entrepreneurship to balance their mission and money. In this chapter Lévi-Strauss' concept of 'bricolage' is applied to analyze multiple case narratives, and an in-depth case study of a small theatre company. Both the use of space, and the use of human resources have been studied. Three factors are identified, that allow creative entrepreneurs to engage in the 'bricolage': flexibility, close-knit personal networking, and use of IT.

Bricolage: Creating with anything available at hand

As small arts organizations (SAOs) navigate institutional and economic constraints, they use creative entrepreneurship to balance their mission and money. Little research has been conducted to determine how SAOs survive in such unfavorable environments and still maintain their creative vitality, particularly how they mobilize their resources. Coined by Lévi-Strauss (1967), 'bricolage' means making do by utilizing the resources at hand. This paper treats bricolage not only as it is practiced in creating, but also in managing and presenting the arts. The quest for creative solutions has become pervasive in the field of business. Many scholars have sought alternative business models, in which managers are also creative artists, making use of their scarce resources (Drucker, 1985; Mintzberg, 1973, 1975, 1989; Reckhenrich, Kupp, & Anderson, 2009; Semler & Mintzberg, 2005). Only recently have a few scholars recognized the use of bricolage in entrepreneurship (Baker, Miner, & Eesley, 2003; Baker & Nelson, 2005; Duymedjian & Ruling, 2010; Garud & Karnoe, 2003; Kincheloe, 2005; Senyard, Baker & Davidson, 2009). This has begun to create a body of substantial descriptions and valuable insights, especially for business administration and entrepreneurship.

The research is based on two qualitative research methods, combined with cross-references: multiple case narratives of 13 SAOs in Columbus, Ohio; and a single in-depth case study of a small theatre company. Weaving these two methods together, a grounded theory was developed of how *bricolage* acts as a legitimating entrepreneurial mechanism for an SAO to defy environmental constraints. In our research a fair number of individuals were interviewed in a variety of SAOs including a gallery, printmaker, orchestra, band, theatre, glass art company, artist collective, dance company, and a heritage preservation organization. For our case study, almost every event and performance was attended and systematically observed, various members were shadowed, and company documents were examined in the in-depth case study.

Despite a scarcity of resources, the majority of SAOs manage to realize their goals. As one respondent noted, his organization *'always gets the job done somehow'*. And this *'somehow'* can be captured in the term *'bricolage'*. Indeed, it can be argued that artists and arts organizations have always practiced bricolage in working with very few resources, rather than accepting limitations.

Bricolage in art production

It is not difficult to find artists who practice bricolage to produce their artworks. Musicians use many everyday objects like trashcans, broomsticks, or saws as musical instruments as in the popular non-verbal musical *'Stomp'*. Using and positioning ordinary objects in the arts has even become a trend in the visual arts, which goes back to 1917 when Marcel Duchamp used a urinal and named it *'Fountain'*, which has been recognized as the most influential modern artwork of all time (BBC News, 2004). As in *'Stomp'* and *'Fountain'*, many SAOs are flexible in using non-arts objects to produce their artworks. I observed a potent example of bricolage in one small theatre production, when they made every kind of sound effect, using daily items that were not necessarily designed for making sounds. In one corner of the stage, the production manager scrunched a handful of dried twigs to create the sound of the city on fire; or he hit the desk with his fist to imitate a giant robot's footsteps.

From the study it was noted that technology expands the pool of SAOs' existing resources, and invigorates the practice of bricolage. Most individuals at SAOs have a 'nothing to lose attitude' that makes them flexible about adopting new technologies early, which in turn collectively informs their innovativeness. Earlier studies suggest that firm innovativeness plays an important role in shaping the outcomes of bricolage (Anderson, 2008; Rogers, 2003). For example, in our study one of the organizations used a presentation software package to create a dynamic background of scenes and various lighting effects. A bandleader used the looping pedal, a digital sampler built into easy-to-use pedals, to create looping layers of beat and melody. By using this pedal to record his voice, beat box, and repeated guitar melody, he created a rich musical effect for such a small band. In a performance of a small theatre company, a one-man band used the looping pedal to create sonorous background music and ear-catching songs. He literally stood alone at a corner of the multi-stage, while he performed not only the vocals, but also all of the instruments, including beat-boxing, guitar, keyboards, and percussions by himself. These are just a few examples of bricolage in creating the arts.

Bricolage in the use of space

Flexibility in the use of space is another example of how SAOs practice *bricolage*, using available artistic and managerial resources. For example, a small theatre company utilized the kitchen and dining area of a local farmer's market as the venue for one of its performances. Members actively used every corner of the kitchen and dining area to create a multi-stage. Alternatively, a small dance company used corners in hospitals, churches, nursing homes, and assisted living centers for its performances. SAOs do not only use public spaces that are meant for other purposes, but also use abandoned places as their stages or studios. For example, a glass cooperative transformed a vacant tire factory into a glass arts facility. Another theatre group turned an auto body shop, which was no longer in use, into a unique and useful theatre venue. Such transformations of abandoned spaces into arts venues have been supported and implemented as a revitalization strategy in many cities. Since many SAOs actually cannot afford to rent an office for their managerial works and meetings, any place where there is a table and some chairs can serve as their office. A coffeeshop is often a good alternative. For example, a small theatre was lucky to rent an office space downtown for a minimal fee from a large arts presenter, while it continued to use a local coffeeshop as its longtime office. A dance company also used a local coffeeshop as its office. For an artist collective, a big room behind a local bar served as an office and meeting room. Using such public spaces as offices provides SAOs with unexpected opportunities to connect with their local communities. First of all, once the owner of the space gets to know the organization, s/he often becomes a staunch supporter. Second, since those spaces like coffeeshops and bars are public spaces, SAOs have opportunities to meet their audiences in person and receive live feedback.

Bricolage in the use of human resources

The most important practice of bricolage in SAOs is their flexible use of human resources. Once SAOs recognize an individual's potential, they are open to giving him/her new tasks. The artistic director of a small theatre company becomes a Jack-of-all-trades. Another member evolved from costumer to actor, to stage manager, and finally to operations manager. Subsequently, she was asked by a local children's theatre to be the stage manager for their upcoming play. SAOs often use amateurs to fill in professional positions. For example, a music director never had any formal music training, but was self-taught. Most of her training was through various church choirs and community arts organizations, with some additional private lessons. The show she directed became a big hit and consequently, she has enjoyed high repute in Columbus's theatre circles. In both of these examples, bricolage of human resources positions SAOs as the incubator of the arts world, providing on-the-job training and professional development opportunities.

SAOs carry out bricolage in human resources through their personal networking. In many cases, they import their managerial experts through their boards. A marketing specialist at a major publishing company was in charge of marketing for a small artist collective where she was a board member. Similarly, another SAO had a sub-committee of its board, comprised of professionals in marketing and communication. A theatre contacted the founder of a marketing and advertising agency, after seeing his blog posting in which he expressed his hope to be cast in Thornton Wilder's 'Our Town'. Thus began their collaboration, and thereby the theatre's fundraiser show was launched. Through this collaboration, the theatre gained marketing/managerial expertise and contributed highly reputable artistic skills. Soon after, the company expanded the one-time fundraiser into its regular program at the beginning of each season so that it could afford to produce the kinds of original works it preferred, even though they were money-losing productions.

Bricolage: An artist's way of entrepreneurship

Through the analysis of a selection of SAOs, three factors were identified that allow them to engage in bricolage: flexibility, close-knit personal networking, and use of IT. These factors are in line with the elements associated with bricolage as identified by Baker and Nelson (2005). Flexibility, which enables SAOs to adapt to fast-changing and uncertain situations, is aligned with what they termed, *'violation of norms'*. Close-knit personal networking with SAOs' constituencies tends to grow into *'multiple networks'* (Baker & Nelson, 2005), which enable SAOs to multiply their existing resources. In addition, IT helps many individuals in SAOs to carry out their artistic and managerial tasks on demand, on the spur of the moment. These three factors work together for SAOs to realize effective results from practicing bricolage.

Bricolage can also have a downside. Engaging in bricolage can prompt SAOs to neglect to plan ahead, believing that they can solve any problems with whatever resources they may have at hand. Indeed, being so accustomed to improvising, many SAOs lack a concrete long-term plan. In some cases bricolage prohibited SAOs from making any plans beyond their immediate projects. Regarding this drawback of bricolage, Baker and Nelson (2005) pointed out that bricolage may be harmful if not used judiciously and that judicious use of bricolage can result in sound growth of the firm.

Bricolage has recently become a topic of discussion in entrepreneurship research; and studies about bricolage have not been developed fully to create any deductive theories yet. However, bricolage offers researchers a useful lens with which to view SAOs' entrepreneurial practices. As my research has shown, artists as budding entrepreneurs in SAOs often practice bricolage. Therefore, as reflected in the title to this paper, I refer to bricolage as 'an artist's way of entrepreneurship', which can provide models for the wider world of arts and business.

References

- Anderson, O.J. (2008). A bottom-up perspective on innovations. *Administration & Society*, 40(1), p. 54-78.
- Baker, T., & Nelson, R.E. (2005). Creating something from nothing: Resource construction through entrepreneurial bricolage. *Administrative Science Quarterly*, 50(3), p. 329-366.
- Baker, T., Miner, A.S., & Eesley, D.T. (2003). Improvising firms: Bricolage, account giving and improvisational competencies in the founding process. *Research Policy*, p. 32, 255-276.
- BBC News. (2004). Duchamp's urinal tops art survey. Retrieved from http://news.bbc.co.uk/2/hi/entertainment/4059997.stm.
- Chang, W. (2011). Small arts organizations: Supporting their creative vitality. Unpublished doctoral dissertation, The Ohio State University, Columbus.
- Drucker, P.F. (1985). *Innovation and entrepreneurship: Practice and principles*. New York: Harper & Row.
- Duymedjian, R., & Ruling, C. (2010). Towards a foundation of bricolage in organization and management theory. *Organization Studies*, 31(2), p. 133-151.
- Garud, R., & Karnoe, P. (2003). Bricolage vs. breakthrough: Distributed and embedded agency in technology entrepreneurship. *Research Policy*, 32(2), p. 277-300.
- Kincheloe, J. (2005). On to the next level: Continuing the conceptualization of the bricolage. *Qualitative Inquiry*, 11(3), p. 323-350.
- Lévi-Strauss, C. (1967). *The savage mind*. Chicago, IL: University of Chicago Press.
- Mintzberg, H. (1989). *Mintzberg on management: Inside our strange world of organizations*. New York: Free Press.
- Reckhenrich, J., Kupp, M., & Anderson, J. (2009). Understanding creativity: The manager as artist. *Business Strategy Review*, 20(2), p. 68-73.
- Rogers, E.M. (2003). *Diffusion of innovations*. New York: Free Press.
- Semler, R., & Mintzberg, H. (2005). Managers, not MBAs: Debating the merits of business education. Retrieved from http://mitworld.mit.edu/video/302.
- Senyard, J., Baker, T., & Davidsson, P. (2009). Entrepreneurial bricolage: Towards systematic empirical testing. *Frontiers of Entrepreneurship Research*, 29(5), p. 1-9.

About the author

Woong Jo Chang (USA) is a post-doctoral researcher in cultural policy and arts management at the Ohio State University. He holds a BA in Chinese Literature, an MA in Performing Arts from Seoul National University, and a Ph.D. from the Ohio State University. Chang was awarded the Barnett Dissertation Fellowship (2011) and the Judith Huggins Balfe Award for Emerging Young Scholars in the field of Cultural Policy (2010). His research is focused on entrepreneurial practices and the uses of IT especially in small arts organizations.

woongjo@gmail.com

More or less governance inside cultural organizations and territories in France

Fabrice Thuriot

Abstract

Governance is not a brand new issue for cultural organizations. Management by public administrations alone or by the private or third sector has been a tempting question for a long time in France. Several solutions were experimented with during the last decades towards a mixed economy, but we can wonder if it is still the case with the new separation of public and private bodies to the detriment of the third sector (such as associations). Governance inside organizations and outside (meaning territories they are acting in) can be distinguished. We identify corporate governance inside organizations (Hagoort, 2005) and cooperative governance in territories. In both cases, questions of legitimacy and efficiency, but also of control, have to be addressed.

Introduction

Firstly, we would like to stress that France has been considered a mixed economy country since the end of the First World War until the 1990s. Public, private and third sectors were all working in a similar fashion for economic and social progress. Nowadays, the third sector (the public/civic sector) has to reduce its spending, while the private sector is encouraged to enhance revenues. This is due to privatization, but also to public procurement contracts.

The third sector is now considered to be a commercial player, unless it can prove its non-profit making activities. During the 19th century until the First World War, the State was not regarded as an economic actor, local authorities were assimilated into private bodies for economic activities until about 1850 and the third sector, replacing charities, entered into competition with public and private organizations. Relations between administration and economic and social sectors were ruled by the regulatory authority on the one hand and competitive biddings on the other hand. This is no longer the case. Public authorities come back on stage to guide the economy, but not to act directly, except when it is necessary or in the administered States. The 'laissez-faire' attitude seems to be over and the consumer is supposed to become again a citizen even as the market still prevails. The sign of the return of public authorities is the multiplication of public service concessions, public procurement contracts and public and private partnerships, and the public management of cultural institutions. They were usually linked to the public authorities by subsidies, sometimes conventions, especially concerning the use of public facilities, and in some cases the State and/or local authorities' partnerships within the Board. The main purpose during the 1960-70's in France was to give cultural leadership to citizens in association with public authorities, but also to let artistic choices be made by professionals. The legitimacy of these associations was not strong at first in terms of democracy, because voluntary administrators were co-opted before enlargement by elections among members.

What is emphasized in these cases is in fact not legitimacy or efficiency, but control over cultural organizations. The efficiency of the private sector is not proven at all. Some public service concessions, handed over to private parties or public procurement contracts, cost more than previous public bodies or association's management. In other sectors, such as water supply for instance, it is known that the cost for public authorities and for citizens is higher when supplied by private companies than by public bodies; private firms aim to generate a profit, unlike public authorities.

Legal status of cultural organizations

In France, several legal statuses with lots of arrangements are possible. Associations can be opened to the general citizens or not, i.e. 'closed' (with no members); they can be private, public or mixed, non-profit but commercial and subject to tax, with volunteers and/or professionals; for the general public interest or a special activity. Companies can be personal or individual; family businesses, with limited liability; public, with quotation or not. Public bodies can be integrated into the administration, financially or also legally autonomous. Public services can have an administrative, non-profit or commercial status, even in a public body.

The question is to determine the degree of governance or influence of the public authorities on the one hand, or the market on the other, and the consequences of different arrangements on the local partnerships.

Governance and dependence of cultural organizations

We have to distinguish the term *governance* from *government*. Governance relates to management, co-operation and leadership processes inside a government, an organism, a territory, or between organizations (Gombault, 2009).

Firstly, we can separate structures without any subsidies from the others. When deciding about subsidies, given the tax system in France and the European Union, legal status is not be taken into account, only activities matter. This means that an association is now considered as an economic actor, except if it can prove its non-competitive activities. The situation is the same for public bodies if their activities are commercial, even if their status protects them from some commercial rules until now. For example, an autonomous public institution is not put in competition with private structures to get some public services.

Partnerships in the local territories: new marketplaces?

In a way, we can say that the cooperative governance has never been so influential. Cultural structures are asked to work with each other in order to reach more people, to develop activities and make cities attractive and, finally, to avoid subsidies divisions.

People can rightly be considered as stakeholders in this kind of policy through consultation processes or by being involved in local committees or boards of partner organizations (associations), especially inside fragile territories such as disadvantaged neighborhoods but also at the municipal level. Even if the collaboration and participation process works well, public authorities use mutual cooperation to reduce the amount of subsidies distributed. For a long time, municipal institutions have been acting only for the communities to which they were attached. Audiences have recently broadened, such as offering students specific rates or fees (for Libraries, Music and Dance Academies...). Agreements between local authorities still support these types of issues. For private, but above all associative or public organizations, partnerships are necessary to get funds but also to develop. Until the 1980s, the State was the main partner of the cities, sometimes helped by the Department (101 in France) for decentralization in a larger urban or rural territory. As they grew, cultural institutions have been invited to contract with other public authorities, Regions (26 in France) or groups of communes during these last years, for other public service missions: territorial decentralization, training, reaching disadvantaged or specific people, with whom these public authorities are concerned. The problem is sometimes for the municipalities to implement their control when giving more money, especially when there is a common committee or status.

Other partnerships are professionally important and allow the reduction of costs, especially for larger projects that cannot be realized alone. Big institutions, whatever their status, such as public authorities, must help smaller ones in providing information, know-how, equipment, sometimes staff, training or money (co-productions). More and more often, small and average cultural associations ask large institutions for these kinds of services or partnerships.

Conclusion

As stated we can identify new structures and developments. It has become compulsory to work together for legitimacy and efficiency from both the private and/or public side. Large subsidized cultural institutions are considered as public bodies, yet often reach only better-off people. Cultural, social, sport, economic or environmental associations give them the opportunity to show they care about other people and parts of the territory in which they are acting. Finally, the main cultural actors have integrated mutual interests for their activities. What was before a guarantee towards their autonomy – several financial partners – is becoming the tool for their dependence, not only financial but artistic and cultural as well. Competition for resources brings out both financial weakness and the necessity of improved partnership projects.

References

- Baron E. & Ferrier-Barbut M, dir. (2005), *Modes de gestion des équipements culturels. Le choix dune structure juridique au service dun projet territorial*, Presses universitaires de Grenoble, 2003, 304 p. (recension par Fabrice thuriot in Pouvoirs Locaux, n° 64, I/2005, p. 158).
- Colbert F. (2007). *Le marketing des arts et de la culture*, 3e édition, Boucherville, Gaëtan Morin éditeur, 302 p. (english version in 2001).
- Colbert F. (2003). Entrepreneurship and Leadership in Marketing the Arts, *International Journal of Arts Management*, Vol. 6, no 1, Fall, p. 30-39.
- Enjolras B. (2009). Une approche des structures non lucratives comme structures de gouvernance, XXIIe colloque de IADDES, *Association pour le développement de la documentation sur léconomie sociale : Gouvernance et performance : quelles exigences de léconomie sociale?*, 10 mars (2009, Paris, 40 p., retrieved from: www.addes.asso.fr (Congress on the third sector).
- Enjolras B. (2000). Coordination failure, property rights and non-profit organizations, *Annals of Public and Cooperative Economics*, 71:3, p. 347-374.
- Gombault A, dir. (2009). Gouvernance des organisations culturelles. Un regard international, *Revue Espaces*, n° 268, mars, p. 50.
- Gombault A., Livat-Pecheux F. & Durrieu F. dir. (2009). *LAlphaBEM des industries créatives*, Bordeaux Management School, p. 359.
- Hagoort G (2005). *Art management. Entrepreneurial style*, Eburon, Utrecht School of the Arts, Netherlands, 5th ed., p. 296.
- Laurin C., Turbide J. (2009). Performance Measurement in the Arts Sector: The Case of Performing Arts, *International Journal of Arts Management*, vol. 11, n° 2, Winter, p. 56-70.
- Laurin C., Turbide J., Lapierre L. & Morissette R. (2008). Financial Crisis in the Arts Sector: Is Governance the illness or the Cure?, *International Journal of Arts Management*, vol. 11, n° 2, Winter, p. 4-13.
- Mickov B., dir. (2010). *European Management Models in Contemporary Art and Culture*, Muzej Savremene, Umetnosti Vojvodine., 2010, 128 p. (in english and serbian).
- Solima, L. (2004). *Limpresa culturale, Processi e strumenti di gestione*, Carocci editore, Roma, p. 309.
- Thuriot F. (2005). « Les salles de musiques actuelles, entre municipalisation et privatisation » in dossier de Richard franco, Lévolution des lieux de musiques actuelles, La Scène, n° 38, septembre, p. 70 ; 2 p., retreived from MAPP : http://www.mapp-web.org/index.php?option=com_content&view=article&id=87:juridique&catid=61:a-voir-ou-a-savoir&Itemid=100.
- Tobelem J-M. (2005). *Le nouvel âge des musées, les institutions culturelles au défi de la gestion*, Armand Colin, Paris, 2e éd., p. 324.

About the author

Fabrice Thuriot (FR) received his Doctorate in Public Law (PhD) on Cultural decentralization and territories (1998). He is a researcher and the coordinator at the Centre of Research on Territorial Decentralization at the University of Reims Champagne-Ardenne and lecturer in public law and cultural policies in France and Europe. Research fellow to the Arts, Culture & Management in Europe Chair, BEM-Bordeaux Management School (France) and to the Fernand Dumont on Culture Chair at the Urbanization, Culture and Society Centre of the National Institute of Scientific Research (INRS, Quebec).

fabrice.thuriot@univ-reims.fr

Coincidences of creativity and entrepreneurship

Jacob Oostwoud Wijdenes

Abstract

The systems theory of creativity (Csikszentmihalyi, 1996) is presented as a powerful instrument
to understand the problems artists and entrepreneurs encounter, when they try to valorise (in an
economical or cultural sense) their ideas, products, or services. Although it is a descriptive theory,
implications can be drawn from it, for the advancement of a climate where creativity can flourish.
Key is the notion of the interdependency of individuals, the relations they maintain and positions
they occupy within the process.

Introduction

'As long as I am painting, I am an artist, when finished I am an entrepreneur'. Thus the Dutch secretary of state for culture, Halbe Zijlstra, cited the 19th century painter Lawrence Alma-Tadema. Zijlstra
used the statement in a letter to parliament, announcing cuts in culture-expenditures. He aims to
introduce a more direct connection between cultural productions, audiences and the economy
and, in line with this, diminishing financial interference of the government with these processes. Citing the artist, he apparently sought legitimacy for this policy.
From this quote it almost seems as if Alma-Tadema considered his artistic and economic activities
as two separate professions. And in holding this point of view, he is in no way an exception. Since
the institution of the *'guilds'*, in particular the St Lucas guild, artists had to behave as entrepreneurs
as much as artists (Gombrich, 1989). Hagoort (2007) is less inclined to look upon these practices
as separate professions. Instead he defines (certain) artists, together with managers of cultural
institutions, as cultural entrepreneurs. Being an artist or a cultural manager implies a reconciliation
of artistic and economic activities. Following this analysis the individual has to overcoming tensions
that arise between the demands of the artistic domain and the demands of the economic domain.

Individualistic conceptions of creativity

Both views concern conceptions artists and politicians hold about the responsibilities of the artist's
profession in relation to conceptions of responsibilities of the government for the arts and the
broader culture in the Netherlands (Oosterbaan, 1990). In the policy of Zijlstra, individual artists and
cultural institutions are addressed as the primary agents for a policy change. Artists and cultural
institutions are committed to the view that they have a responsibility to deliver the products to the
market. According to Apple folklore, Steven Jobs adhered also to this view. Jobs is supposed to have
called this quality 'shipping': 'Real artists ship' (Jobs, 1983). In other words, for an artist to be successful it is not sufficient to have creative ideas and to make creative products, there is also a need to take
care of (economic and cultural) valorization. An important consequence of this view is that acquiring
recognition for artistic endeavors, in combination with the commercial aspect of bringing products
to the market and selling them, should be at the forefront of the concerns of cultural entrepreneurs.

In the encompassing study of the entrepreneurial dimensions of the cultural and creative industries
(HKU, 2010) this very issue is formulated as follows.
*'In essence, a cultural and creative entrepreneur can be understood as someone who creates or
innovates a cultural or creative product or service and who uses entrepreneurial principles to organize and manage his/her creative activity in a commercial manner.'*

Fundamental to these analyses is a coincidence or concurrence of artistic creativity and creative entrepreneurship. It amounts to an individualistic conception of artists and of entrepreneurs: some persons have artistic qualities, and some persons have entrepreneurial qualities, and an intrapersonal amalgamation of these traits is needed to have success in the cultural and creative industry. This line of reasoning complies with mainstream theories on the topic of creativity as well as on the topic of entrepreneurship. Sternberg (1999) identifies seven out of eight research traditions in creativity being individualistic. The exception is the confluence model, also known as systems theory of creativity. More or less the same observation can be made for the concept of entrepreneurship that is also seen as a personal quality. According to Schumpeter (1942), an entrepreneur is a person who is willing and able to convert a new idea or invention into a successful innovation. In more recent formulations risk taking, creativity, corporate activities, acquisition of investments and dealing with contextual constraints are included in defining entrepreneurs (Scott, 2004). According to the literature, the importance of entrepreneurship for a successful business culture can hardly be underestimated.

Other conceptions of creativity

In other sciences this individualistic line of approach to creativity and innovation is lacking. In history and economics the concepts of creativity and innovation are often used to qualify changes that take place in the organization of communities or in the organization of labor. Biology, for example, has done away with the concept of creativity as an exclusively human faculty.

The position of creativity and innovation as individual properties is reminiscent of the *'lone genius'* concept: an autonomous creator who masters not only the art of creating new products or services but also has the capacity to create cultural or economic value with them. This *'individualistic'* view however, is more and more considered a myth (e.g. Weisberg, 1993; Kelley, 2001; Bilton, 2007; Johnson, 2010; Berkun, 2010). For mankind it actually is impossible to create from nothing. In early life children are very dependent upon parents and teachers who introduce them into the world. Learning from others is prerequisite to become humane. In later life new ideas find their origin in accepted concepts or in a new combination of existing ideas. People always make use of the teachings and creations of their processors.

The systems theory of creativity

As mentioned above, only one out of eight research approaches to creativity does not view creativity as a personal trait or capacity. This tradition is sometimes named *'confluence theory'* but more often *'systems theory of creativity'*. There are a number of researchers in psychology that have come to the insight that creativity cannot fully be understood from an individualistic perspective (e.g. Amabile, 1996; Gardner, 1993; Sternberg, 1999). Here the systems theory of creativity, as formulated by Csikszentmihalyi (1996), is used to clarify the coincidences of the concepts of creativity and entrepreneurship.

According to this theory creativity is considered to be a social phenomenon, arising from the interaction of individuals, domains and fields. Attempts to come to grips with an individual or psychological explanation of creativity have failed to isolate criteria by which creative contributions can be defined. The systems theory recognizes that creative achievements are not limited to artists or scientists. People can be creative in any domain of human accomplishments; including domains entrepreneurs are active in, creating a business, innovative products or new business models. It was often observed that creativity is not a general trait like intelligence. Instead it is rather dependent upon structural characteristics of a particular domain. E.g. creativity in the domain of music differs from creativity in the domain of the visual arts and both differ again from the domain of mathematics. Innovations or new discoveries in one domain seldom lead to parallel innovations in other areas. It is also necessary to recognize that domains change and that creativity is connected to that change. Besides the contribution of individuals and the specificity of their domain, it is unavoidable to take a third element into account to understand the character of creativity, i.e. the field. It was often observed that many ideas, artifacts or services that are absolutely new are not considered to be creative. It seems theoretically impossible to connect novelty alone to creativity. Innovation is often defined by combining novelty with value creation. The systems theory resolves this problem in a fundamental way. The selection of creative accomplishments out of the large number of new ideas, products and services, lies within society. There is nothing in the power of individual innovators that can guarantee that their innovation will be recognized as being creative. Put in other words: the justification of creativity is up to the field. Creativity thus interpreted is equivalent to accepted novelty. Innovations, changes or novelties have to be socially adopted otherwise they are forgotten.

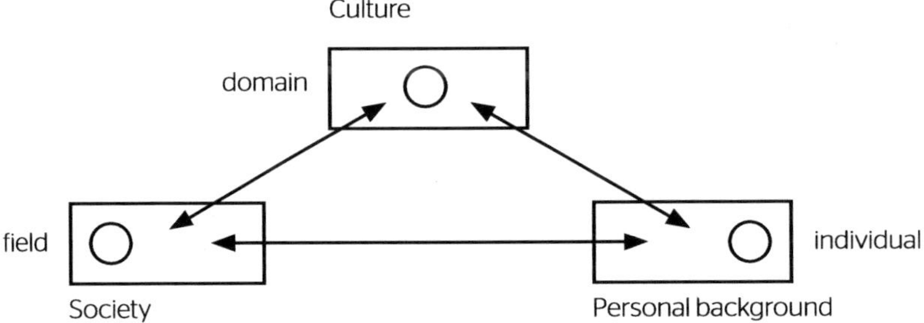

Figure 1. The systems view of Creativity.

For creativity to occur, a set of rules and practices must be transmitted from the domain to the individual. The individual must then produce a novel variation in the content of the domain. The field for inclusion in the domain must then select the variation.
Selection and adoption of ideas is a complicated interactive process. In order to be adopted, an idea or product has to be sanctioned by some group that is entitled to make decisions as to what should or should not be included in the domain.

Legitimacy of creativity

Csikszentmihalyi (1996) stresses that a field has to be relevant to the topic at hand. Artistic artifacts require specific fields and so do scientific results and economic commodities. The field can be a small part of society but also society at large. At the outset scientific, artistic or business innovations will be recognized only by a small group of experts, but later on larger audiences may catch up. Usually only a few specialists decide whether a scientific article is being published and poems have an audience of only a small group of connoisseurs. Business, science and art have different and intricate mechanisms to evaluate innovations and expertise is needed to operate successfully in these domains.

Of course selection need not be a passive process: normally facts or artifacts don't speak for themselves. Anyone with a good idea, product or service has to convince the relevant field of its worth. This struggle for recognition is intrinsic to the concept of creativity. Many artists understand this requirement very well and actively cultivate an image to support the communication with the public about their art (Kisters, 2010). Convincing others that they have an outstanding business plan, product or service is the one qualities entrepreneurs are most renowned for. Spotting opportunities, taking risks and marketing are the essential tools of entrepreneurs.

In studies concerning artistic creative processes, much attention is paid to the inception of creation, finding ideas, getting inspiration, etc. In terms of the systems model this regards communication between individual in relation to domain. Quite contrarily, studies of entrepreneurial creativity often concentrate on the creation of value, in other words, the interaction between individual and field. In the case of entrepreneurs, this field is called the market. In the case of artists, this field consists of critics and connoisseurs. Only by considering both functions in relation to each other can the production of creativity be understood. From systems theory it can be understood that productive qualities and valuing qualities cannot be united in one person. It is vital that the two functions are brought together in one system.

In this way, the systems theory of creativity can be understood as creativity growing in a network of interdependent individuals each with supplementary qualities maintaining particular relations with each other. The idea is not that the whole is more than the sum of its parts, but that the relations between the participants have an influence on the qualities of the participants (Goudsblom, 2011). Creativity evolves within a context of interdependencies.

Implications

It may be useful to realize that the systems model of creativity is a descriptive model and not a prescriptive one. It doesn't provide a formula for creativity or innovation. Most probably a formula for creativity cannot exist at all. Hofstee (1987) properly observed: *'Suppose that someone would contend to posses a recipe of the following kind: 'if you do this or that, in this or that way, I predict it will result in something creative.' At best we would admire this person for his sense of absurdity'.* Nevertheless, what we want to stress in this article is that the systems theory of creativity offers a way out of the individualistic view on creativity. It frees artists and entrepreneurs from the impossible compilation of capacities and responsibilities they are often expected to exhibit. Despite its descriptive character, a number of consequences for artistic and entrepreneurial practices can be drawn from the model.

1   Creativity is a result of a social process.

The systems theory makes it obvious that creativity always involves more than one person. Both conceptions of domain and field imply that others are part of the game. The domain is defined as a knowledge part of culture and thus it rests with people practicing that domain. The field is defined as a group of relevant experts who can judge whether the novelty will be accepted. This notion does in no way diminish the uniqueness and value of individual contributions. It does not deny the existence of geniuses; it merely contends that cooperation lies at the heart of creativity and innovation.

2   Creativity allows for division of labour: group genius

At the base of creativity lies a division of labor. The lone genius is a myth on both theoretical and empirical grounds. Even geniuses make use of others, although this may not be obvious at first glance. Because more systems are involved, more than one person is required for creativity to happen. This division of labor is however not restricted to a division by the systems. Cooperation is also possible within each part of the system (Oostwoud Wijdenes, 2009). At the same time this implies that besides personal qualities, personal relations (communication) form a crucial factor in generating creativity.

3 Creativity allows for multidisciplinary cooperation

The systems theory of creativity recognizes that the nature of innovations in the arts differs from innovations in business. When professionals with diverse specialisms cooperate, everyone makes a contribution that may or may not be innovative in its own field. Sometimes the novelty is of a conceptual nature, but it can also be only the design that is new. On another occasion the production process may be innovative or the marketing can be brand new. Of course it is possible that a novelty contains more than one innovation that originates in different disciplines.

4 Creativity asks for interdependent cooperation

In studies of individual productive processes it was found that there is no prescribed order in the proceedings. Very often a conceptual idea lies at the base, but the innovation process may also start from a design as well as from an external demand or a financial source (e.g. available money to invest). This relative anarchy in proceedings, or freedom in sequencing, is one of the characteristics of creative processes in general. Plans are revised, rewritten, redone, adapted, accommodated or done away completely. And the same happens to designs, business plans and marketing strategies. Iterative movements may be observed as well as recursive ones.
Normally when different specialists have to work on a problem the strategy recommended is to organize the work by dividing the case in discrete elements and putting them together in the end. These strategies are very useful in production chains: when the target is clear and it is known how to divide and assign the tasks. When this knowledge is not available, in case the goal is not yet known, then the cooperation has to be of the interdependent kind: participants need to communicate almost continuously about their own conception of the problems to solve. Every participant needs 'room to move' and needs to leave room for others to move (Saywer, 2007).

5 Creativity regards qualities and relations

The systems theory of creativity forces us to think in structures that foster dynamic developments. The structure consists of the professionals with their knowledge, skills and attitudes (or qualities) who play particular roles in interaction with each other (relations). This interactive development has a special nature. In productive thinking every step is conditional and can be revised. To be able to solve problems that rise, it sometimes is necessary to accept a problem as a solution and redefine the goal. It must be possible to interchange means and ends. Such a process cannot be qualified as linear, nor as recursive but rather as interdependent. Flexibility forms the best condition to allow for serendipity to be grasped: coincidental events that can be put to good use.

6 Individual motivation in relation to system drives

In psychology thought processes of the individual are considered the origin of the creative process. This is not necessary so. The individual does not inevitably stand at the beginning of a creative process. Sometimes ideas or problems originate in a domain or in a field. E.g. clients can order works or services. Nowadays customers expect that products will be improved every time a new series is fabricated. The drive underlying this kind of creativity is primarily rooted in competition, and not in an individual motivation to create. Innovation has become a survival strategy in some parts of our industry.

7 Management for creativity

From the systems model of creativity it can be understood that collaboration for innovation may need management. The model clarifies the importance of establishing and maintaining good relations between productive contributors. It may well be that a key to creative performances of groups can be found in the quality of the on-going conversation (Sawyer, 2007). Managers should particularly be aware of the constraints of this communication. If creative solutions are wanted, managers should strive for a culture that brings together experts from different domains and then foster improvisation and open communication. A consequence of the field factor is that is not appropriate to speak of management of creativity. The ultimate decision whether an innovation is creative lies beyond the competences of the participants including managers. Therefore 'management for creativity' (to happen) is the appropriate phrase.

8 Learning for creativity: in contexts

An identical implication that holds for managing should be drawn for education: creativity cannot be learned, but teaching and learning can be directed for creativity to happen. The systems theory of creativity specifies the elements education for creativity should encompass: individual competences, domain knowledge and skills, and a deep understanding of the function of a highly selective field. The theory forms an educational foundation and frees higher arts education from the endless stacking of supposed competences their students have to digest. It becomes obvious that students have to be highly skilled in a certain domain to become experts with an individual twist who master communicating with others.

9 Creativity is heavily dependent on contextual factors

The concept of a field that is decisive for success or failure of innovations draws attention to the fortuitous character of an undertaking that aims for creative renewal. An enlightening example of this influence is the relative age effect.

In a study after the determinants of talent in sports Dudink (1994) observed that there is a correlation between birth date and sporting success. The birth dates of professional soccer players in the Netherlands fell mainly in August, September and October. This is an unforeseen consequence of the fact that in the past the selection date for young talents was August 1st. Talents born near that date have a developmental advantage on their competitors of the same cohort born months later in the same year. In other countries the phenomenon is confirmed in sports and also in education caused by arbitrary selection dates. The relative age effect in this case caused by arbitrary selection dates, brings about life long lasting (dis)advantages.

The recognition of a contextual determinant sheds light on the actual risks for entrepreneurs and artists alike when trying to valorize their innovations and creative artifacts. From the perspective of the science of history comes the notion that creativity may be an important factor explaining the rise and fall of cultures. This implies that the cultural environment may have stimulating and supporting effects on creative expression or may contrarily have negative and inhibiting effects (Lubart, 1999).

Conclusion

This article aims to present the systems theory of creativity as a fruitful source for understanding the intricacies artists and entrepreneurs likewise encounter when they strive to realize innovations. According to the systems theory, creativity should not be treated as an individual or organizational assignment but rather as the outcome of a collective mission: creativity materializes in a context of interdependencies. Overcoming tensions between (artistic) values and (economic) demands lies within the collective not within the individual.

In the UNCTAD report on the creative economy (Dos Santos, 2010) much attention is devoted to a search for national and international conditions that are favorable for the creative industries. By appointing the creative industry as one of the top sectors for innovation, the Dutch government (Ministerie EL&I, 2011) seems aware of the same urgency. At any rate it is recognized that a context of interdependencies is necessary for creativity to thrive.

To promote creativity, a communal perspective is more appropriate than an individualistic view. With the Dutch policy paper on top sectors the government acknowledges that a shared responsibility for the development of the creative industry is needed. In this perspective to cut expenditures on the arts, being part of the top sector 'creative industry' is like putting the cart before the horse. Luckily the systems theory of creativity also clarifies the fact that the whole process is very robust. With a little variation on a quote from Friedrich von Schiller we can conclude that: *against creativity even the gods themselves contend in vain'*.

References

- Amabile, T.M. (1996). *Creativity in context*. Boulder, Westville Press.
- Berkun, S. (2010). *The myths of innovation*. O'Reilly Media.
- Bilton. C. (2007). *Management and creativity. From creative industries to creative management*. Oxford, Blackwell Publishing.
- Csikszentmihalyi, M. (1996). Creativity: *Flow and the psychology of discovery and invention*. New York: HarperCollins.
- Dudink, A. (1994). *Birth date and sporting success*. Nature, 368, 592.
- Gardner, H. (1993). *Creating Minds: an anatomy of creativity seen through the lives of Freud, Einstein, Picasso, Strawinski, Eliot, Graham and Gandhi*. New York Basic Books.
- Dos Santos Duisenberg, E. (Ed). (2010): *The creative economy report 2010*. UNCTAD United Nations, Geneva. Retrieved from: ISBN 978-0-9816619-0-2 http://www.unctad.org/creative-economy.
- Gombrich, E.H. (1989). *The story of art*. London, Phaidon Press (15th edition).
- Goudsblom, J. (2011). *Stof waar honger uit ontstond. Van biologische evolutie naar sociaal culturele ontwikkeling*. Olympus (2e druk).
- Hagoort, Giep: *Cultural Entrepreneurship. On the freedom to create art and the freedom of enterprise*, Inaugural Lecture, UU/HKU, 2007.
- HKU (2010). *The entrepreneurial dimension of the cultural and creative industries*, Hogeschool voor de Kunsten Utrecht, Utrecht.
- Jobs, S. (1983). Retrieved from: nhttp://www.folklore.org/StoryView.py?story=Real_Artists_Ship.txt . http://c2.com/cgi/wiki?RealArtistsShip.
- Johnson, S. (2010). *Where good ideas come from : the natural history of innovation*. Penguin. London.
- Kelley, T. (2001). *The art of innovation, lessons in creativity from IDEO, America's leading design firm*. With John Littmann. New York Doubleday.
- Kelley, T. (2005). *The ten faces of innovation: IDEO's strategies for defeating the devil's advocate and driving creativity throughout your organisation*. With John Littmann. New York Doubleday.
- Kisters, S. (2010). *Leven als een kunstenaar*, proefschrift Vrije Universiteit Amsterdam.
- Lubart, T. I. (1999). Creativity across cultures. In: Sternberg, R.J. (Ed.) (1999). *The nature of creativity*. Cambridge University Press.
- Ministerie van Economische Zaken, Landbouw en Innovatie (2011). *Naar de top: het bedrijvenbeleid in actie(s)*. Rapport, 13-09-2011, EL&I.
- Oosterbaan Martinius, W. (1990). *Schoonheid, welzijn, kwaliteit. Kunstbeleid en verantwoording na 1945*. Gary Schwartz / SDU, Den Haag .

- Oostwoud Wijdenes, J. (2009). Creativity in collaboration. Implications of the systems model of creativity for its management. In.: Hagoort, G. and R. Kooyman (Ed) (2009). *Creative Industries, colourful fabric in multiple dimensions.* Delft, Eburon.
- Sawyer, R. K. (2007). *Group genius, the creative power of collaboration.* New York, Basic Books.
- Schumpeter, J. A. (1942). *Capitalism, Socialism and Democracy.* New York, Harper Torchbooks.
- Shane, S. (2004). *A generals theory of entrepreneurship: the individual-opportunity nexus.* Edward Edgar Pub.
- Shapiro, S.M. (2011). *Best practices are stupid: 40 ways to out-innovate the competition.* Portfolio / Penguin.
- Sternberg, R.J. (Ed.) (1999). *The nature of creativity.* Cambridge University Press .
- Weisberg, R.W. (1993). *Creativity: beyond the myth of genius.* W. H. Freeman, New York.
- Zijlstra , H. (2010). Kamerstuk, 06-12-2010, OCW, *Uitgangspunten cultuurbeleid.*

About the author

Jacob Oostwoud Wijdenes (NL) studied psychology at the University of Amsterdam. He worked as a researcher in the field of arts education at the SCO Kohnstamm Institute of the University of Amsterdam. Since 2000 he works at the Utrecht School of the Arts (HKU) as Policy Advisor of Quality Assurance for Education and Research. He has published about higher arts education, e.g. on the transition from higher arts education to the labor market, on the impact of the three cycle system for arts education and on creativity.

jacob.oostwoudwijdenes@central.hku.nl

Creative networks: complexity, learning and support across creative industries

Roberta Comunian

Abstract

In the discussion about the Creative Industries often the concept of 'clusters' is being used. This article analyses the complexity and the role of the cluster concept within the CCIs. There has been a growing interest in the way that social and cultural dimensions are intertwined with the sites of exchange and consumption, but also with the value of production systems and supply-chains. The research presented points at the role of networks as learning infrastructures and support.

From clusters to networks and complexity

Most authors looking at creative industries at local and regional levels have used some kind of cluster approach, on the basis that clustering plays an important role in these industries. Authors have focused on the analysis of clustering in different sectors: film and media (Coe, 2000; Turok, 2003); design; advertising (Grabher, 2001); software and new media (Christopherson (2004); music (Gibson, (2005); Brown, O'Connor, and Cohen 2000) and others.

The overlap between physical clustering of organizations and companies in the creative industries is explained in a variety of ways: from supply chain relation and product innovations, to access to specific knowledge resources and labor markets.

However, it is often the case that these 'cluster' benefits are not simply delivered by mere co-location of organizations, but more strongly developed through the establishment of collaborative networks. This new focus on connections (across space and time) has been recently presented as a new 'relational turn' in our understanding of economic geography (Sunley, 2008).

In the context of creative industries, there has been a growing interest in the way that social and cultural dimensions are intertwined with the sites of exchange and consumption but also with the value of production systems and supply-chains. This is not a new theme for researchers in the field, but it can be argued that very little attention has been directed towards understanding the nature and dynamics of these networks.

Using the classification of models of clusters developed by Gordon and McCann (Gordon and McCann 2000) it can be argued that much of the research around the creative industries production clusters has been concentrating on the first two models; *pure agglomeration economies'*, placing emphasis on the importance of external economies and agglomeration, and the *'industrial complex'* model, instead focusing on the role of input-output connections between firms in the cluster (Grabher, 2001; Coe, 2001; Scott, 2002; Wood & Taylor (2004)). Although many studies have touched on the *'social network model'* only few have explicitly focused on it (Julier (2005); Kong (2005); van Heur 2009). While the use of industrial data and exchanges has been the main methodology for the industrial mapping, the social network aspect has been mainly investigated through qualitative interviews with people in the creative sector.

Although not much research has been conducted on the actual structure and organization of these networks, a large part of the literature related to clusters and regional economic development within the creative economy makes claims about their importance within particular sectors case studies and investigations (Ettlinger, 2003; Mossig, 2004); Neff, 2004). These arguments have been, on various occasions, interconnected with the urban cultural infrastructure through terms such as cultural quarters or cultural milieu.

Nevertheless, arguments in favor of prioritizing a network approach over a co-location understanding of the creative industries have emerged recently (Chapain and Comunian 2010) and a new understanding of the importance of scale within the creative economy has expanded this framework .

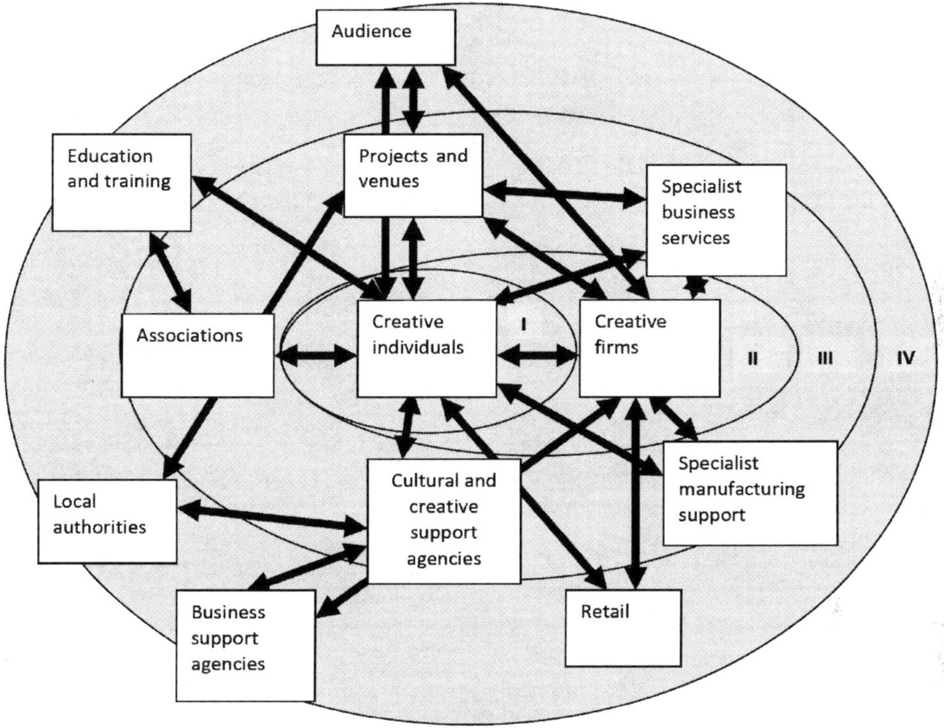

Figure 1. The Creative Knowledge Pool Model (CURDS 2001, p.11). The circles / levels added in the background are an elaboration of the model by Chapain and Comunian (2010, p. 722).

Key research issues and case study

In previous work (Comunian 2010) it is argued that understanding the role played by these networks and their interaction with local and global stakeholders in the creative economy benefits from adopting a complexity theory perspective. There is a large literature emerging on the role of networks in general in various economic contexts (Grabher, 2004), and some older theoretical frameworks, such as clusters and industrial district analysis, place considerable importance on the networks and interactions. However, the dynamics and interactions which might emerge in the context of the creative economy seem to provide an interesting setting to test further and explore in more detail how individuals use networks in their creative and cultural practice, often managing not only a business but the progression of their knowledge and artistic practice. In particular we aim to explore:

- **The role of network as learning infrastructure**

Learning is a key dynamics in the development of the creative and knowledge economies. There is a growing literature exploring the concept of 'learning region'. Regions are repositories of knowledge and ideas, a specific symbolic capital and specialised skills and practices. The region needs to create an infrastructure (often linked to the social capital and local networks) through which this knowledge is shared, flows and becomes a driver of further learning processes. This can ultimately create space for possible innovation and specialisation which will create a competitive advantage on other places (Florida 1995; Hudson 1999; Capello 1999; Morgan 1997; Lundvall & Johnson 1994). Glaeser (1999) specifically links this to the learning opportunities to the new role of cities *'the primary informational role of cities may not be in creating cutting edge technologies, but rather in creating learning opportunities for everyday people. Dense urban agglomerations provide a faster rate of contact between individuals and each new contact provide an opportunity for learning'* (Glaeser, 1999, p.255).

- **The role of network as support infrastructure**

While there are many studies exploring the economic and social outputs of the creative industries, there is very little recognition of the role that support infrastructure has played in developing and fostering the creative industries. As Holden (2007) states, while there are clear overlaps and interconnections between creative industries and the publically-supported cultural infrastructure (as well as the public agencies and bodies who fund culture), *'the connections and economic linkages between publicly-funded culture and the creative industries are not yet well understood'* (p. 32). Networks analysis can provide us with a better understanding of these overlaps and interconnections.

- **The overlap between social and professional networks in the creative economy**

Another characteristic that adds to the complexity of understanding creative networks is the complex nature of these relations, often stretching across friendships and business transactions. As O'Connor ((2002)) suggests, these networks are underpinned by infrastructures of knowledge and expertise which do have formal, institutional dimensions, but equally are embedded in more amorphous social and cultural infrastructures – described as *'soft infrastructure'*, or *'critical infrastructure'*, or *'creative infrastructure'*. These last terms concern those informal networks, those place specific cultural propensities, those *'structures of feeling'* which are very difficult to grasp, let alone strategically direct, but which nonetheless are crucial to the urban regional *'innovative milieu'* (O'Connor, (2002), p.27). Understanding that the structure of certain networks is often to be found in friendships and social relations, rather than economic reasoning, is important in this field.[1]

Understanding creative networks

The role of network as learning infrastructure

The link between knowledge exchange and place is further explained by Pratt ((2002)) and these general socio-organisational location factors are further tightened by the particular mode of production of new media products that involve tacit and situated knowledge. Tacit knowledge is usually

---

[1] The results presented in this chapter were gathered over two years of research carried out in Newcastle-Gateshead and the North East region of England between (2004) and 2006. For a details discussion about merits and limits of social network analysis, please see Comunian R., (2011), Social Network Analysis, Regional Insights, Volume 2, Issue 2 Autumn 2911, p. 3.

encompassed by a range of learning by doing, learning by watching, and simply learning by *'being there'* (Pratt, 2002; p. 40)

Song, Almeida and Wu (2003) investigate the conditions under which knowledge transfer can take place through learning-by-hiring. In the CCIs it can be argued that this is further facilitated by the high degree of freelance and project-based work. These can provide a seedbed for the development of knowledge exchanges and social networks that are central in the CCIs economy. This is further highlighted by Grabher (2001), who considers how projects provide a focus for learning best practices and *'learning-by-watching': 'provides side for training and for gaining access and, at their core, they provide the organisational context for gaining reputation'* (Grabher, 2001, p.368). Part of the overlapping of activities and collaborations, also depends upon the change in peoples' careers and movements from organisation to another. People tend to remain and work in the region for a long time and they tend to maintain their contacts throughout their diverse activities or diverse career paths.

Wenger (1998, p. 251) describes communities of practice as the 'social fabric of learning'. This is a very good description of how learning seems to happen within the creative industries, both in terms of learning how to run a business, but also learning from different sectors and organizations within the creative industries.
Peer-to-peer support and review also seem to be an important structure for the development of innovation. *'The learning and innovation capacity of CI businesses depends to a high degree on the wider learning and innovation capacity of these surrounding networks'* (O'Connor, 2002; p. 9). Creative industries hardly identify themselves with mainstream business support. This could be based on their experience; if they find a person competent and useful they will rely on business support; if they find somebody who is not familiar with their issues, they will dismiss all the business support as being not adapted to their needs. Indeed, they believe that the best people to provide support or business advice are the people who practice their work and have experience in their field; therefore the peer-to-peer support through formal and informal networks and advice seem to be a means to create the personal support infrastructure that a creative industry needs.

Network and public support infrastructure

The fact that most creative industries are small companies and often sole traders also creates a need for creative practitioners to establish a platform of cultural exchange and an opportunity to share ideas. However, alongside the more personal support, business support and valuable business directions are passed on within the networks of the public and not for profit sector and play a valuable role in this.

The results from the social network analysis questionnaire highlight this. Figure 2 and Table 1 provide the breakout in reference to the direction of the relationship mapped by the questionnaire. As we can see, there are strong interconnections across all the three sectors (public, private and not for profit), which highlights the role played by the public and not for profit sector in the creative economy. But more interestingly, we need to explore what kind of relations interconnect these sectors.

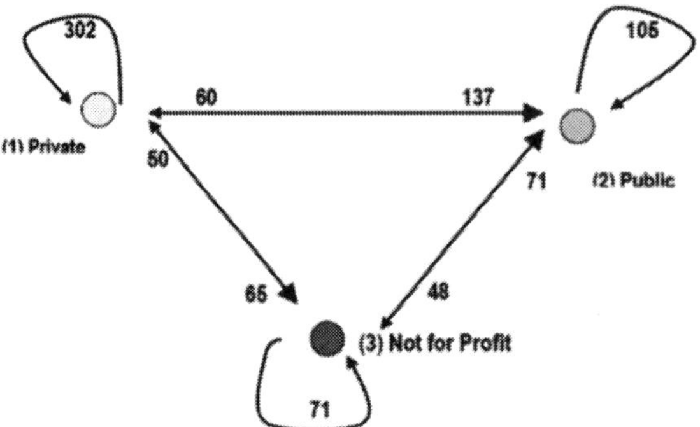

Figure 2. Interconnections between public, private and not for profit in the creative industries

Sometimes the involvement of the public sector can be even more direct, through commissioning and public funding. Public funding and public sector collaboration are also used to define the strategy and give recognition to organizations.

Many of the networks that connect creative practitioners have received public sector support as they are considered to be a strategic way to support and sustain the practitioners.

Many respondents highlighted the role of public sector institutions and support in the running or support of networks. Also not-for-profit organizations and networks seem to play a vital role in this respect.

Nodes and interconnections	Value (absolute=n. of interconnections)
Private (415 nodes)	
• Private to Private	302
• Private to Public	137
• Private to Not for Profit	65
Public (232 nodes)	
• Public to Public	105
• Public to Not for Profit	48
• Public to Private	60
Not for Profit (153)	
• Not for Profit to Not for Profit	71
• Not for Profit to Public	71
• Not for Profit to Private	50
Total	909

Table1. interconnections across sector amongst the sample.

Blurring boundaries: professional and social networks

As part of the social network analysis questionnaire, in our research interviewees were asked to categorize the contacts they provided in three groups: whether the nature of the relationship with the person was solely professional, solely social or both professional and social. As we can see from the results in Table 2, respondents have a social or both social and professional relationship with half of their named people that is important for their work.

Nature of the relationship	Frequency	Percentage
Professional	Professional	50.7%
Social	Social	9.5%
Both	Both	39.8%
Total	Total	100.0%

Table 2. Nature of the relationships with key contacts.

The network seems to rely, build and strengthen within the social infrastructure. Alongside these dynamics, there is a recognition both in the literature and among the research participants that the formal or informality of networks is important. So, it is not just about networking but the nature and structures of networks and how individuals feel about these interactions. For example, the fact that a network is organically developed by practitioners (rather than established by an institution) seems to make it more relevant to the sector's activities.

Although networking is often considered part of a business practice, people working in the creative industries do not always perceive the need to network as part of their business development. The formal networking is often boring and implies mixing with people sometimes from very different contexts or business sector. On the other hand, the social dimension is perceived as very important for the person and their work, so often networking is a matter of social interactions, common space sharing, or even meeting in the pub.

Overall, respondents showed a high degree of awareness with respect to their network strategies and in relation to how grassroots /organic networks might provide different and often complementary opportunities to institutional or structured networks. One element that seemed central is the social dimension of the network and the type of bond and experience that holds the people together. In this respect, it is often the case that within large formal networks people develop active smaller and closer social networks.

Conclusions

Networks seem to play a central role in the development of sustainable creative production systems in the urban economy. Of course, the relevance of networks might depend on the size of companies involved and different sectors of the creative economy might rely on networking activities for different reasons or with different effects.

This chapter aimed to provide a first exploration in these specific dynamics that closely connect economic, cultural and social exchanges and interactions. In particular, we highlighted the role of networking in supporting the learning process of creative practitioners, regarding both business knowledge and sector specific know-how. We also described the important role played by public and not-for-profit organizations in providing frameworks, funding or networking opportunities for creative practitioners. Finally, we considered the importance of understanding the interaction between social and business dynamics in the creative economy and between social and informal versus business and formal networks and the different role they can play.

Looking at this from a policy perspective, networks seem to be a key player in the delivery of a better and more sustainable support systems which provide answers to the needs of the creative industries. Nevertheless it seems important not to limit the support to mainstream and established networks and also to support the more hidden or temporary ones, which for many people can be the first step into the sector.

References

- Christopherson, S. (2004). The Divergent Worlds of New Media: How Policy Shapes Work in the Creative Economy. *Review of Policy Research* 21 (4):543 - 558.
- Coe, N.M. (2000). The view from out West: embeddedness, inter-personal relations and the development of an indigenous film industry in Vancouver. *Geoforum* 31:391-407.
- Coe, N. M. (2001). A Hybrid Agglomeration? The Development of a Satellite-Marshallian Industrial District in Vancouver's Film Industry. *Urban Studies* 38 (10):1753-1775.
- Comunian R. (2011). Social Network Analysis, *Regional Insights*, Volume 2, Issue 2 Autumn 2911, p. 3.
- Comunian, R. (2008). The weakest link: creative industries, flagship cultural project and regeneration. In: ICCPR 2008 - *Fifth International Conference on Cultural Policy Research*. Istanbul (Turkey).
- Comunian, R. (2010). Rethinking the creative city: the role of complexity, networks and interactions in the urban creative economy. *Urban Studies* 48 (6):1157-1179.
- Comunian. R. (2010). Enabling and Inhibiting the Creative Economy: The Role of the Local and Regional Dimensions in England. *Regional Studies* 43 (6):717-734.
- CURDS. (2001). *Culture Cluster Mapping and Analysis*. Newcastle Upon Tyne: Prepared by CURDS, Centre for Urban and Regional Development Studies for ONE North East.
- Ettlinger, N. (2003). Cultural economic geography and a relational and microspace approach to trusts, rationalities, networks and change in collaborative workplaces. *Journal of Economic Geography* 3:145-171.
- Florida, R. (1995). Toward the learning region. *Futures 27* (5):527-536.
- Gibson, C. (2005). Recording Studios: Relational Spaces of Creativity in the City. *Built Environment* 31 (3):192-207.
- Glaeser, E. (1999). Learning in Cities. *Journal of Urban Economics* 46 (2):254-277.
- Gordon, I. R., and P. McCann. (2000). Industrial Clusters: Complexes, Agglomeration and/or Social Networks? *Urban Studies* 37:513-532.
- Grabher, G. (2001). Ecologies of creativity: the Village, the Group, and the heterarchic organisation of the British advertising industry. *Environment & Planning* A 33:351-374.
- Grabher, G. (2004). Learning in projects, remembering in networks? Communality, sociality and connectivity in project ecologies. *European Urban and Regional Studies* 11 (2):99-119
- Holden, J. (2007). *Publicly Funded Culture and the Creative Industries*. London: DEMOS
- Hudson, R. (1999). The Learning Economy, the Learning Firm and the Learning Region: A Sympathetic Critique of the Limits to Learning. *European Urban and Regional Studies* 6 (1):59-72
- Julier, G. (2005). Urban Designscapes and the Production of Aesthetic Consent. Urban Studies 42 (5/6):869-887
- Kong, L. (2005). The sociality of cultural industries. International *Journal of Cultural Policy* 11:61-76

- Lundvall, B, and B Johnson. (1994). The learning economy. *Journal of Industry Studies* 1:23-42
- Matarasso, F. (2000). *Bringing the city together.* A discussion paper on the potential of a bid by Newcastle and Gateshead for the title of European Capital of Culture in 2008. London: Comedia
- Miles, S. (2005). Understanding the Cultural 'Case': Class, Identity and the Regeneration of NewcastleGateshead. *Sociology* 39 (5):1019-1028
- Minton, A. (2003). *Northern Soul: Culture, Creativity and quality of place in Newcastle and Gateshead.* Published by DEMOS & RICS
- Morgan, K. (1997). The Learning Region: Institutions, Innovation and Regional Renewal. *Regional Studies* 31 (5):491-503.
- Mossig, I. (2004). The Networks Producing Television Programmes in the Cologne Media Cluster: New Firm Foundation, Flexible Specialization and Efficient Decision-making Structures. *European Planning Studies* 12 (2):155-171.
- Neff, G. (2004). The Changing Place of Cultural Production: The Location of Social Networks in a Digital Media Industry. *Annals,* AAPSS.
- O'Connor, J. (2002). Public and Private in the Cultural Industries. In: *Lifestyle, Desire and Politics: Contemporary Identities,* edited by T. Johansson and O. Sernhede: Centre for Cultural Studies, University of Gothenburg.
- Pratt, A. C. (2002). Hot jobs in cool places. The material cultures of new media product spaces: the case of the south of market, San Francisco. *Information, communication and society* 5 (1):27-50.
- Scott, A. J. (2002). A New Map of Hollywood: The Production and Distribution of American Motion Pictures. *Regional Studies* 36:957-975.
- Song, J, Paul A, & Wu, G. (2003). Learning-By-Hiring: When is Mobility More Likely to Facilitate Interfirm Knowledge Transfer? *Management Science* 49 (4):351-365.
- Sunley, P (2008). Relational Economic Geography: A Partial Understanding or a New Paradigm ? . *Economic Geography* 84 (1):1-26.
- Turok, I. (2003). Cities, Clusters and Creative Industries: The Case of Film and Television in Scotland. European Planning Studies 11 (5):549-565.
- Van Heur, B. (2009). The Clustering of Creative Networks: Between Myth and Reality. *Urban Studies* 46 (8):1531-1552.
- Wenger, E. (1998). *Communities of Practice: Learning, Meaning and Identity.* MA: Cambridge University Press/
- Wood, P, & Taylor, C. (2004). Big ideas for a small town: the huddersfield creative town initiative. In *Local Economy.*

About the author

Roberta Comunian (UK) is Creative Industries Research Associate at the School of Arts, University of Kent. She holds a European Doctorate in Network Economy and Knowledge Management. She is interested in the creative industries and the relationship between public and private investments in the arts. She is currently researching the role of higher education in the creative economy.

R.Comunian@kent.ac.uk

Publishers as cultural intermediaries; the cultural and economic importance of personalties

Barbara Heebels, Oedzge Atzema, Irina van Aalst

Abstract

There is growing support to define cultural product industries in terms of networks instead of products (Caves, 2002; O'Connor, 2007; Potts et al, 2007). In this chapter the role of book publishers as brokers between authors, press and bookstores and colleagues is explored.
Publishers govern networks not just by pecuniary incentives. Networks consisting of personal ties function as channels for the exchange of symbolic knowledge of which the cultural meaning has to be (re)created continuously. Most social network research is too focused on institutionalized collaborations between organizations and on the functional attributes of communities of practice. As a consequence, underlying (informal) personal ties are neglected. In this respect, different types of personal ties can be distinguished; communality, sociality and connectivity ties. Furthermore the multiplexity of network logics of persons is underestimated, i.e. the obligation and loyalty of persons to projects and firms in which they are engaged as well as their role as entrepreneur of their own human capital. They show that multiplexity and strength of ties differ between cultural product industries.

Cultural product industries and social networks

From inter organizational trust to multiplex personal ties

Networks of interpersonal relations are imperative when doing business to generate trust and avoid wrongdoing. In his seminal paper on the problem of embeddedness, Granovetter (1985) argued that the social context of economic action is crucial. Moreover, those networks facilitate the exchange of information and knowledge. In line with these ideas, economic geographers have conducted many empirical studies on clusters of knowledge-intensive firms where inter-firm knowledge spillovers and face-to-face contacts are at the centre of their interest. Whereas strong ties are based on mutual experience and the development of shared norms and values over time, weak ties are more ephemeral, and are less intense with respect to emotional attachment and the time invested. Grabher and Ibert (2006) have extended this dichotomy with a categorization based on what they call *'the multiplexity of ties'*. This multiplexity refers to the extent to which a network involves different types of ties ranging from private friendships to business partnerships. They distinguish between three types of networks (see Table 1):

a   network communality; strong ties and high multiplexity of ties
b   network sociality: weak ties and high multiplexity of ties, and
c   network connectivity: weak ties and low multiplexity of ties

	Communality	**Sociality**	**Connectivity**
Nature of ties	Lasting, intense	Ephemeral, intense	Ephemeral, weak
Social realm	Private cum professional	Professional cum private	Professional
Governance	Trust	Networked reputation	Professional ethos, peer recognition
Focus	Relationship-oriented	Career-oriented	Task-oriented

Table 1. Three types of personal networks and characteristics of their ties. Adapted from Grabher (2004a, b).

When we look at the literature on cultural product industries, we see that both strong and weak ties are considered to be important. Strong ties within a local milieu are necessary for developing trust, reducing risk and stimulating interactive learning (Banks et al., 2000; Basset et al., 2002) and play an important role in coordinating exchange of knowledge (Uzzi, 1997). Weak ties are essential for building credibility within the industry community/ cultural field and for coming up with new ideas (Currid, 2007).

Cultural intermediaries as brokers engaging in multiple networks

Just like music producers (Lingo & Mahony, 2010), publishers combine different brokering strategies to cope with the uncertainties in making a cultural product. Besides producers of books they are cultural gatekeepers and intermediaries between authors, designers, booksellers and people from the press. They are responsible for the creative part of making the book: they help the author to create the content of the book and together with cover designers they decide on the looks of the book. In addition, publishers are responsible for selling the idea to bookstore and press. The book has to get into the stores, and both book and author should receive (positive) attention.

Because the added value of publishing lies in this double role of being creative and integrating/ implementing this creativity into a good-selling product, personal networks and brokering are vital to be successful as a publisher. In addition to personal networks with authors, press and booksellers, publishers also have personal ties to their fellow publishers. Publishing is a competitive field in which judging and being judged plays an important role (Heebels & Boschma, 2011; Heebels, 2011). The cultural field or professional community is important in the creation of art and cultural products such as books (DiMaggio, 1987). In such communities, a continuous process of judging and being judged takes place and gatekeepers or certifiers can make or break a product and its creator(s) (Caves, 2000; Currid, 2007), and reputation is a significant strategic tool (Anan & Peterson, 2000; Lingo & Mahony, 2010).

Publishers and their personal networks

The variety of network strategies used by publishers was investigated by means of 21 semi-structured interviews with publishers of public books in the Netherlands. After open coding to identify the themes discussed, codes were placed in a hierarchical code structure. By means of this code structure and memos, themes were sharpened and related to one another and to the existing literature (Corbin & Strauss, 2008). The result is a conceptual scheme (Table 2), which identifies different network strategies of book publishers (in the columns) for the most important personal ties of book publishers (in the rows).

In publisher's contacts with authors, communality and sociality strategies play a dominant role. Sociality ties are important in establishing contact, communality ties are important in developing trust. Regarding sociality strategies, publishers for instance organize informal meetings with promising potential authors and with journalists. They try to bind new authors through their other authors. Swift trust and networked reputation make sure that the author and the content he/she will provide fits the publishing house. Moreover, publishers bring their different authors together in the hope that this leads to cross fertilization and an overall stronger bonding with the publishing house. After establishing contact, developing personal ties based on communality are important to build trust in competences and intentions. The combination of personal ties within and outside the work atmosphere, as noted by Ettlinger (2003), leads to empathy or identification based trust (Nooteboom,

	Communality	Sociality	Connectivity
Authors	Investing in author/ making book, 'strategic friendships', trust	Acquiring authors and keeping in touch	
Press		'Moulding', don't come across as pushy	Professionalization press contacts
Booksellers		'Keep them on', thinking along, get books in store	Partnerships, extensive network
Fellow publishers	Advisers, brotherhood of same thoughts	Acquiring authors, practical experiences, career	(Conglomerate) strategies, extensive networks on book fairs

Observability
Keeping an eye on each other ('s list)

Table 2. The role of different network strategies in publishers' personal ties with authors, press, booksellers and fellow publishers.

2006). Although a number of publishers jocularly compare the bond between publisher and author to a love affair, the majority of publishers refer to their relationship with authors as a 'mix of business and friendship'. Emotionally based relations are less important as suggested by Ettlinger (ibid.), but relations between author and publisher are also not purely professional. One might qualify such relations as strategic friendships, in which business is what connects publisher and author, but in which support and mutual trust are crucial as well. The business aspect and the power relationship between publisher and author make it difficult to be friends:

> *'Trust is essential. Of course, it is a 'peoples-business', so you should like the other, there must be mutual sympathy. (...) It is hard, real hard to be friends with writers though. Of course many writers are friends of mine, but you have to be real careful, because there is always a commercial, business side to it. It is hard to say to a friend 'we are not going to publish this'.*

Whereas contact with authors ranges from preliminary friendly to quite professional, it is always important to be 'same minded' to a certain degree to be able to work on a creative project together and 'to achieve the best possible results with your collective brain'. To commit authors to the publishing house, communality ties are important during a project. Sociality ties, i.e. 'keeping in touch', are more vital during the periods in between the publishing of two books and when authors seclude themselves to work on a manuscript.

The kind of personal ties with press and bookstores is quite different. Here personal ties are complementary to business contacts outsourced to press departments and salesmen of the publishing house. By consequence, for publishers of smaller independent publishing houses, these complementary personal ties are more important than for larger publishing houses that are part of a conglomerate. Sociality ties with press and book sellers are important for promoting books and authors on the one hand, and in pitching ideas on design and marketing on the other hand. Coincidental meetings or passing by at each other's office are instrumental to *'mould'* the press and to avoid coming across as too pushy. Dropping by at bookstores helps to *'keep booksellers on'* and supports getting books (in a prominent place) in their store.

However, the importance of sociality ties in respect to booksellers and people from the press should not be overestimated. Connectivity ties and extensive networks with a great number of booksellers are more important to put books on the market. Publishers speak of partnerships with book sellers (see also Kaye, 2003) and personal relations are based on common (business) interests and/or are more task oriented; they involve consulting about the cover of a book for example. Press contacts are a combination of professional contact and more informal chats. There is even a growing tendency for professionalization of press contacts:

> *'In a sense it has become 'not done' for reviewers to mingle too much with the people who they have to review. That used to be very different by all means. I would say it is a good thing. Of course it is possible that you see each other at parties, but I think it is not unhealthy that there is somewhat more distance now.'*

Although book publishers rarely cooperate with publishers outside their own house, they often have personal contact with their colleague publishers, in particular in the field of literature publishing. Contacts with fellow publishers have three related purposes: they can be helpful in acquiring content, they are used to develop (common) strategies and they can be supportive in one's career.

Publishers use all three types of network strategies with fellow publishers, as well as a fourth network strategy, which we have called *observability*. Communality is least common but, in a number of cases, publishers who started their own firm used befriended publishers as advisers. Sociality networks are more usual but it is important to note that these revolve much more around competition than cooperation. Sometimes practical experiences are shared and occasionally people grant each other projects, but mostly these networks are used for a publisher's own career. This is different for the personal contacts with foreign publishers. These publishers are not direct competitors and keeping in touch and networked reputation are important to acquire new content (both through tips and more chances at auctions).

Publisher's personal ties with colleagues most often involve connectivity. The publishing community is small and quite organized: practical experiences are shared and joint stakes are looked after together in publishing associations. However, most exchange occurs between publishers who are part of the same conglomerate. Another important connectivity network is the contacts with foreign publishers with overlapping interests at book fairs and other scheduled meetings. This is both instrumental in acquiring new books and getting Dutch authors translated abroad. Within the Dutch publishing community, it is observability rather than sociality that is important for acquiring new books. Publishers keep an eye on each other and exchange book lists with one another to see what the competition is doing, either to imitate this or to distinguish themselves from their competitors:

> *'We have sort of a gentleman's agreement to send each other the brochures, so that you know what others are doing in the upcoming months and which books will arrive, and everybody participates in the digital book magazine, where you follow each other's news. It is easy to keep track of each other because it is a quite limited group of people.'*
> *'My biggest competitor is [xxx], a very nice and decent fellow, if we meet each other on the street, we always have a chat. At the same time, we keep an eye on each other and our [book] lists.'*

Conclusion and discussion

As can be concluded from Table 2, all three types of network ties identified by Grabher (2001) – communality, sociality and connectivity – are used by publishers. Moreover, we discovered a fourth network tie: observability.
Personal ties instead of inter-organizational networks are crucial for publishing firms to successfully develop and sell books. This does not mean that business in publishing is grounded on emotions and friendships, as Ettlinger (2003) seems to suggest. Rather, personal ties are used for business purposes. The multiplexity of networks of personal ties is a vital strategy in publishing. Publishers strategically use different types of personal ties as cultural intermediaries. In their relationships with authors, communality and sociality are important, in their contacts with booksellers and press sociality and connectivity are vital and in relation to their fellow publishers all three kinds of personal ties are used.

The literature on cultural product industries has mainly stressed the importance of sociality ties within geographical clusters, like the cluster of publishers in Amsterdam. This study gives rise to two points of critique on this emphasis. First, communality and connectivity ties are at least as important in publishing as sociality ties. It even seems that these ties are gaining in importance in recent years: book publishing is becoming more commercial and this seems to reflect in more connectivity ties on the one hand and to a revaluation of communality ties with authors in literature publishing on the other hand. Second, many studies focus on the exchange of symbolic knowledge within a cultural field and these sociality ties often have a very positive connotation: networks are good. However, it is more about keeping an eye on each other than about exchanging in the field of book publishing. Whereas sociality ties are important for selecting content, ties between publishers are mainly based on observability. These network ties are both a blessing and a burden. Publishing is highly competitive and publishers keep an eye on each other in an informal way and exchange specific content in a more formal way.

With these insights, it is interesting to reflect on the function of (policies on) clusters of cultural product industries. The role of communality and connectivity might make other places important: is hanging in the right bars really what matters?
We expect that this is not the case. Competition and observability rather than sociality might be the mechanisms behind the clustering of cultural product industries. This also impacts the evolution of clusters, because observability and imitation do not lead to self-augmenting processes (Brenner, 2005). In publishing, networks are not primarily used to exchange established routines. Instead, book publishers use a combination of personal ties to distinguish themselves and to establish trust, reputation and recognition.

References

- Anand, N. & Peterson, R.A. (2000). When market information constitutes fields: sensemaking of markets in the commercial music industry. *Organization Science*, 11 (3), p.270-284.
- Banks, M.,Lovatt, A., O'Connor, J. & Raffo,C. (2000). Risk and trust in the cultural industries. *Geoforum*, 31(4), p. 453-464.
- Bassett, K., Griffiths, R., Smith., I. (2002). Cultural industries, cultural clusters and the city: The example of natural history film-making in Bristol. *Geoforum*, 33, p. 165-177.
- Brenner, T. (2005). Innovation and cooperation during the emergence of local industrial clusters: An empirical study in Germany. *European Planning Studies*, 13 (6), p. 921-938.
- Caves, R. E. (2000). *Creative Industries: Contracts Between Art and Commerce*. Cambridge: Harvard University Press.
- Corbin & Strauss (2008). *Basics of qualitative research: techniques and procedures for developing grounded theory.* 3th ed. London: Sage.

- Currid, E. (2007). *The warhol economy: how fashion, art, and music drive New York city.* Princeton (NY).: Princeton University Press.
- Di Maggio, P. (1987). *Classification in Art.* American Sociological Review, 52, p. 440–55.
- Foster, P. ,Borgatti, Stephen P. ,Jones, C. (2011). Gatekeeper search and selection strategies: Relational and network governance in a cultural market. *Poetics* 39, p. 247–265.
- Grabher G. & Ibert O. (2006). Bad company? The ambiguity of personal knowledge networks. *Journal of Economic Geography,* 6(3), p. 251-271.
- Grabher, G. (2004a). Temporary architectures of learning: knowledge governance in project ecologies. *Organization Studies,* 25, p. 1491-1514.
- Grabher, G. (2004b). Learning in projects, remembering in networks? Communality, sociality, and connectivity in project ecologies. *European Urban and Regional Studies* 2004 11: p. 103.
- Granovetter, M. (1985). Economic action and social structure: The problem of embeddedness. *American Journal of Sociology,* 91, p. 481-510.
- Heebels, B. & Boschma, R.A. (2011). Performing in Dutch book publishing 1880-2008: the importance of entrepreneurial experience and the Amsterdam cluster. *Journal of Economic Geography,* 11 (6), p. 1007-1029.
- Heebels, B. (2011). Place-making from publishing house to publishing hub: Dutch book publishers and the role of place in establishing trust and reputation. Working paper (under review).
- Kaye, L. (2003). Publisher–Bookseller Cooperation in the UK Book Industry. Unwin Trust UK-Australian Fellowship. Retrieved from: http://www.publishers.asn.au/emplibrary/Unwin_Trust_Fellowship_Report_2003.pdf.
- Lingo, E.L. & O'Mahony, S. (2010). Nexus Work: Brokerage on Creative Projects. *Adminstrative Science Quarterly.* 55 (1), p. 47-81.
- Nooteboom, B. (2006). Innovation, learning and cluster dynamics. In: Martin, R. Asheim, B. Cooke, P. (Eds.). *Clusters and Regional Development; Critical Reflections and Exploration,* London: Routledge, p. 137-163.
- O'Connor, J. (2007). *The Cultural and Creative industries. A Review of the Literature.* London: Creative Partnerships/ Arts Council England.
- Potts, J., Cunningham, S. Hartley, J., Ormerod, P. (2008). Social network markets: a new definition of the creative industries. *Journal of Cultural Economics,* 32(3), p. 67-185.
- Uzzi, B. (1997). Social structure and competition in interfirm networks: The paradox of embeddedness. *Administrative Science Quarterly,* 42, p. 35-67.

About the authors

Oedzge Atzema (NL) works as professor in Economic Geography at the Urban and Regional Research Centre of Utrecht university. He has done research in many fields, among which evolutionary economic geography, ICT and geography of production, urban labor markets, economic restructuring of cities, regional effects of economic globalization, regional aspects of firm demography, migration and urbanization and creative economies and urban development.

Irina Van Aalst (NL) is assistant professor Urban Geography at the Urban and Regional Research Centre of the Utrecht University. Her research and publications focus on urban nightlife and the night-time economy, the (re-)development of public spaces and the clustering of creative industries.

Barbara Heebels (NL) is currently working on her PhD on the role of place and personal network ties in the functioning of cultural intermediaries. She is affiliated to the economic and urban geography departments of the Urban and Regional Research Centre of Utrecht University (the Netherlands). Her research interests include the geography of networks, cultural product industries, urban nightlife and the night-time economy and urban redevelopment.

b.heebels@gmail.com (corresponding author)

Unlocking the Symbolic Value of the Creative Industries

Alain Guiette, Sofie Jacobs, Ellen Loots, Annick Schramme and Koen Vandenbempt

Abstract

Looking at the CCIs we have to note that the other-than-economic value of the creative industries is wide-ranging and labeled in different ways. A generic kind of value is not connected to objects or attributed to it by an actor, but different 'sorts' of value originate from the interaction or experience with art, culture and creative products or services; instances such as efficiency, games, beauty, status or ethics can come to mind.

The research presented here discusses and confronts the intrinsic value of the creative industries on the one hand, versus extrinsic value allocated by both individuals and society, on the other.

Introduction

Creative industries[1] are increasingly positioned as an engine of value creation for society. The value of creative industries, however, extends beyond their purely economic impact. Some attempts have been undertaken to describe this value (European Commission, 2006; Dos Santos, 2008), which is referred to as *symbolic value*. However, consensus on the content, components and positioning of this construct appears lacking Nonetheless, clear constructs are the building blocks of theory, facilitate communication and allow empirical explorations of phenomena (Suddaby, 2010). To our knowledge, there is no clear agreement on the substantive definitional content of the construct *'value'* in general, and on the *'value'* generated by creative industries in particular. What we do see is that a distinction between economic and *'other value'* is often made, but that a consensus on the content of this complement to economic value appears lacking.

The entwinement of the economic and symbolic value of an object, or their reciprocal influencing, is suggested in the expression *'twin concepts'* of value by Hutter & Throsby (2008), linked to the exploration of different disciplinary approaches to the valuation of art and culture. The authors state that value is *'multidimensional, qualitative, shifting, and contested, without an agreed unit of account by which it can be measured'* (Hutter & Throsby, 2008, p.13). Furthermore, value is dynamic and relative, with value regimes changing in time and shifting on the individual and societal level.

Value in literature

From a literature review we note that the other-than-economic value of the creative industries is wide-ranging and labeled in different ways. David Throsby bestows a *'cultural value'* to the artistic or cultural object next to an economic value. On several occasions he uses that term, referring to a long-standing tradition of cultural modernism and humanism in which the true value of an object is to be found within the intrinsic qualities of that object: in the aesthetic, artistic or more wide-ranging cultural value that it possibly possesses (Throsby, 2000). In addition, Throsby assigns a *'symbolic value'* to an object or experience that rests in its capacity to transmit symbolic messages and to reveal symbolic meanings (Throsby, 2000).

A second finding, also proclaimed by Throsby, is that a distinction between an intrinsic and extrinsic dimension of symbolic value can be made. Hence, in addition to a value that is intrinsic to an art object or experience, David Throsby claims that *'cultural'* value also *'reflects assessments of the significance or worth of the work judged against aesthetic and other artistic or cultural criteria (...)'* (Throsby, 2008, p.76). What

---

[1] We defined creative industries as 'those sectors and activities relying on the input of human creativity to produce economic, societal and symbolic value - throughout the links of creation, production, dissemination and consumption in the value chain – and contributing to the expansion of Flanders' creative advantage.' Based upon this demarcation, the creative industries have been divided into 12 separate sectors: architecture, audiovisual industry, communication & advertising, cultural heritage, design, fashion, gaming, music, new media, performing arts, publishing, and visual arts (Guiette et al., 2010).

surfaces from this outlook is a twofold approach of value: first, value is an attribute intrinsic to the object (Ginsburgh & Weyers, 2008; Throsby, 2008); second, value is anchored within the utility or significance that an individual user or a community or society experiences from it (Marx, 1867; Throsby, 2000; Frey, 2008). A third consideration directly follows from this. One attribute of value, raised by e.g. Hutter & Throsby (2008), is that the value of creative industries is *'relative'*. This means that value tends to depend on who is assigning value to something and tends to vary and fluctuate in significance over time. Focusing on the *micro level*, objects that have a major value to an individual are not necessarily those objects with considerable (aesthetic, monetary, etc.) value.

The value experienced is not inherent to the object, but it fully resides within the individual that attributes the value affectively or cognitively. On a *meso level*, Anand and Jones (2008) have developed insights in within-industry valuation processes. More authors ally the individual, industrial and societal (macro) roles in the creating or assigning of value that is extrinsic to objects (e.c. Boztepe 2007)

Finally, a fourth finding relates to the filling-in of the concept *'value'*. A generic kind of value is not only connected to objects or attributed to it by an actor, but different *'sorts'* of value originate from the interaction or experience with art, culture and creative products or services; instances such as efficiency, games, beauty, status or ethics can come to mind (Holbrook,

Value dimension I	Value dimension II	Value component	Operationalization
Intrinsic	Related to object	Aesthetic	- Aesthetical quality - Quality of intrinsic beauty - Technical-artistic qualities
		Historical	- Contribution to history, tradition - Cultural-historical contribution
Extrinsic	Instrumental	Experience	- Entertainment quality - Stimulating, fun experiences
		Educational	- Intellectual / cultural capital creation - Short and long term cultural education
		Spiritual	- Existential meaning - Enhancing consciousness - Generation of flow, happiness
		Identity	- Individual identity creation - Sense of belonging - Identification of social status
	Individual perception	Emotional	- Flow experience - Welfare effects, insight - Longer term health effects
		Cognitive	- Wellbeing through knowledge - Mental capability development - Learning & educational performance
	Societal perception	Social	- Social interaction - Societal integration - Repeated cultural exposure

Table 1 Symbolic value typology.

1999[2]. Boztepe (2007) clusters values into four major categories: use value or utility, social value, emotional value and spiritual value, some of which are akin to Frey (2008), who distinguishes existence, option, bequest, education and prestige value. Also Throsby (2000) has deconstructed the non-economic value of arts into components: an aesthetic value (beauty and harmony), a spiritual value (understanding, insight), a social value (connection, identity), a historical value and a symbolic value (a repository or conveyer of meaning).

Symbolic value typology

In the model developed, we discern first between two major dimensions of value: intrinsic value of the creative industries on the one hand, versus extrinsic value allocated by both individuals and society, on the other hand (value dimension 1). Within the extrinsic value approach, a second-level fragmentation can be made (value dimension 2): one dimension is the instrumental value, i.e. the ability to move, to educate, to make aware, etc.; another is related to the perception or reception of value on both the individual level and the societal level (see Table 1).

Expert focus groups

In order to seek acceptance of the symbolic value typology presented, three moderated focus groups were conducted. For the purpose of this exercise, the twelve creative industry sectors have been grouped in three clusters (Rutten, 2010): Arts & Patrimony, Media & Entertainment, and Creative Services
During moderated focus groups, experts were asked to *describe what they understood by the symbolic value of creative industries in general and of their cluster in particular*. Accumulated responses were then compared with the presented typology in mind. In a second phase,

Cluster	Arts & Patrimony		Media & Entertainment		Creative services	
Significance	Higher	Lower	Higher	Lower	Higher	Lower
Aesthetic		■		■	■	
Historical	■			■		■
Experience		■	■		■	
Educational		■	■			■
Spiritual	■		■			■
Identity		■	■		■	
Emotional		■		■	■	
Cognitive	■		■			■
Social	■		■		■	

Table 2. Experimental measure of relative importance of value component.

[2] For reasons of space, we have chosen not to go into detail on this viewpoint of value.

based upon the narrated frequency of value components, their relative importance has been deduced.

Based upon the analysis of the focus groups we deduce that the symbolic value typology has gained widespread acceptance amongst the participating experts. The analysis furthermore revealed the following findings per cluster.

- Key value components for the Arts & Patrimony cluster include historical value (through the potential of art to create history and facilitate dialogue across generations), spiritual, cognitive and social value (arts representing 'social glue' and a vehicle of societal cohesion).
- The Media & Entertainment cluster is characterized by a higher diversity of values labelled as important: experience, educational, spiritual, identity, cognitive, and social values. Their contribution to identity building and effective usage of spare time appear to be key characteristics.
- Creative Services are characterized by five important values: esthetical, experience, identity, emotional and social (See Table 2).

Conclusion

The analysis and measurement of symbolic value is controversial. The expert focus groups demonstrated for all creative industries clusters the significance of social, cognitive and spiritual value. More important, however, was the widespread acceptance gained for the proposed symbolic value typology validation of the conceptual framework by the experts.

In this research we focus on a possible (sociological, philosophical, societal) description of the notion 'symbolic value', whereby the creative industries are differentiated from other industries. The concept 'experience economy' could also be an interesting viewpoint. Further research on the role and impact of this experience economy could produce relevant information in the area of strategic marketing and management of the creative industries.

References

- Anand, N., Jones & Brittany C. (2008): Tournament Rituals, Category Dynamics, and Field Configuration: The Case of the Booker Prize. *Journal of Management Studies* 45 (2008): p. 1036-1060.
- Boztepe, S. (2007): User Value: Competing Theories and Models. *International Journal of Design*, p. 155-63.
- Dos Santos Duisenberg, E. (Ed). (2008): *Creative Economy Report 2008: the challenge of assessing the creative economy: towards informed policy-making.* UNCTAD United Nations, Geneva.
- European Commission. (2006): *The economy of culture in Europe.* Brussels: Directorate-General for Education and Culture, KEA European Affairs.
- Frey, B. S. (2008): What Values Should Count in the Arts? The Tension between Economic Effects and Cultural Value. In *Beyond Price. Value in Culture, Economics and the Arts*, edited by Michael Hutter, and David Throsby, p. 261-269. Cambridge: Cambridge University Press.
- Ginsburgh, V. & Weyers, S. (2008): Quantitative Approaches to Valuation in the Arts, with an Application to Movies. In *Beyond Price. Value in Culture, Economics and the Arts*, edited by Michael Hutter, and David Throsby, p. 179-199. Cambridge: Cambridge University Press.
- Guiette, A., Schramme, A. & Vandenbempt, K. (2010): *Creative Industries in Flanders anno 2010: a preliminary study.* Antwerp: Antwerp Management School – Flanders DC Knowledge Centre, (in Dutch).
- Holbrook,Morris B. (1999): *Consumer value: a framework for analysis and research.* New York: Routledge.
- Hutter, M. & Throsby, D. (2008) Value and Valuation in Art and Culture: Introduction and Overview. In *Beyond Price. Value in Culture, Economics and the Arts*, edited by Michael Hutter, and David Throsby, 1-22. Cambridge: Cambridge University Press.

- Marx, K. Capital. (2011): A critique of political economy. Volume One: The process of production of capital. Moscow: Progress Publishers, 1867. Accessed October 3; http://www.marxists.org/archive/marx/works/1867-c1/index.htm
- Rutten, P., Koops, O. & Roso, Monique. (2010): *Creatieve Industrie in de SBI 2008 bedrijfsindeling.* Leiden/Delft: TNO
- Suddaby, R. Editors comments: Construct clarity in theories of management and organization. *Academy of Management Review* 35 (2010): 346-357.
- Throsby, D. (2011): Economic and Cultural Value in the Work of Creative Artists. In: *Values and Heritage Conservation.* Research Report, edited by Erica Avrami, Randall Mason, and Marta de la Torre, 26-31. Los Angeles: The Getty Conservation Institute.

About the authors

Alain Guiette (BE) is PhD Candidate and Teaching Assistant at the University of Antwerp at the Department of Management (Faculty of Applied Economics).

Annick Schramme (BE) has a PhD in Contemporary History. She is Academic Coordinator of the Master of Cultural Management (Faculty of Applied Economics of the University of Antwerp).

Koen Vandenbempt (BE) has a PhD in Applied Economics and Management. He is professor Strategic Management (Faculty of Applied Economics of the University of Antwerp) and also responsible for the Master of Management and the Executive MBA at Antwerp Management School

Ellen Loots (BE) is PhD Candidate at the University of Antwerp at the Department of Management (Faculty of Applied Economics)

Sofie Jacobs (BE) is researcher Creativity & Creative Industries at Antwerp Management School.
sofie.jacobs@ams.ac.be (corresponding author)

Approaches to stimulate and support the cultural entrepreneur – the case of Denmark and Norway

Trine Bille and Donatella De Paoli

Abstract

There is a growing realization in many countries that the existing public and state support mechanisms, systems and incentives are not well adjusted for the growing cultural and creative entrepreneurs. There is a demand and need for developing new kinds of state support mechanisms and incentives directed specifically to the special needs of cultural entrepreneurs residing between art and commerce, being small and independent, lacking commercial knowledge and the right networks. Although there are expectancies in many European countries for the cultural and creative economy to grow, there is little research and cases showing how this sector can be stimulated and supported in the best way. The purpose of this paper is to put the issue of state support mechanisms towards the cultural and creative industries on the research agenda, and discuss the experiences from Denmark and Norway. Challenges and solutions in stimulating the CCIs are discussed.

Introduction

The Northern countries have traditionally had strong public subsidizing of the arts and culture, a so-called social democratic cultural policy approach. This means an abundant financing of varied arts and cultural expressions of high quality for all groups of citizens. Denmark and Norway have strong and influential educational institutions of art and many talented artists, as well as functioning networks, good arenas and infrastructure for arts and culture. These publicly funded art worlds can be important assets in developing the creative and cultural industries in the Scandinavian countries, but the challenge is how?

Both in Denmark and Norway, the state policies and support mechanisms for the cultural and creative industries are in general two-fold. The Ministry of Culture supports art and cultural production through general art schemes, but here the primary reason for support is the quality of the arts, and not the commercial potential (actually rather the opposite). On the other hand, the Ministry of Economics and Business Affairs support general schemes and framework conditions for business support, but these policies are not especially directed towards the cultural and creative industries. The question is: Are special state policies, incentives and support mechanism necessary for the cultural and creative industries? If this is the case, why do we need special treatment of these industries? And how do we build policies that can best stimulate the cultural and creative industries?

Definition of cultural and creative industries

The definition of the creative and cultural industries has been discussed in many contexts (Bille, 2011; Bille & Lorenzen, 2008; Throsby, 2007). A common list includes the following industries: publishing, advertising, architecture, art and antiques, arts heritage, handcraft, design, fashion design, film & video, computer games, software, music, performing arts, publishing, TV & radio (Towse, 2003). Several analyses define the sector as a growth sector, but also point to large variations between the different sub-sectors. In Norway the cultural and creative industries employ 4% of the total workforce, in total 75.000 persons in 27.000 firms and 42 billion NKK in value added, which is about 4 % of the total value added in the country (Menon & Perduco, 2011). In Denmark the cultural and creative industries account for 175 employees (7.5 % of the total employment), and 108 billion DKK in value added, which is about 12 % of the total value added in Denmark (Danish Enterprise and Construction Authority, 2011).

Special characteristics of the creative industries

There have been some attempts to describe the special characteristics of the creative industries (e.g. Caves, 2000;, Power & Scott, 2004; Hesmondhalgh, 2002; Pratt, 2004). Power and Scott (2004) mention 9 characteristics that the creative industries have in common:

1   Production of symbolic content
2   They employ a highly skilled and highly
    motivated labor force which often works on
    flexible project contracts
3   The use of advanced technology in the
    production process
4   They tend to agglomerate in geographical
    clusters
5   There are often a strong association
    between place and products (e.g. Danish
    furniture, Italian shoes)
6   They are often connected to public authori-
    ties' local and regional development strate-
    gies
7   Their global connectedness
8   The market is characterized by monopolistic
    competition.

Other authors come to some of the same conclusions but also suggest different characteristics of the cultural and creative industries based
on the purpose of their research. What they
have in common is, however, that all the characteristics mentioned may be true for the creative
industries (but not all of them), but many of
them may also be true for industries outside the
cultural and creative sector.

Special political initiatives towards the cultural and creative industries in denmark and norway

Some special initiatives towards the creative
industries have been initiated in *Denmark*. The
first concrete initiative to be mentioned is the
Center for Culture and Experience Economy.
The center is an independent government
funded agency opened in 2009 and financed
by the Ministry of Culture and the Ministry of
Economics and Business Affairs. One of the
purposes of the center is to strengthen the creative sector's business understanding through
strategic collaboration with the business world.
The second initiative is the so-called *experience
zones*, where four zones have been established:
the zones for food culture, music, fashion
and computer games. An experience zone

is a network, where firms, organizations and
institutions join to create growth, innovation and
knowledge within the creative industry throughout the whole country. Finally, the Ministry of
Foreign Affairs has created a special program
call Born Creative to support export development in the creative industries.
Since 2007 the cultural and creative industries
in *Norway* have been stimulated and supported
by a centralized State owned agency called Innovation Norway (hereafter called IN), the basis
for this being an action plan developed jointly
by the Department of Commerce, the Department of Regional and Communal authorities
and the Department of Culture in 2005. The
cultural industries have been one of the 10
target businesses that IN has focused upon. The
measures, grants and support offered to artists
and cultural entrepreneurs are similar to those
offered to other businesses and entrepreneurs;
Financial aid and grants (such as aid for start-
offs and financial aid to business development),
Network oriented competence development
(FRAM Culture, special program directed to
entrepreneurs situated regionally in Norway).

The cultural entrepreneur

The large majority of firms in the creative and
cultural industries in Denmark and Norway
follow a European trend; they are relatively small
firms with a large part of them being one-man
firms or freelancers, so called *'new independent
entrepreneurs'* (Leadbeater & Oakley, 1999).
Entrepreneurs in the creative and cultural
industry do not respond to grants, loans, information and resources in the same way as other
entrepreneurs (De Paoli & Hansen, 2010). The
cultural entrepreneur is often an independent
actor, often operating alone or in networks with
others. Although the artist role has changed
and is influenced by artists searching for other
arenas and incomes, the traditional notion of
the artist still prevails and influences values and
identities of the cultural entrepreneur (Mangset
& Røyseng, 2009). The cultural entrepreneur
sees himself or herself more as an artist than

as a business person and is often influenced by the charismatic and romantic artist role and values (Mangset, 2003), well conserved in traditional art and design schools. In reality, in Norway artists and cultural entrepreneurs that spent more than half of their working time on art production earn a relatively smaller part of their income from the arts (De Paoli and Hansen, 2010).

Special need for support from the cultural and creative industries

In Denmark a report from the Center for Culture and Experience Economy (2011) shows that some of the needs in the cultural and creative industries are different from the needs in all other industries. The results show - among other things - that a larger share of the creative industries are internationally oriented; that immaterial rights are extremely important for the business models; and that financing is a huge challenge in many cultural and creative industries compared to other industries.
In *Norway*, experience shows that despite the many measures and grants for the cultural industry offered, there were relatively few artists applying for the support measures. An evaluation report (De Paoli & Hansen, 2010) concluded that these general support mechanisms, developed for general business, were not working to stimulate the cultural industries. Research amongst artists and cultural entrepreneurs confirmed that they did not find the support understandable, relevant and in a language that appealed. They also found that it was difficult to obtain support (although IN considered that their problem was lack of applicants), and they thought that IN consultants did not have the right competence and insight about the cultural field. Many artists gain money to survive in other fields and activities. Artists report that lack of financing, lack of skills and lack of resources in marketing and administration are the main reasons for not earning higher incomes. They also report that the main sources for increas-

ing incomes are additional sales of products or performances and selling their competences and services.

Challenges and solutions in stimulating the cultural and creative industries

The cases from Denmark and Norway show that the cultural and creative industries are special in some sense, and the cultural entrepreneurs especially need policies concerning financial start-up, how to deal with immaterial rights and exports. The general business support measures have not functioned well in Norway, as cultural entrepreneurs do not respond to these kinds of initiatives in the same manner as general business entrepreneurs (De Paoli & Hansen, 2010).
The common view is that business support needs to be as general as possible. Denmark has partly chosen a 'pick the winner' strategy with focus at four experience zones: food culture, music, fashion and computer games. Norway has chosen for a typically democratic strategy, spreading the support evenly across all cultural fields. In Denmark the special initiatives have not yet been evaluated, but it seems that the 'pick the winner strategy' may function better in regard to meeting each cultural industry's needs. Based on the evaluation of support mechanisms in Denmark and Norway, cultural industries seem to have different needs for support. Even though they have several characteristics in common, they do also differ with regard to various dimensions; institutional support, size, competence level and need for financing.

References

- Birch, S. (2008): *The political promotion of the experience economy and creative industries* – Cases from UK, New Zealand, Singapore, Norway, Sweden and Denmark, Forlaget Samfundslitteratur and CBS, Copenhagen.
- Bille, T. and M. Lorenzen (2008): *Den danske oplevelsesøkonomi – afgrænsning, økonomisk betydning og vækstmuligheder.* Forlaget Samfundslitteratur and CBS, Copenhagen .
- Caves, R. E. (2000): *Creative Industries. Contact between art and commerce,* Harvard University Press, Cambridge.
- Center for Culture and Experience Economy (2011): *Behovsanalyse. Kreative Erhverv i Danmark,* del. 1, Copenhagen
- Danish Building and Construction Authority (2011): *Vækst via oplevelser,* Copenhagen.
- Danish Government (2003): *Danmark i kultur og oplevelsesøkonomien – 5 nye skridt på vejen,* Copenhagen.
- De Paoli, D. & T. Hansen (2010): *Competence about public measures directed towards the cultural industries – An evaluation of the Norwegian Art Council and State Innovation Bureau,* A report for the Norwegian Department of Commerce.
- Hagoort, G. & Kooyman R. (Ed). (2010): *The Entrepreneurial Dimension of the Cultural and Creative Industries.* Utrecht School of the Arts HKU, Utrecht.
- Hesmondhalgh, D. (2002): *The Cultural Industries,* Sage Publications.
- Leadbeater, C. & Oakley, K. (2001): *The independent. Britain's new cultural entrepreneur.* Demos, London.
- Mangset, P. (2003): *Jeg må! Jeg må; så byder meg en stemme. Om kunstneroller i endring,* Nordisk Kulturpolitisk Tidsskrift 2, p 127-167.
- Mangset, P. & Røyseng S. (Ed.)(2009): *Kulturelt entreprenørskap.* Fagbokforlaget.
- Menon & Perduco (2011): *The role of the cultural industries for Norwegian economy.* Report Nr. 9, Menon Business Economics, Oslo.
- Pratt, A. (2004): Mapping the cultural Industries: Regionalization: The Examples of South-East England, In: D. Power and A. J. Scott: *Cultural Industries and the Culture of Production,* Routledge, London.
- Power, D. & Scott. A.J. (2004): *Cultural Industries and the Production of Culture,* Routledge, London.
- Throsby, D. (2007): Paper presented at the conference: Cultural Industries Seminar Network: *New Directions in Research: Substance, method and Critique,* Edinburgh.
- Towse, R. (2003): Cultural industries. In R. Towse (ed.): *A Handbook of Cultural Economics,* Edward Elgar, Cheltenham.

About the authors

Trine Bille (DK) is Associate Professor, Ph.D. at Copenhagen Business School (CBS), Department of Innovation and Organizational Economics, and Senior Researcher II at Telemarksforskning, Norway. She got her Ph.D. from University of Copenhagen, Department of Economics. Her main research interest is cultural economics and she has published many books and articles within this field.
tb.ino@cbs.dk

Donatella De Paoli (NO) is Associate Professor, Ph.D. at BI Norwegian Business School. She got her Ph.D. from the Norwegian School of Economics (NHH) and was visiting scholar at Stanford University during her doctoral work. Her main research interest is cultural management and leadership, but also the role of aesthetics and art for business. She has published several books and articles within these fields.
donatella.d.paoli@bi.no

Abstract

Creativity plays an important role in modern society and so do the creative industries. This role should change distinctively if we recognize the urgency of a sustainable society. Ten different reasons to pursue sustainability are given. Among them, climate change and the addiction to economic growth. Transition theory is used as a means to organize the road to sustainability. A possible role of the creative industry in this transitional process is indicated. In conclusion, the idea of a slow creativity movement is initiated, and proposals for further research on this matter sketched.

Creative in modern society

Being creative usually means that you have reached an original solution for a problem. But being creative may also involve an artistic view or product for the sake of itself: art for art's sake, or in the original expression in French: *'l'art pour l'art'*. The cultural and creative worker or entrepreneur combines elements of both problem solving and of making for art's sake. As Giep Hagoort noted (Hagoort, 2007), the cultural entrepreneur combines two freedoms: artistic freedom as immaterial content oriented value, and entrepreneurial freedom as material value, supportive to immaterial (cultural) values. For a better understanding you could – as UNCTAD does (Dos Santos Duisenberg, 2010) - distinguish between two types of creative & cultural activities: *'upstream activities'* (traditional cultural activities such as performing arts or visual arts) and *'downstream activities'* (those closer to the market, such as advertising, publishing or media related activities).

It is widely recognized that cultural and creative activities are important in modern society. On this subject there are numerous publications. Governments and international agencies, like the OECD, the EU and UNCTAD realized the importance of creativity for the development of new policies. An OECD study: *The creative society of the 21st century* points out the role of creativity in the knowledge society (2000). Starting with Richard Florida's Rise of the creative class (2002) and followed by many articles, actions on a local scale promoted these ideas as is shown further on in this article.

Important reasons for a growing interest in the creative industries and in creativity in general are:

- Creativity and art leads to new solutions; gives new interpretations or new ways of looking at complex matters.
- The growing attention for the creative industries in recent years by governments and the EU establishment. This attention is mainly focused on its contribution for growth-oriented innovation. It expresses the acknowledgement of the role of the cultural and creative industries (CCI) to attract new knowledge based industries.
- In rankings of *'cool'* cities to live in; a large and active CCI is supposed to contribute strongly to a good living climate in the city. The EU even has a site: creativemetropoles.eu. It states about Amsterdam: *'A thriving creative sector itself brings new entrepreneurship, innovation and employment. Amsterdam is the place where your ideas, and your dreams, can really flourish.'*

Figure 1. creativemetropoles.eu.

Those reasons are based upon the notion that innovation is important to stay in the front line in the race of the metropolises.

The so-called Lisbon agenda, followed by Europe 2020 (EU, 2010), concentrates on growth and jobs. Included in this strategy are sustainable objectives (like clean energy and electrical cars). However in due time growth of gross national product (GNP) as a value in itself became the single goal. Nevertheless the knowledge society and education and training are keywords as well.

A second foremost reason is the continuation of the promotion of ICT projects. An important element for the growing role of the CCI in modern society can also be found in wealth: in short, higher income means a diminishing percentage that is needed for fundamental living conditions, such as food, insurance and primary housing conditions. As a consequence we can identify a growing spending on fashion, design products, art and culture in general.

Creativity is the *'ability to produce something new through imaginative skill, whether a new solution to a problem, a new method or device, or a new artistic object or form. The term generally refers to a richness of ideas and originality of thinking'.*[1] The cultural & creative industries are defined in the same kind of terms: industries in which the product or service contains a substantial element of artistic or imaginative endeavor. The product is usually subject to intellectual property rights.

The urgency of sustainability

On the urgent need for sustainability there is a rising number of books and articles. Some deal more with the aspects of nature and the loss of bio-diversity, like: Growing within Limits (2009) a report for the Global Assembly of the Club of Rome, others deal with aspects of the economy unsustainable conduct like Tim Jackson (2009) or Alejandro Nadal, or specifically with strategies Like Lester Brown (2009). Inequality is also an important aspect of sustainability, as in Tony Judt or Stewart Lansley, or Zygmunt Bauman (2011). Focusing on the Netherlands I wrote, with co-author Lou Keune, an oversight on the relevant factors (2011).

To understand the possibilities for the CCI on the road to a sustainable society, I will take sustainability more seriously and more urgently than the EU establishment and the governments of the member states. We have 10 to 20 years to organize and execute the transition to a sustainable society. I give 10 reasons as a short overview:

1 **Overshoot day and footprint:** overshoot day in 2010 was august 21. This means 'once we pass this day, humanity will have demanded all the ecological services – from filtering CO2 to producing the raw materials for food – that nature can provide this year. From that point until the end of the year, we meet our ecological demand by liquidating resource stocks and accumulating carbon dioxide in the atmosphere'.[2] Overshootday in 2011 was September 27. Related to overshoot is the concept of the human footprint. The average footprint of a Dutchman is 6.2 hectares while the average footprint for humanity is 1.8 hectare per person.

2 **Climate change:** If we do not succeed in bringing back the CO2 emissions below the 350 PPM limit global warming may cause a tipping of the climate system. Instability, food shortage, desert formation, the disappearance of islands etc. follows (Guardian, 2009).

[1] See: http://www.answers.com/topic/creativity.

[2] http://www.footprintnetwork.org/en/index.php/GFN/page/earth_overshoot_day/.

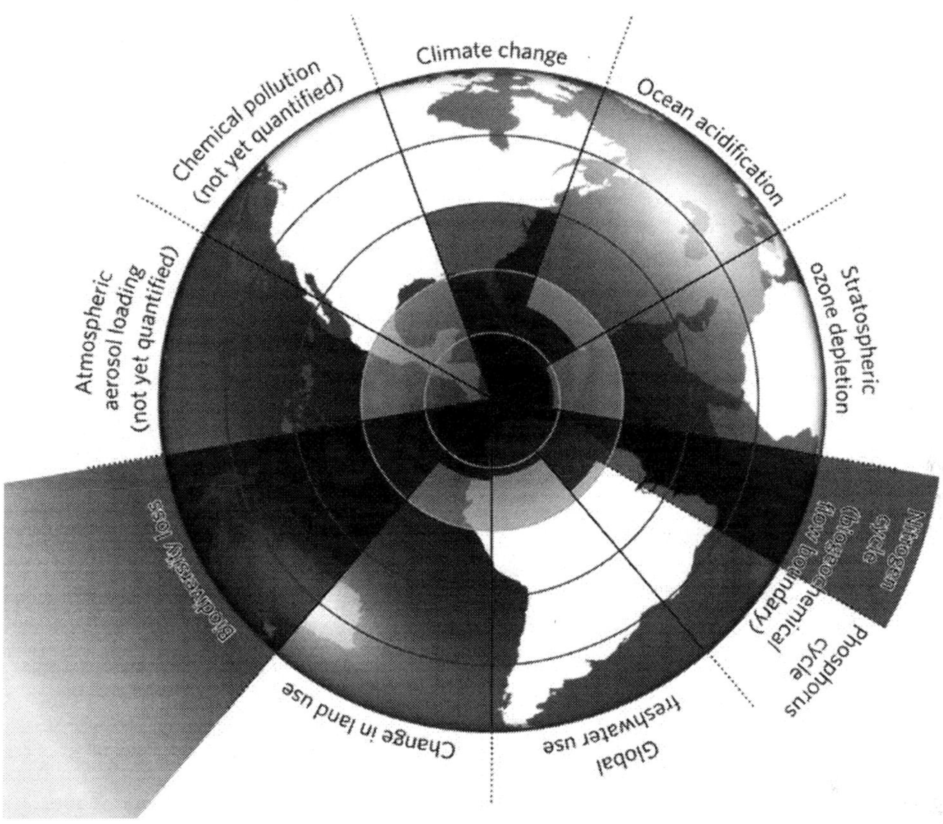

Figure 2. Rockström: http://climatesafety.org/great-johan-rockstrom-presentation-on-planetary-boundaries-concept

3   **Raw materials and energy:** Peakoil is a well known phrase. From now on it is going to be less. That not only holds for oil, but for most non-renewable energy sources. To compensate for the use of new materials *Cradle to Cradle* (MBDC2012) is an important new way, but it is not enough.

4   **Biodiversity and land use:** Today the rate of extinction of species, is estimated to be 100 to 1000 times higher than would be considered a natural rate of loss. The loss of biodiversity on a world scale is 70%, on the European scale it is 50% (in the Netherlands even 70%)[3] This loss is very clear in figure 2. Land use is another huge problem. We are losing arable land for new roads, for cities, but mainly because of degradation, and we need more because of the rise in food demand (growing population and growing income).

5   There is nothing wrong with **globalization** in the sense of world solidarity. But the current globalization process is mainly a profit driven monopolistic action to promote international trade, foreign direct investment flows and financial transactions. Land grabbing is one of the examples by which large corporations buy large pieces of Africa for less than nothing (FAO 2011). The only ecological and social alternative is to promote a regional

[3] http://www.pbl.nl/publicaties/2010/State-of-the-Environment-Report-2010-SOER-2010.

economy in the high-income countries as well as in developing countries. International solidarity then means that the rich countries establish a system for basic secure livelihoods. A tax on financial transactions (FTT) could provide the necessary finance.

6 **Addiction to growth.** Growth of GNP is in all countries a major policy goal. It is also the main future problem. Since growth leads to a worsening of an unsustainable situation. It leads to more energy consumption, to the use of more raw materials, to the use of more land etc. To step out of the growth cycle is difficult: growth is good for corporations (more profit); good for trade unions (higher wages); good for government (more spending > more votes); good for consumers (more income> more goodies). To step out of the growth addiction means: dematerialized consumption, more free time, more time for culture etc.

7 The **world population** is growing fast towards 8.9 billion people (UN 2004). In this prognosis is already reckoned with a diminishing growth! This growing population also will want to consume like we do. Population policies are tricky. They are about personal freedom, but it has been argued that each 7 $ spend on family planning in the years 2010 – 2050 leads to a lesser CO2 emission of one ton. Also education for girls and economic chances for women are important.

8 The present economic crisis originated as a **crisis of financial institution**s, of major banks. Banks should go back to their original role of service institutions for the economy. For a sustainable economy we don't need banks that go for the highest profits, but banks that support community oriented business.

9 Let's be short about **warfare**. War tends more and more to be civil war (with outsiders involved). If we had spent all the dollars, euro's, and pounds on development and sustainability programs we would have had a totally different world.

10 For a new start we need **transparent governance**, more influence of the population in actual policies and we need leadership: leaders that are not afraid of the next election and are concerned with the urgency to create opportunities for a transition to a sustainable world.

On these ten needs there is much debate. On some of them progress has been made, but the important thing is that we need progress on the whole of this complex set of requirements.

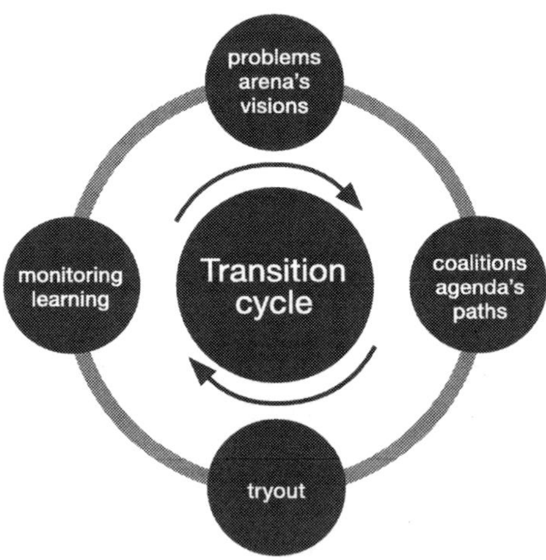

Figure 3. Transition cycle.

The contribution of creativity towards a sustainable transition

In history there have been many examples of the uses of artists and creatives in phases of transition. During the Second World War, for example, the UK Government employed the creative community to encourage changes in consumption not possible by rationing alone. President Roosevelt pumped millions of dollars into the arts. Drawing inspiration from the Mexican mural movement of the 1920s, the New Deal put socially conscious murals in public buildings across the country. An ambitious oral history project documented national history including the first-person accounts of former slaves. The Federal Music Project employed around 16,000 musicians at its peak, who gave an estimated 5,000 performances to audiences of around three million people each week. In 1939, around 132,000 children and adults in 27 states received music lessons every week. I found these examples in: The Great Transition, published by the New Economics Foundation. They call themselves an *independent do and think tank*[4].

One of the authors mentioned before: Lester Brown (2009) argues that there are three models for social change:

> 'One is the catastrophic event model, which I call the Pearl Harbor model, where a dramatic event fundamentally changes how we think and behave. The second model is one where a society reaches a tipping point on a particular issue often after an extended period of gradual change in thinking and attitudes. This I call the Berlin Wall model. The third is the sandwich model of social change, where there is a strong grassroots movement pushing for change on a particular issue that is fully supported by strong political leadership at the top' (Brown, 2009).

Before Fukushima or Lehman Brothers we could not think of these disasters. And so we did't know what was to come. The best guarantee is to start working on a transition towards a sustainable and solidary society. Transition theories have become quite important in the area of sustainable research. A recent overview states that over 1000 scientific publications have been written on this subject (Loorbach, 2012).

The transition to a sustainable society is a long and complex process. But a general model of transitions is usually drawn as a cycle. Each of the phases of that process has its own dynamics. And it is recognized that transitions take place on many levels and in many places by various actors (Loorbach, 2007).

Artists, Cultural and Creative workers (CCW's) have the qualifications to make an important contribution to such a transition. As we saw before the imaginative skills of the CCW's are their core business. They are trained and experienced people who bring new solutions to a problem, develop new methods or devices, and create new artistic objects and or forms.

I'll describe some of the roles of the CCI and its workers in this transition process:

1 **To develop a new vision** for a sustainable society means new images have to be developed. New narratives have to be created. In this area videos, film, architects and many others from the CCI can play a role.
2 To create an agenda and / or a transition path is something for the information sector, to act the possibilities of various paths is theatre.
3 For trying out, for experiments we need to **reconceptualize design & production processes** (C2C). In the process of sustainability we need to focus on new differences in expression and on the benefits of diversity. The CCI in various sectors can contribute to

[4] http://neweconomics.org/publications/great-transition

these experiments for a 'cultural' turn. The CCI are experts in processes of new cross overs.

4 Media are **experts in monitoring**, in reporting on new developments in society. Experimenting in processes of new cross overs is a piece of cake for the CCI's.

5 Lastly: if we thrive for a dematerialized society, **material downshifting** will be part of the process. Cultural workers and artists can put in their personal experience with downshifting .

Slow creativity

When the primary interest of the CCW´s shifts towards a role in promoting a sustainable society, they will look more like the so-called *'cultural creatives´* (cc's) as defined by Ray & Anderson (2000). They are described as caring: ...*'deeply about ecology and saving the planet, about relationships, peace, and social justice, about self-actualization, spirituality, and self-expression.'*
Giving urgent attention to these values, and especially about ecology and saving the planet, the main future role for CCW´s (and their qualifications as making new images and new creative solutions) should focus more on maintaining and restoring old values, to maintaining and restoring diversity (in society as in nature), slowing down the path of economic growth etc. In this way they can be part of the *'slow movement´*.

This movement originates from the *slow food* as a protest against mass consumption (profit driven, unhealthy, destroys local cultures, diminishes bio diversity). As an alternative they promote: local food, food of the season, better energy uses, local markets and economy, more bio diversity, more quality, endeavors fair prices, and community building. This also is a movement restoring old values but in a very exciting way. It is against standardization of taste and culture. Slow Food believes in the strong connections between plate, planet, people and culture (Slow Food, 2012).

The same holds for slow cities: Slow cities are characterized by a way of life that supports people to live slow. Traditions and traditional ways of doing things are valued. These cities stand up against the fast-lane, homogenized world so often seen in other cities throughout the world. Slow cities have less traffic, less noise, fewer crowds.

Along the same line of thinking, I think a *slow creativity movement* can play an important role in our striving for a sustainable society. It is a movement to promote a better & creative living, with a large impact of cultural and creative people, against mass consumption and standardization, supporting people to live slow, to live with communal values. The artist, the creative and large parts of the creative industry can thus play a major role in the promotion, in experiments for sustainability, in the realization of a sustainable society. But we must realize that creativity can only produce new ideas, new products, new art through imaginative skill and through a persistent critical attitude. In short the *slow creativity movement* means: to work for a creative & sustainable society; that is a better society.

A lot of themes I discussed in this article/chapter can be processed in further research activities. It is my observation that the cultural and creative industries lack a research agenda on these themes. We have to collect information about artistic practices which have their focus on sustainability and we have to study the position of main cultural institutes within a slow creativity movement - and their new role in city marketing? We can also pay attention to the pioneers in this experimental field: green designers, community artists, directors who realize sustainable and environmental friendly festivals. The aim of this new research is quite clear: to work on a creative and sustainable society. And that is - according to Unctad (Dos Santos 2010) - a more human society.

References

- Bauman, Z. (2011) *Collateral Damage, social inequalities in a global age*, Polity Press, Cambridge.
- Brown, Lester (2009). *Plan B 4.0, mobilizing to safe civilization*, W.W. Norton & Company, New York.
- Dos Santos Duisenberg, (Ed.) (2010). *Creative Economy Report 2010. E feasible Development Option.* Geneva: UNCTAD.
- EU, (2010). *From the Lisbon Strategy to "Europe 2020".* Retrieved from: http://ec.europa.eu/education/focus/focus479_en.htm.
- FAO (2011): *Land grab or development opportunity?* Retrieved from: http://www.fao.org/docrep/011/ak241e/ak241e00.htm.
- Florida, R. (2002). *The Rise of the Creative Class.* New York: Basic Books.
- *Growing within Limits,* a report to the global assembly of the Club of Rome, Netherlands Environmental Assessment Agency, 2009.
- Guardian Environment Network (2012). Retrieved from: http://www.guardian.co.uk/environment/2009/aug/26/pachauri-350ppm-breakthrough-climate.
- Hagoort, Giep (2007) *Cultural Entrepreneurship. On the freedom to create art and the freedom of enterprise,* University Utrecht.
- Jackson, T. (2009). *Prosperity without Growth, economics for a finite planet.* Earthscan, London.
- Judt, T. (2010). *Ill Fares the Land,* Penguin, London.
- Lansley, S. (2011). *The cost of inequality, three decades of the super-rich and the economy,* Gibson Square, London.
- Loorbach, D. & Rotmans, J. (2012). *Transities en transitiemanagement, Oorsprong, status en toekomst,* Drift, Dutch Research Institute For Transitions, Creative Commons, Rotterdam.
- Loorbach, D. (2007). *Transition Management; new mode of governance for sustainable development,* International Books, Utrecht.
- *Mondiale Voetafdruk.* Global Footprint Network. Retrieved from: http://www.voetafdruk.eu/, feb 2012.
- MBDC (2012). *Cradle to Cradle Framework.* Retrieved from: http://mbdc.com/detail.aspx?linkid=1&sublink=6.
- Nadal, A. (2011). *Rethinking macroeconomics for sustainability,* Zedbooks, London.
- NEF (2010). *New Economics Foundation.* Retrieved from: http://neweconomics.org/publications/great-transition.
- Ray, P. & Anderson, S. R. T*he Cultural Creatives: How 50 Million People Are Changing the World,* 2000, Three Rivers Press, New York.
- *Slow Food.* Retrieved from: http://www.slowfood.com/international/2/our-philosophy, feb 2012.
- *The creative society of the 21st century,* OECD 2000.
- United Nations (2004). *World Population to 2300.* UN Economic and Social Affairs. New York. Retrieved from: http://www.un.org/esa/population/publications/longrange2/WorldPop2300final.pdf.

About the author

John Huige (NL) is a political economist. He researches and publishes on sustainability and works as an independent consultant. Before that he used to be director of two large Dutch NGO's and he taught economics and labor relations.

johnhuige@planet.nl

Creative Urban Renewal
Evaluating Cultural and Creative Entrepreneurial Development
Rene Kooyman

Abstract

Almost all larger cities have to cope with the never-ending cycle of attracting new entrepreneurial activities, economic growth and decay. When trying to renovate run-down quarters, city planners look at the creative industries.
In order to evaluate urban area developments, the Creative Zone Innovator (CZI) Model has been developed. The CZI identifies four dimensions within the Creative Zone; the development of the Learning lab, a Cultural Value Chain, the Flow of Diversity, and Cultural Business Modeling (CBM). These dimensions have resulted in a system of measurable indicators. The CZI Model will be tested and amended in the EU Creative Urban Renewal project.

Introduction

The changing dynamics of our industrial societies have an impact on our built environments. Urban areas that once served as industrial quarters, are abundant and become derelict areas, once the original entrepreneurs have left and moved to more attractive quarters.
Entrepreneurial behavior is driving these local developments. Almost all larger cities have to cope with the never-ending cycle of attracting new entrepreneurial activities, economic growth and decay. When trying to renovate run-down quarters, city planners look at the creative industries. It is seen as a win-win situation. Creative entrepreneurs, often in their start-up phase, are looking for low-cost working spaces, and the city planners want to attract new initiatives, visitors and users, in order to create a viable, urban creative zone.

The creative economy, urban area development and the entrepreneurial dimension

When examining the Cultural and Creative Industries (CCIs) one is confronted with a complex, multi-layered discussion. One is not only discussing the built environment; the 'bricks and mortar'. The city-developer has in addition to deal with the social dimension. And one is confronted with cultural policies; does it stimulate art production and art-participation, and if so should it be supported by governmental financial funding?
The concept of the 'creative economy' is an evolving one that is gaining ground in contemporary thinking about economic development (Dos Santos-Duisenberg, 2008). It entails a shift from the conventional models towards a multidisciplinary model dealing with the interface between economics, culture and technology and centered on the predominance of services and creative content. Given its multidisciplinary structure, the creative economy offers a feasible option as part of a results-oriented urban development strategy for different policy actors.
Urban Planning starts with the assumption that social, economical and environmental developments can be identified by analyzing the territorial consequences (World Planners Congress, 2006). For several decades there has been a discussion amongst urban planners regarding the paradox of (a) developing urban areas on the basis of rational processes, and (b) the place and position of the creative sector. Part of these discussions is based on the question whether developments can be invoked by rational planning mechanisms (Etzioni, 2009).
More persistent is the debate about the social characteristics of the cities developed. Jane Jacobs was one of the first who pointed to the contribution of creativity regarding the vital characteristics of a neighborhood (Jacobs, The death and life of great American cities, Feb 1993 [1961]). In her view, cities are the unique places where innovations are promoted. In her book *The Economy of Cities* she

describes that cities – by nature – have the capability of supporting creative potential, because they can build upon the various diversified environments (Jacobs, 1970). Attracting the creative class can put a hold on the ongoing decay of underprivileged neighborhoods. Richard Florida (Florida, 2006) struggles to grasp why creative and talented people settle in a certain city or region. He uses the sociological concept of the 'cultural class' introduced by Pierre Bourdieu (Bourdieu, 1984). Bourdieu makes a distinction between 'financial capital' and 'cultural capital' and put these two on an equal footing. In Florida's view, what cities and regions should attract is not the creative companies, but the people that work for these companies or might start such companies themselves; the creative class. Referring to Jane Jacobs (1961; 1970) as one of his main inspiration sources, Florida claims that creative and talented people prefer to live in cities with a diverse population and a tolerant atmosphere. In more recent work Florida (2006) added that *talent is not a stock, it is flow*. Talent can move from one place to another.

Clustering of socio-economical development

Since the 1990s, the importance of geographic location and context has enjoyed a revival in economic and economic-geographic theories (Gritsai, 2007). Phelps and Ozawa (Phelps, 2003) have highlighted the main shifts in agglomeration factors from the late industrial to the post-industrial era. They refer amongst others to shifts in geographic scale (from town with suburbs to the global city-region), shifts in the intra-regional structure (from hierarchically organized monocentric structures, to polycentric structures that have a more complementary organization), shifts in economic specialization (from manufacturing to services), and shifts in the mode of production and the division of labor (applying new principles and increasingly complex labor inputs with major impacts for labor composition within firms and for relations between firms, within and between sectors and within and between cities and regions).
Few of the concepts referred to above have been as influential in the academic and political debate as the cluster concept. The cluster concept as defined by business economist Michael Porter. Porter points at the emergence of clusters as *critical masses – in one place – of unusual competitive success in particular fields'* (Porter, 1998, p. 76). More specifically he states: *'Clusters are geographic concentrations of interconnected companies and institutions in a particular field. Clusters encompass an array of linked industries and other entities important to competition'* (p. 78). The cluster concept has, however, been repeatedly criticized (Turok, 2004).

Sustainable urban development

There is an ongoing debate about how creative industries contribute to sustainable and evenly distributed economic and urban development (Musterd c.s., 2007). At first sight, the emerging 'creative class' seems to be synonymous with a new bourgeois-bohemian component of the population with individual and protective values (Brooks A. C., 2001). This would have repercussions both at the production and consumption levels in cities. Concerns about creative knowledge strategies for social cohesion should be taken seriously. Yet it is important to stress that a creative knowledge economy offers chances to people of all socio-economic and educational strata to profit from their talents. An economy focusing on creativity does not need to be an elitist economy. It can also offer new chances to marginal groups that have been unable to participate in urban and regional economic progress (Musterd c.s., 2007, p. 64).

The current trend of policy initiatives to create or enhance creative quarters reminds one strongly of the heated debate on gentrification in social science and society. Gentrification is a general term for the arrival of wealthier people in an existing urban district, a related increase in rents and property values, and changes in the district's character and culture. The effects of gentrification are complex and contradictory, and its real impact varies (Pekarchik, June 11, 2001):

- Demographics: An increase in median income, a decline in the proportion of racial and cultural minorities, and a reduction in household size, as low-income families are replaced by young singles and couples.
- Real Estate Markets: An increase in rents and home prices, increases in the number of evictions, conversion of rental units to ownership (condos) and new development of luxury housing.
- Land Use: A decline in industrial uses, an increase in office or multimedia uses, the development of live-work "lofts" and high-end housing, retail, and restaurants.
- Culture and Character: New ideas about what is desirable and attractive, including standards (either informal or legal) for architecture, landscaping, public behavior, noise, and nuisance.

Butler (2003) found that gentrifiers largely live in their own world (or 'bubble' as he phrases it) and almost exclusively mingle with 'people like them' in all aspects of social life. These findings comply with the cultural distinction created by those who create the class of 'cultural capital' (Bourdieu, 1984).

The entrepreneurial model

Seen from an occupational perspective creative entrepreneurs own and manage their own business enterprise (Hagoort & Kooyman, 2011). In essence, the creative entrepreneur is a creator of economical value (Sternberg, 2005). Yet, in addition they have to balance the entrepreneurial targets with the cultural ones (Hagoort, 2007).

A number of activities embody entrepreneurial behavior:

- Developing new and innovative products;
- Proposing new forms of organization;
- Exploring new markets;
- Introducing new production methods;
- Searching for new sources of supplies and materials (Schumpeter, 1975).

They share *the willingness to assume risk*s in the face of uncertainty. For example, risks such as a possible loss of business capital or the personal financial security, risk associated with the uncertain outcome of an entrepreneurial undertaking (Knight, 1921). *The alertness of opportunity*, the focus on the detection of entrepreneurial opportunities either for financial profit, or content based. This alertness allows the entrepreneur to exploit market opportunities that have been overlooked or gone undiscovered by others (Kirzner, 1973). As other entrepreneurs they share the change perspective. *'Entrepreneurs see change as the norm and as healthy'* (Drücker, 1985).

Entrepreneurs are involved in networks of multiple and changing clients, competitors, colleagues, etc. (Gardner, 2007). However, there are a number of entrepreneurial aspects that set the CCIs apart. One can identify differences in the labor market. The cultural fabric of the CCI is complex and thrives on numerous very small initiatives (Reidl & Steyer, 2006); a conglomerate of individuals and free lancers; the *'nano-enterprises'* (Kooyman, Preliminary Inventory of existing literature, aug 2009). In addition, one can identify specific product characteristics and differences in production methods (Christiane Eisenberg, 2006), in market conditions (Montmarquette, 1996).

The creative urban renewal (cure) model

Recently six mid-sized cities in the North West of Europe have combined their effort to renovate local underprivileged areas.[1] The CURE Project aims to develop innovative solutions to the question how the creative economy can play an active role in urban renewal processes in medium-sized cities in NW Europe (Koppejan, 2011). Creative Urban Renewal (CURE) is meant to facilitate triggered allocation of the creative economy in decayed urban areas. Once it is decided to use cultural and creative entrepreneurs in order to develop urban neighborhoods, the basic problem is how to evaluate the developments that take place. When is the process a success, or how to look at failures? What model can we use, in order to evaluate creative urban development?
Urban interaction can be divided into four dimensions that can be translated into 'Sub-values' and 'Indicators' to initiate strategic measuring and monitoring activities. The four dimensions constitute the Creative Zone Innovator (CZI) conceptual model. They represent the dynamics of the functioning of C SMEs in a particular context (Utrecht School of the Arts (HKU, 2010).

- **Learning lab**: The Creative Zone Innovator (CZI) aims to create a learning environment, which enables entrepreneurs to continually expand their capacity, to create the results they want and remain innovative and creative. The knowledge dynamics of a creative quarter is the combination of individual and networked learning; to facilitate people to develop their skills and capacities to be able to respond flexible and imaginatively to the opportunities and difficulties faced as a creative entrepreneur.
- **Cultural Value Chain:** The CZI aims to stimulate and strengthen the networked alliances of the creative entrepreneurs with gatekeepers, (co-)producers, distributers and costumers in the creative quarter. An enhancement of the infrastructure by filling the gaps in the supply chain improves sustainable development of the entrepreneurs and the value of creative products and services.
- **Flow of Diversity:** The CZI aims to create a natural flow with an emphasis on diversity offering continuous new impulses and avoiding the creation of a non-commercial bubble. By combining commercial with subsidized entrepreneurs, start-ups with established firms, or combining different functions and stimulating embedded networking diversity generates a natural stream of new and spontaneous encounters.
- **Cultural Business Modeling (CBM):** The CZI aims to describe the specifics of the creative workforce and the dynamics of urban planning, including specific alternative networking and financing structures in order to accelerate the successful development of entrepreneurial companies. The creative zones are strongly focused on the entrepreneurial spirit of the creative professionals (C SMEs).

[1] City of Hagen, Dinslaken & Kettwig (BRD), Brugge (BE). ; Colchester & Edinburgh (UK); Lille (FR)

A graphic illustration of the four dimensions showing the accompanying goals and objectives is presented here.

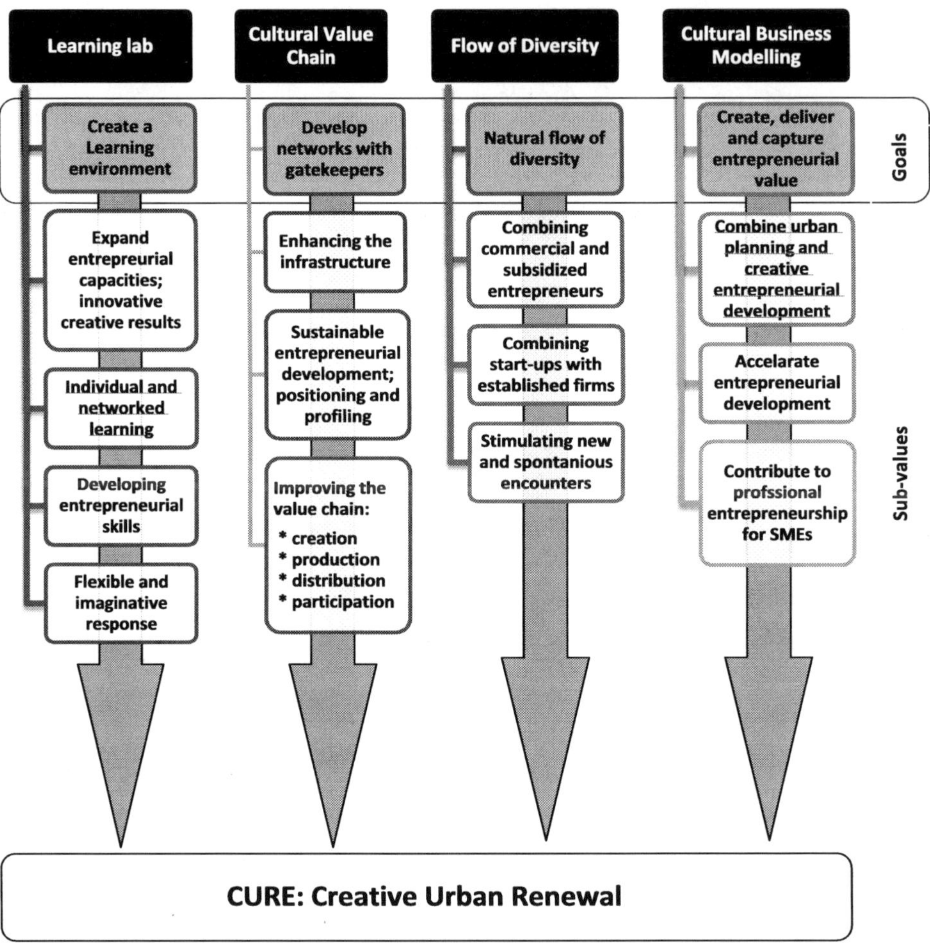

Figure 1. CURE Conceptual Model: the Creative Zone Innovator (CZI).

The need for and use of indicators

Investing time, money and commitment in a project has to be justified in several ways. Evaluation is part of this justification process, both at the beginning, during and at the end of a project. In order to create a fair, clear and easy to communicate opinion regarding the development of a project one needs explicitly defined indicators, applicable to all partners in the project.

An indicator can be defined as *'a characteristic or attribute which can be measured to assess an intervention in terms of its outputs or results'* (EU, 2009). A good indicator should provide simple information that both the supplier and the user can easily communicate and understand. This is, however, a necessary but not sufficient quality. Indicators are signs of progress and change that result from your project. They provide some guidance about what would be useful evaluation information to collect. Some of this will involve collecting information along the way, which help you to gauge how well things are going, and possibly enable you to make improvements throughout the project. Others will involve collecting information at the start, during and end of the project (Feuerstein, 2006).

The system of Indicators developed within the CURE Project produce quantified or qualitative information, with a view to helping actors concerned with public interventions to communicate, negotiate or make decisions. Within the framework of evaluation, the most important indicators are linked to the success criteria of project interventions. Within the CURE Project, the Creative Zone Innovator model will be further tested and - if needed - amended.

A system of quality control has been introduced. A continuous assessment process has been planned; at the start (the zero-state assessment), at the mid-term, and the final assessment. A separate Monitoring Board has been appointed, in order to guarantee external reflection and quality checks. The conclusions derived from the project will lead to the development of the Creative Zone Innovator Index; an overview of the different projects and activities, and an evaluation of the final results.

References

- Bourdieu, P. (1984). Distinction. *A social critique of the judgement of taste.* New York/Paris.
- Brooks A. C., R. J. (2001). Cultural Districts and Urban Development. In: *International Journal of Arts Management* (No 2).
- Christiane Eisenberg, R. G. (2006). From Gentlemanly Publishing to Conglomerates: The Contemporary Literary Field in the UK. In S. Gesa, *Cultural Industries: The British Experience, in International Perspective.* Berlin: Humbold University.
- CURE (2009). *INTERREG IVB North West Europe Application 7th Call.* Hagen: HKU Utrecht School of the Arts.
- Dos Santos-Duisenberg, E. (Ed) (2008). *Creative Econmy Report 2008.* United Nations Committee on Trade, Aid and Development. Geneva, CH: UNCTAD.
- Drücker, P. (1985). *Innovation & Entrepreneurship.* New Yorh: Harper and Row.
- Etzioni, A. (2009). Mixed scanning; a third approach to Decision Making. In A. C. Coates, *Strategic decision making paradigms.* USAWC.
- *EU MEANS programme* (Means for Evaluating Actions of a Structural Nature). (2009). Retrieved from: http://ec.europa.eu/regional_policy/sources/docgener/evaluation/evalsed/index_en.htm. February 2012.
- Feuerstein, R. &. (2006). *La pédagogie à visage humain.* Paris: Le Bord de l'Eau.
- Florida, R. (2002). *The Rise of the Creative Class.* New York: Basic Books.
- Florida, R. (2006). *The Flight of the Creative Class: The New Global Competition for Talent.* New York: Harper Collins.
- Gardner, W. (2007). 'Who is an entrepreneur?' is the wrong question. *American Journal of Small Business*, 12 (4), p. 11 - 32.
- Gritsai, O. (2007). *Target group importance in the Barcelona Case Study.* Amsterdam: UVA.
- Hagoort, G. a. (2011). *On the principles of cultural entrepreneurship. Balancing between imagination and financial profit.* Utrecht, the Netherlands: Utrecht University/HKU.
- Hagoort, G. (2007). *Cultural Entrepreneurship. On the freedom to create art and the freedom of enterprise Utrecht:* Utrecht University, the Netherlands.
- Jacobs, J. (1993 [1961]). *The death and life of great American cities.* New York: Random House.
- Jacobs, J. (1970). *The Economy of Cities.* New York: Random House.
- Kirzner, I. M. (1973). *Competition and Entrepreneurship.* Chicago IL: University of Chicago Press.
- Knight, F. H. (1921). *Risk, Uncertainty, and Profit. Library of Economics and Liberty.* Retrieved 07 11, 2011, from http://www.econlib.org/library/Knight/knRUP1.html.
- Kooyman, R. (2009). Preliminary Inventory of existing literature. In *The entrepreneurial dimension of cultural and creative industries.* Utrecht: HKU School of the arts.

- Kooyman, R. (2011). Creative Zone Innovator: Conceptual Framework, Sub-values and Indicators. *Theoretical notions.* Utrecht: HKU.
- Koppejan, G.H. (2011). *CURE Project Kick-off Document.* Utrecht: HKU School of the Arts.
- Montmarquette, G. L. (1996). *A micro-econometric study of theatre demand.* 20 (1).
- Musterd c.s., S. (2007). *Accommodating Creative Knowledge.* Amsterdam: ACRE University of Amsterdam.
- Pekarchik, K. (2001). Alphabet City: The ABCs of Gentrification. In: *Businessweek* , (June 11, 2001)
- Phelps, N. a. (2003). Contrasts in agglomeration: Proto-industrial, industrial and post-industrial forms compared. In: *Progress in Human Geography* (5), p. 583 - 604.
- Porter, M. (1998). Clusters and the new economics of competition. In: *Harvard Business Review* , 76 (6), p. 77 - 91.
- Reidl Sybille, F. S. (2006). *Zwischen Unabhanginkeit und Zukunftangst. Quantitatieve Ergebnisse in der Wiener Creatieve Industries.* Wien.
- Schumpeter, J. (1975). *Capitalism, Socialism, and Democracy.* New York: Harper.
- Sternberg, R. &. (2005). Determinants and effects of new business creation using global entrepreneurship monitor data. *Small Business Economics* , 24 (3), 24(3), 193-203.
- Turok, I. (2004). Cities, regions and competitiveness. *Regional Studies* , 38 (9), p. 1069 - 1083.
- Utrecht School of the Arts (HKU). (2010). Study on the *Entrepreneurial dimension of cultural and creative industries.* Progress and Interim Report, Utrecht.
- World Planners Congress. (2006). *Reinventing Planning: A new governance paradigm for managing human settlements.* Vancouver: American Planning Association.

About the author
Rene Kooyman (NL) graduated with a major in Urban and Regional Planning. He received a Diplôme Educations Approfondies (DEA) from the University of Geneva and a Master in Urban Area Development (MUAD). Recently Rene Kooyman has been Managing Editor for the EU EACEA Research Project on the Entrepreneurial dimensions of cultural and creative industries. He is Project Manager and Executive Secretary at the CURE Monitoring Board.
rkooyman@rkooyman.com

Abstract

'Cultural routes' can be defined as paths or routes of historical significance with a common, thematic, denominator. Cultural Routes allow and aim for cultural *consumption* that goes beyond place-based enjoyment of cultural goods, events or heritage. The Council of Europe (CoE) has put in place a system through which it certifies itineraries as Cultural Routes on the basis of their ability to help in preserving and showcasing Europe's cultural identities and historical legacies, and fostering wider territorial development and cohesion in Europe.

In this article both a network assessment and market failure are being analyzed. The article concludes that a narrow approach is a rather standard practice to promote only parts of the CRs. This leads to piecemeal and patchwork marketing, which does not help in the branding and awareness raising of the CRs as a whole.

Introduction

'Cultural routes' can be defined as paths or routes of historical significance with a common, thematic, denominator. Similarly, they can be viewed as routes that *'have a cultural value or have elements of cultural heritage as their focus and that assign a key role to cultural attractions'* (Puczko & Ratz, 2007).

Due to their itinerary-based character and the possibility of travelling along the routes, Cultural Routes (hereafter referred to as CRs) allow and aim for cultural *'consumption'* that goes beyond place-based enjoyment of cultural goods, events or heritage (cf. KEA, Oct 2006, p. 56). Similarly, for the development and innovation of CR-related products and services, the travelling or itinerary dimension is also important. An analogy to the term *'slow food'* is useful and one could argue that CRs are for *'slow tourism'*. And just like 'slow food' has a growing number of followers, so can 'slow tourism' (Kühn, 2010).

In fact, the Gottlieb Duttweiler Institute (2006) identified a set of tendencies that create opportunities for the further development of cultural tourism, which can thus give a push to CR-based innovation and entrepreneurial initiatives. Among them are the transition from unskilled to skilled forms of consumption (Scitovsky, 1976); a rising demand for authenticity among consumers (Zukin, 2010); a progression in the production of culture (Pine and Gilmore, 1999); and an integration of cultural tourism and creativity (Frey, 2009).

To leverage such opportunities, the Council of Europe (CoE) put in place a system through which it certifies itineraries since 1987 as Cultural Routes on the basis of their ability to help in: (a) preserving and showcasing Europe's cultural identities and historical legacies, and (b) fostering wider territorial development and cohesion in Europe. Since 2012, it has tried to raise the impact of CRs through setting up joint initiatives with the European Commission (CoE, 2011; EC, 2011).

Methods and sources applied

In dealing with the question of *'do CoE-certified Cultural Routes provide a climate that encourages innovative and entrepreneurial practices'*, we analyze whether the CRs suffer from network and market failures, as typical impediments for entrepreneurial and innovative initiatives and for bringing their outcomes successfully to the demand side.

Network failures (see e.g. Carlsson et al., 2002; Drejer 2004; Gustafsson and Autio, 2006) refer to a lack of, or ineffective, liaising activity among market actors – be it on the supply and or demand side; I.e., if there is little contact between complementary service deliverers or product suppliers, or between the former and (specialized) support providers. This is notably an issue in sectors where the final consumer prefers integrated packages of services and co-development of such packages (Dixon, 2000). In addition, due to a lack of or ineffective liaising activity, network failures can also be a consequence of missing nodes on either the demand or supply side (Oxera, 2005).
Market failures (see e.g. Arrow, 1962; Carlsson and Jacobsson, 1994; Parsons, 1999; Oxera, 2005; Gustafsson and Autio, 2006) refer to the lack of view on demand characteristics (product features, volumes, etc.) on behalf of the supply side to markets (typically companies and other kinds of product/service providers) as per information shortages. This may lead to the offering of products or services with 'incorrect' characteristics and or a mismatch between quantities requested and supplied. Moreover, a blurred sight on demand may lead to a lack of efforts (or wrongly directed efforts) to develop new products and services, to invest in product/service innovation and or to develop new entrepreneurial initiatives (Williamson, 1981; Rabin and Thaler, 2001; Gilovich, Griffith and Kahneman, 2002; Mani, 2002). As such they can constitute severe market barriers.

In detecting market and network failures, there is a ground for policy intervention (Arrow, 1962; Carlsson & Jacobsson, 1994; Parsons, 1999; Oxera, 2005; Kamp & Bevis, forthcoming). In our study we used case studies to diagnose whether market and network failures prevail regarding CRs, carried out with regard to the following CRs: Hansa League network, Via Regia, Via Francigena, TransRomanica, and the Pyrenean Iron Route. For these case studies, a questionnaire-based survey and telephone interviews provided the main inputs. The former has been complemented by secondary analysis of expert papers on these CRs. In addition, for a wider sample of CRs, similar expert papers as well as documentation on the different CRs from the European Institute of Cultural Routes have been reviewed. Furthermore, internet-based desk research on the various CRs was undertaken.

Assessing cultural routes

Network failure assessment
Most of the Cultural Routes harness cultural riches and heritage from areas that have preserved an air of authenticity and virginity. Their nature and architectural patrimony has remained relatively untouched and the areas in question count typically with a low density of population – leaving aside that there are CRs that run through bigger cities as well. Consequently, the lion's share of the CRs run through peripheral areas across Europe that do not offer a wealth of agglomeration economies. Moreover, these areas tend not to be richly endowed with (large-scale) lead firms that can act as finding customers for an advanced creative services industry serving cultural tourism in a placed-based or itinerary-based manner. Therefore, the CRs typically thrive on SMEs and micro-enterprises interacting on an individual and non-strategic basis vis-à-vis the demand side, and with little contact with complementary service deliverers or product suppliers and (specialized) support providers.[1] The former hampers the development of user-responsive products and services that require collaborative processes.

---

[1] In fact, whereas many SMEs have a strongly developed client orientation and ditto feeling for market trends (largely as an outcome of their proximity to nearby and reduced markets), most of them lack the capacities to develop and apply this vocation in a more integral manner. That is, applied to a broader (client) environment and in a more strategic manner.

In sum, large geographical parts of the CRs do not shelter an industrial texture that allows seizing advanced innovation and entrepreneurial opportunities that cultural tourism can generate; i.e., many areas thrive on mature or declining industries, on crafts, and on small-scale artisanal activities in the tourism and cultural sector. Hence, the local supply side often lacks the means to provide a significant pull (or push) to cultural tourism in the areas concerned. As a consequence, business opportunities for the development of knowledge-intensive services, products or applications, which require teaming up with providers of advanced and creative services, tend to spill over to better endowed places that are often situated outside of the CR's course.

The former implies that businesses from the regions involved are able to fulfill the basic needs of the travelers wandering along the Routes (lodging, transport, subsistence, souvenirs, …), but that the provision of higher end artifacts often passes them by. That is especially a problem if companies look for partners in their proximity and then plow back on themselves when they do not find the necessary complementarities. This causes regional lock-ins and business entropy (Rosenfeld, 2002). The fact that business relations between SMEs typically do not stretch out along the CRs means that gaps in networks remain unfilled, which perpetuates the lack of business and innovative muscle.

The former leads to missed opportunities, since the CRs as a whole could provide a context in which 'missing links and missing nodes' situations can be overcome in view of fortifying and completing supply side issues. Evidently, the reality of missing nodes in rural areas inside the CRs' realm, and the subsequent difficulty to capitalize on opportunities for business and innovation, could give way to entrepreneurial initiatives to fill up the gaps. But regularly the necessary entrepreneurial intent for that is absent. Consequently, such initiatives are often taken up in cities inside or outside the CRs' course, from where a wider demand can be served and where there are superior agglomeration advantages (Wilson, 2010).

A further source for network failures along the CRs stems from the cross-border aspect that characterizes the Routes. This poses challenges to their overall governance and in getting stakeholders and agents from distant places to act together. The difficulty in developing network effects along many of the CRs is further aggravated by the following factors.

On the one hand, there is the geographical 'archipelago' character of many CRs (Veltz, 1996). When Routes are not chain - or corridor - shaped, they quickly suffer from substantial 'missing links', which constitute de facto a geographical network failure. This not only forms a handicap for their stakeholders, but it often also holds travelers back from traversing considerable parts of the CRs. On the other hand, there are CRs that are not based on a shared, historical, bond. This also complicates a united approach towards valorizing the CRs as a touristic attraction and as a trigger for business initiatives. If there is no shared identity and a weak sense of belonging, the CRs easily turn into artificial constructs, especially when (external) funds are lacking. Lastly, network failures can be a consequence of an absence of coordination or leadership vacuum for the CRs as such, making them just a theoretical and virtual concept.

Considered together, there is an arguable case of network failures with regard to the Cultural Routes. To overcome them, it is recommended to link up SMEs from segments along the Routes with counterparts from elsewhere and to embed them into trans-regional value chains, instead of building up full-fledged autochthonous business systems for cultural tourism in each place. To avoid that geographical fragmentation erodes the CRs as such, it is also recommended that institutional stakeholders provide the necessary glue for the CRs as a whole. If such a reuniting force is absent, it can be expected that the CRs as a whole become a side-cause and riparian regions along the CR let the marketing of the local assets prevail over the promotion and development of entire Cultural Routes.

Market failure assessment

Among several of the CRs and the stakeholders governing them (tourism boards and similar), there exists a certain aversion towards promoting and opening up the CRs to a wider public. Under the mantra of avoiding over-exploitation of the Routes and their cultural treasures (Devine & Devine, 2011), it is reserved to a cultural in-crowd. Consequently, many events related to those CRs obtain a *'happy few'*: insiders-only sometimes with an elitist touch (see e.g. the Olive Tree Route and Mozart Ways). This hampers the creation of a fertile climate for innovation and entrepreneurship; in the way that it limits the possibilities to cater for large groups and achieve economies of scale. Also, it limits the interaction with more progressive market segments, and thus deprives business actors from developing economies of scope and from receiving strong and targeted innovation stimuli. This makes it difficult as well to engage the demand side in the conceptualization and development of products and services.

Moreover, most of the CRs apply rather 'low tech' and narrow approaches to their marketing activities and thus only expose themselves to, and manage to reach out to, a limited audience. The low tech approach also hampers reaching out to the most advanced customer segments and further source from the most demanding and ingenious consumers. Although there are some timid and small-scale experiments, they typically fail to excel in visibility and traceability and they insufficiently leverage possibilities that web-tools and web-cam solutions can offer in this regard. Web-tools could promote a cultural tourism network in an interactive way with visitors (e.g. the Odyssea network), endowed with an interactive and knowledge-intensive tourist web portal, where Google maps allow navigators to trace virtual routes, to geo-locate , to be able to gather info in a coherent way on tangible and intangible heritage assets, etc.

Piecemeal marketing

The narrow approach indicated above also means that it is rather standard practice to promote only parts of the CRs. This leads to piecemeal and patchwork marketing, which does not help in the branding and awareness raising of the CRs as a whole. Moreover, it also refers back to the issue of targeting niche markets and insiders, instead of addressing the wider public, which leads to further missed opportunities for business initiatives. Consequently, even when interesting initiatives are undertaken, the impact is confined in the first place to the area that is promoted, and not to the CR as a whole. This, again, means that the sight on the Routes as such is blurred from a demand perspective, making it once more difficult to unlock and spur an interest among larger communities of interest. The absence of more holistic promotion campaigns and branding of the CRs, also means that one fails to create a kind of 'internal market' for services and products to be developed and sold in relation to the CRs as such. Instead, the outcome is mostly local-for-local initiatives with few scaling possibilities.

All in all, the low profile and secular promotion of the CRs aggravates the problems for companies to open a window to wider demand. At the same time, and although it can be attributed to a deliberate choice in some cases, it also reveals a lack of marketing skills on behalf of those bodies that oversee and coordinate the CRs, and thus capacity building in this field is required. The impression is that more systematic use of new media can be developed by the CRs; not just for plain marketing purposes, but also to tap into the possibilities social media offer for interacting with (potential) user groups. The latter allows engaging potential consumers into the creation of the offer to be supplied along the CRs.

References

- Arrow, K.J. (1962) 'Economic welfare and the allocation of resources of invention', in R.R. Nelson (Ed.) *The Rate and Direction of Inventive Activity: Economic and Social Factors*, Princeton, NJ: Princeton University Press for the National Bureau of Economic Research, p.609-625.
- Carlsson, B. and S. Jacobsson (1994), Technological Systems and Economic Policy: The Diffusion of Factory Automation in Sweden, *Research Policy*, 23, p. 235-248.
- Council of Europe (2011), *Study on the impact of European Cultural Routes on Small and Medium-Sized Enterprises' innovation and competitiveness - Transversal Themes guidance document*, Council of Europe & European Institute of Cultural Routes, Strassbourg/Luxembourg.
- Devine, A. and F. Devine (2011), Planning and developing tourism within a public sector quagmire: Lessons from and for small countries, *Tourism Management*, 32, p. 1253-1261.
- Dixon, N. (2000), *Common knowledge: How companies thrive by sharing what they know*, Cambridge, MA: Harvard Business School Press.
- Drejer, I. (2004), Identifying innovation in surveys of services: A Schumpeterian perspective, *Research Policy*, 33: p. 551-62
- EC : European Commission – DG Enterprise and Industry (2011), *Call for Proposals : Trans-national cooperation projects on European Cultural Routes*, Brussels : EC.
- Florida, R. (2002), *The rise of the creative class*, New York: Basic Books.
- Frey, O. (2009), Creativity of Places as a Resource for Cultural Tourism, In: G. Maciocco & S. Serreli (eds) *Enhancing the city, urban and landscape perspectives*, 6: p. 135-154, Berlin: Springer.
- Gilovich, T, D. Griffith, D. Kahneman (eds) (2002) Heuristics and biases: *The psychology of intuitive judgment*, Cambridge: Cambridge University Press.
- Gottlieb Duttweiler Institute (2006), *The Future of Leisure Travel – Trend Study*, Zürich: Gottlieb Duttweiler Institute.
- Gustafsson, R. and E. Autio (2006): Grounding for Innovation Policy: The Market, System and Social Cognitive Failure Rationales. Paper presented at *Innovation Pressure – Rethinking Competitiveness, Policy and the Society in a Globalised Economy* – International ProACT conference, Tampere, Finland, March p. 15-17, 2006.
- Kamp, B. and Bevis, K. (forthcoming), *Knowledge transfer initiatives as doorstep formulas to open innovation*, Int. J. Automotive Technology and Management.
- KEA (Oct 2006), *The economy of culture in Europe*, Brussels : KEA European Afairs.
- Kühn, K. (2010), *Services innovation in tourism niche markets*, Paper prepared for Seminar on Service innovation, sustainable tourism and rural regions , organized by DG Enterprise and Industry of the European Commission, p. 22-23 November 2010, Saint Vincent, Valle D'Aosta, Italy.
- Mani, S. (2002) *Government, Innovation and Technology Policy, An International Comparative Analysis*, Cheltenham: Edward Elgar.
- Oxera (2005), *Innovation market failures and state aid: developing criteria*, Report prepared for European Commission, DG Enterprise and Industry, November 2005, Brussels: EC.
- Parsons, W. (1999), Public policy – *An introduction to the theory and practice of policy analysis*, Cheltenham: Edward Elgar.
- Pine, J. & Gilmore, J. (1999), *The experience economy*, Boston: Harvard Business School Press.
- Puczko, L. and Ratz, T. (2007), Trailing Goethe, Humbert and Ulysses Tourism: *Cultural Routes in Tourism, Cultural Tourism: Global and Local Perspectives*, New York: Haworth Press.
- Rabin, M., Thaler, R (2001) , Risk aversion, *Journal of Economic Perspectives*, 15(1), p. 219-232.
- Rosenfeld, S.A. (2002), *Creating smart systems: A guide to cluster strategies in less favoured regions*, Carrboro: RTS Inc
- Scitovsky, T. (1976), *The Joyless Economy*, New York: Basic Books.
- Veltz, P. (1996), *Mondialisation, Villes et Territoires*, Paris : Presses Universitaires de France.

- Williamson, O.E. (November 1981), The economics of organization: The transaction cost approach, *American Journal of Sociology*, 87 (3), p. 548-575.
- Wilson, J. (2010), *Creative and Cultural Industry Clusters in Tourism Niche Markets: Framework Conditions for their Competitiveness*, Presentation held at Seminar on 'Service innovation, sustainable tourism and rural regions' organized by DG Enterprise and Industry of the European Commission, p. 22-23 November 2010, Saint Vincent, Valle D'Aosta, Italy.
- Zukin, S. (2009), *Naked City: The Death and Life of Authentic Urban Places*, Oxford: Oxford University Press.

About the author
Bart Kamp (BE) is Head of the Strategy Department at ORKESTRA: the Basque Institute of Competitiviteness (Spain). In addition, he is a lecturer in the strategic management of start-ups at the Université Catholique de Louvain-la-Neuve (Belgium). Kamp has written extensively on overcoming market and network imperfections in the field of entrepreneurship and innovation policies.
bart.kamp@orkestra.deusto.es

Redefining creativity in a diversified cultural setup: an urban design approach

Adarsha Kapoor

Abstract

Asian urbanism has been an outcome of efforts put in by the creative industry taking clues from the prevalent *culture*. This socio-cultural setup of Asian cities and urban centers is largely shaped by the unorganized worksector of the society. This unorganized sector has redefined creativity to such an extent that it has become an important factor in the changing urban environments of urban centers.

Developing nations respond to the recent economic recession by the virtue of their unique economically sustainable ways of development. In the present cities and urban centers small - yet significant - initiatives by end users give an idea of their aspirations fueled by the city and its physical fabric. The case of Calcutta and Mumbai are discussed

Introduction

Asian urbanism has been an outcome of efforts put in by the creative industry taking clues from the prevalent *culture*[1] Constantly going through peaks and depressions, this process has reached a point where political decisions related to urbanism are now based on the socio-cultural setup of the geographical areas under consideration (Chatterjee, 2009). This socio-cultural setup of Asian cities and urban centers is largely shaped by the unorganized work sector of the society. This unorganized sector has redefined creativity to such an extent that it has become an important factor in the changing urban environments of urban centers. This has been the focus of discussions regarding unorganized work sectors of creative industries, evolving socio-cultural setup of the place and resultant changing patterns of Asian Urbanism; primarily due to various forms of diversity in the user groups and communities involved in this debate.

Increased globalization and the recent economic recession have shifted the focus of planners, policy makers and researchers with varied areas of interest, towards understanding the ways in which Asian economies have responded to the crisis (The Economic times, 2009). This article attempts to initiate appreciation of the role of the above-mentioned creativity of the unorganized sector in generating 'recession-proof' ways of shaping urban environments, derived out of their culture of creativity. As a result of globalization; the intertwined web of cultures, creative ways of space formulation and changing life styles give an insight into the direction that economies need to take to understand the benefits of the 'bottom to top approach' of physical planning.

Creativity and complexity

Creativity is a way in which the human mind tries to divert its potential towards evolving a physical or a virtual experience. The case of cultural creativity, arising from needs based aspirations of the developing nations, is an approach to appreciate its impact on the urban settlements. Cities and urban settlements are an outcome of spatial planning, based on future needs that subsequently manifest into execution with a significant influence of the local culture. The policies of spatial planning become an overriding framework for development of the city, while the local culture and its unique ways of urban development help in evolving ways of executing the policies of spatial planning.

In the book, *The Cultural Economy of Cities* Allen Scott (1990) talks about the possibilities of symbiotic relationship between culture and economy in shaping cities and urban environments.

In the process of creation of urban environments, the role of individuals and institutions is significant. *The Rise of the Creative Class* (Florida, 2002), discusses the role of creative

---

[1] *Culture and Creativity* as defined by Oxford Dictionary, 2011.

professionals and formal creative education in shaping environment. Creative professionals such as planners, architects, policy makers and institutions play an integral role in understanding the context, projecting future directions of growth and creating a policy framework for spatial planning and guiding execution. *The Creative City* (Landry, 2000), talks about the need for a paradigm shift to understand the ways in which the emerging culture of creativity shape and re-shape the cities. He emphasizes a basic need of understanding the role of changing urban dynamics in its course to address urban issues and problems. The realization of a spatial plan of a city is significantly influenced by realities on the ground, local cultural influence, political parameters and ecological considerations. Out of which, the influence of local culture on the physical development of Urban Fabric needs better understanding, as there are no unique set of standards or parameters under which it can be studied. The case gets complex when the local culture of an urban area under consideration is a web of various cultures and practices. In order to device an algorithm, to study the influence of local culture on growth of urban environments, one has to understand all such sub-cultures, their role in the mother culture of the city, and their ways of influencing urban growth both individually and collectively. Developing nations respond to the recent economic recession by the virtue of their unique economically sustainable ways of development. The same ways of development might have reduced their pace of reaching the status of a developed nation in the pre-recession years, and proved to be a blessing in disguise at the time of recession. In the book, '*The Work of Nations: Preparing Ourselves for 21st century Capitalism*', while talking about the changing work culture and the subsequent rise of working class, Reich describes them as problem-solvers, problem-identifiers, and brokers of information. Through this he brings out a very significant aspect of any physical change (Reich, 1991.) In the developing countries, the basic need for something encourages even the financially weakest members of society to find their own ways to fulfill their need. Arising due to sheer necessity, this form of true creativity shapes our urban environments.

The case

Developing nations of Asia and Africa, thrive on their culture and diversity. Throughout their past and even in their present the economically weakest, yet largest percentage of their population, try to meet their needs through ways which are beyond the imagination of skilled professionals. Their ways are developed through the process of trial and error, and as such, the most suitable ones have passed all the tests of culture, financial feasibility and adaptability, ecological influence and workmanship. There might be some short comings in their approach to resolving issues and concerns, yet it is important to understand their response, to evolve a better way forward towards culture-specific ways of urban development and growth. Dharavi is a slum in the city of Mumbai in India, developed as a fishermen's squatter settlement in the late 19th century. Subsequently, it evolved into a settlement with a unique urban fabric. The local typology of building blocks, referred to as chawls, were defined, redefined, modified and morphed into various other typologies, beyond the scope of formal studies and understanding. The construction materials like bricks, steel, wood and concrete were questioned, experimented, reused and re-invented in order to suit the needs of the people. Houses attached to each other, due to shear density of irregular squatted ownerships, made out of mud bricks, plastic sheets, metal foils or sheets, gunny bags, etc., create an urban fabric unique to such a 'place'. Even services devised here gave an insight in the pattern or design of services needed by the users of the settlements. Though when looked at these critically, one might have an opinion about the pros and cons of the development, the ways in which the design has come about gives rise to a unique approach in city design.

The city of Kolkata, formerly known as Calcutta (West Bengal, India), has a rich culture of creativity integrated with the day-to-day life of people (Kapoor, 2009). A grocer uses cane, jute and banana leaves to make his baskets for fruits and vegetables. The eateries use specially designed packages made out of reused article sheets and small cast in-situ podiums to seat their costumers and use hand drawn wall paintings for advertising their products to improve their sales. The shoppers stitch their carrying bags from old rags and clothes both to reuse otherwise useless household items and to save money. The streets lined with small shops and eat outs reform into a necklace of nooks and corners created by, adjoining building owners, shop owners and street furniture. The blocks are defined and characterized by the local population and their influence on the built form. The culture of social u form and give birth to 'rowak', 'modh', 'chowk', 'gali', 'para', 'football ground'[2] and many such components which have not found their way into formal texts about the urban form of the city. It should also be noted here that all these initiatives have no mention in the planning principles and building bylaws of the city, yet these are the most important components of the city, defining its physical environment. In the world's largest democracy, 'India', the war of political parties after every fixed intervals, or public functions related to religious or local customs, also bring out people's creative self. The creation of bamboo platforms for public gatherings or worships, hand drawn posters or paintings, souvenirs and many such things created specifically for the occasion will all be designed by the members of the party or their relatives and friends. These objects or activities are all done outside the purview of local construction or planning norms.

Conclusion

In the present cities and urban centers small yet significant initiatives by end users give an idea of their aspirations fueled by the city and its physical fabric. Until recently, these smaller creative initiatives were not part of the mainstream city planning and design. It is now time to study all grassroots' initiatives to find out ways to involve the economically weakest yet large urban population in the process of physical development. The globalized world of today and the future has given birth to hybrid cultures, which will make the task of planners, designers and administrators difficult. They will now have to devise their ways of understanding creativity, culture, and peoples' aspirations to decide the way forward.

The pace of change in all the spheres has left professionals struggling to find the ways to address issues and look for better solutions. It is an immediate necessity to learn from the on-going processes of 'jugad' and harness its potential to develop culture and resource specific responses to urban issues typical of Asia.

[2] Following are the local names of some physical components of the public spaces in the city of Kolkata:
Rowak: A small cast in-situ platform for sitting, adjoining the frontage of a building.
Modh: Street crossing, acting as a public plaza.
Chowk: A courtyard formed out of a street and adjoining buildings.
Gali: A narrow lane
Para: A community which also represents a cluster of houses.

References

- Asia. (2009) An Astonishing Rebound, In: *The Economic Times*, 13th August.
- Chatterjee S. (2009): *Conservation of Indo- Danish British heritage of Serampore*, Unpublished thesis, School of Planning & Architecture, New Delhi
- Florida, R. (2002): *The Rise of the Creative Class: And How It's Transforming Work, Leisure, Community and Everyday Life*. New York: Basic Books
- Kapoor A. (2009): *Revitalization of social spaces of College Street Precinct, Kolkata*, Unpublished thesis, School of Planning & Architecture, New Delhi
- Landry, C. (2000): *The Creative City: A Toolkit for Urban Innovators*. London: Comedia
- Reich, R. (1991): The Work of Nations: Preparing Ourselves for 21st century Capitalism. New York: A. A. Knopf.
- Rida A. & Radjawali S.I. (2004): *Creative culture and Urban Planning: The Bandung experience*, Institute of Technology, Bangdung, Indonesia
- Scott A.J. (1990): *The Cultural Economy of Cities*. Thousand Oaks: Sage. Siregar, S.A.

About the author

Adarsha Kapoor is a practicing architect (Thesis Gold medalist), and an Urban Designer with a deep interest in issues pertaining to public participation through urban spaces. He has been involved in a series of publications regarding politics, public participation and urban spaces of developing countries.
adarsha47@hotmail.com

Towards a creative city? Problems and prospects of Istanbul's creative sectors

Yigit Evren and Zeynep Merey Enlil

Abstract

This paper examines Istanbul, one of Europe's mega cites, in the light of the creative city discourse. It focuses on Istanbul's creative industries tendency to clustering within the city and discuss clustering with reference to the challenges that these sectors face. At this point, the question is centrally concerned with the extent to which spatial clustering can help Istanbul to become a creative city. Our findings show that most of Istanbul's creative sectors enjoy localisation economies arising from clustering, nevertheless have not yet reached a capacity to benefit from the positive externalities arising from co-location with other clusters, plus a broad array of externalities related to urban location, namely urbanisation economies.

Introduction

The creative city, creative sectors and cultural industries since the mid 1990s, have been amongst the most popular and central themes in the literature of cultural studies, planning and geography. In particular, the role of creative and cultural sectors in local economic development and creative clusters have attracted considerable interest (Fleming, 1999; Scott, 2000; Power & Scott, 2004; Cooke & Lazzeretti, 2008).

At the risk of oversimplifying the relevant literature we can argue that there have been two differing conceptual definitions of the creative city (Smith and Warfield, 2008). The first definition concerns the culture-centric orientation of the creative city. According to this view, the creative city appears to be a place of diverse and inclusive arts and culture. The second definition, on the other hand, sees local economic development and growth as primarily important, and is therefore labeled as econocentric conception. In this context, creative cities are the places of *economic innovation, creative talent and competitive creative industries.*

An econocentric view of the creative city discourse

When we examine the econocentric framework of the creative city in detail, we observe that it consists of three main interrelated theoretical strands (Costa, 2008).

a   The first strand represents a widespread focus on the production, distribution and consumption of products, whose economic value is constituted mainly from their cultural value. These economic activities, namely creative and cultural industries, include the production of traditional cultural products as well as a wide palette of design activities, requiring creative ability and skill. In this context, places or cities in which creative sectors locate are considered to be the centers of creativity and economic growth (Pratt, 2004).

b   The second strand concerns the importance of a people-climate in the economic competitiveness of cities. Underlying this argument is the creative class, which is derived from the popular writings of Richard Florida (2002, 2003). According to Florida, the creative class is the engine of creativity and innovation, and it comprises the top qualified and innovative people including artists and scientists. He argues that cities which have the capacity of attracting and retaining creative human resources also attract companies. In other words, the 'creative age' brings a people-driven system in the economy, rather than a corporate-centered one where people move to jobs

c   The third strand centers the creative city notion on the idea of creativity as a toolkit for urban development. This is based on Charles Landry's (2000) book entitled *The Creative City: A Toolkit for Urban Innovators.* Contrary to Florida, Landry uses the creative city notion in a broader sense. His approach is a more holistic understanding of creativity, which includes social and political reform in addition to artistic and technological innovation. According to this view, creativity is not only generated through a distinguished class; ordinary people who can introduce imaginative approaches to everyday urban problems may very well be the sources of creativity. Therefore creative cities, according to this view, are those able to motivate their citizens to produce alternative solutions to their problems.

The common message from the above-said theoretical strands is that, as Costa rightly argues '...*creative process is clearly related to urban space, particularly to agglomeration effects...*' (Costa, 2008, p. 183). When we turn our attention to creative sectors, the most distinguishable spatial form defined by these sectors is clustering.
Yet, why do creative sectors cluster? This has been perhaps one of the most popular debates in the economic geography literature. Bathelt (2004), for instance answers this question by referring to various *dimensions of clustering*. Porter (1995) on the other hand, highlights the *competitive advantages* of the inner city, which make the city centre a magnet for these sectors. Scott (2006) introduces the notion of creative field to explain the multi-faceted processes of learning and innovation in clusters. Lorenzen and Frederiksen (2008) focus on the positive externalities creative sectors enjoy and explain the reasons of clustering by referring to *localisation* and *urbanisation* economies.

Creative sectors in istanbul

Istanbul is the ultimate centre of Turkey for various creative sectors to locate. Take jewellery making, for instance, which boasts a history of more than 500 years in the city; the Istanbul sector comprises 79% of manufacturing firms and 85% of all employment in the Turkish jewellery sector. This sector also generates 96% of national jewellery value-added (Evren, 2011). Similarly, in the filmmaking industry there is a significant concentration in Istanbul (Tore, 2010). Furthermore, 59% of total employment in the advertising industry is located in Istanbul.

In publishing and printing, Istanbul covers 45% (Aksoy & Enlil, 2011). In architecture, Istanbul accommodates 42% of architects and is home to more than one-fourth (27%) of all architectural offices in the country (Seckin, 2011). In the software design industry 47% of the qualified workforce is located in Istanbul (Uckan, 2011). In terms of the number of registered industrial designs certified by the Turkish Patent Institute, Istanbul, with a share of 50%, remains far ahead of many other greater cities in Turkey. Istanbul is also the primary centre of the Turkish fashion design industry; a large majority of independent fashion designers have set up their offices in Istanbul (Kozaman, 2011).

This clustering gives Istanbul some competitive advantages. First of all, these sectors cultivate the creative and innovative environment and enable Istanbul to maintain its role as an incubator of creativity and innovation.
Secondly, with their creative capacities in design, branding, advertisement and marketing, creative sectors carry the potential of contributing to the conventional manufacturing industries' ability to compete internationally and access global markets. The local economy of Istanbul, until the late 1980s, was dominated by conventional manufacturing. Since the 1990s, however, we have been witnessing a slow but steady change in the economic base of the city, and there has been a shift from manufacturing to services. Additionally, many of Istanbul's conventional manufacturing industries have lost their previous competitive advantages, which were mainly based on cheap labour costs. In this context, creative sectors open up new possibilities for the trajectory of Istanbul's traditional economy. In short, the growing creative economy in Istanbul has increased its capacity to act as an interface between the conventional sectors and the global economy.

Is agglomeration enough? Some concluding remarks on the creative city nexus

There is no doubt that clustering of creative and cultural sectors offers Istanbul various positive economic externalities. But is that enough to make the city creative? Inspired by Lorenzen and Frederiksen's conceptualisation (2008), we can argue that most of Istanbul's creative sectors enjoy localisation economies arising from clustering. Nevertheless they have not yet reached a capacity to benefit from the positive externalities. The creative economy of Istanbul is capable of making incremental innovations but fails to produce cultural products which are differentiated through novelty and generate radical innovation. Most of Istanbul's creative and cultural sectors are locked in their local trajectories. These industries have not yet become global players. In other words, they fail to set new global trends and are mostly associated with the production of relatively low value-added and/or fake designs.

There are several reasons for this. One possible explanation is the fact that the creative economy in Istanbul has not yet fully achieved the necessary threshold which allows it to take off and reinforce itself. As of 2008, the cultural economy employment in Istanbul stands far behind other leading cities in Europe (Aksoy & Enlil, 2011). Second, local demand and consumer expenditures for cultural and creative industry products are considerably low. Furthermore, the conventional industry's demand for creative input still remains limited. Another handicap of Istanbul's creative and cultural sectors is the insufficiency of channels through which creative ideas and capital are brought together (Enlil and Evren, 2011). Nevertheless, there are various promising developments, yet they are all quite new and still in their formative stages.

To this end, we can argue that geographical agglomeration is by itself is not a sufficient precondition towards a creative city. In developing this point it is rather naive to adopt 'one size fits all' cluster development policies for the development of creative sectors. What we need, as Enright notes, is '...*careful identification and characterization of local clusters in all dimensions, explicit recognition of their needs, and programs that clearly target specific market failures*' (Enright, 2000; p. 327).

References

- Aksoy, A. & Enlil, Z. (2011). *Cultural Economy Compendium: Istanbul 2010*. Istanbul: Istanbul Bilgi University Press.
- Bathelt, H. (2004) 'Toward a Multidimensional Conception of Clusters: The case of the Leipzig Media Industry, Germany.' In: *Cultural Industries and the Production of Culture*, edited by D. Power and A.J. Scott, p. 147-168. New York: Routledge.
- Cooke, P. & Lazzeretti, L. (2008). *Creative Cities, Cultural Clusters and Local Economic Development*. Massachusetts: Edward Elgar Publishing.
- Costa, P. (2008). 'Creativity, Innovation and Territorial Agglomeration in Cultural Activities: The Roots of the Creative City.' In *Creative Cities, Cultural Clusters and Local Economic Development*, edited by P. Cooke ve L.Lazzeretti, p. 183-210. Massachusetts: Edward Elgar Publishing.
- Enlil, Z. and Evren, Y. (2011). 'İstanbul için Yaratıcı Kent Söylemini Tartışmak.' In *Yaratıcı İstanbul*, edited by Z.Enlil and Y.Evren, p. 19-30. Istanbul: Istanbul Bilgi University Press.
- Enright, M. (2000). 'The Globalization of Competition and the Localization of Competitive Advantage: Policies Towards Regional Clustering.' In *The Globalization of Multinational Enterprise Activity and Economic Development*, edited by N. Hood S. Young, p. 303-331. London: MacMillan Press.
- Evren, Y. (2011). 'Fordizm Yeniden? İstanbul Kuyumculuk Sektöründe Yapısal Dönüşüm Süreci, Yaratıcı Kapasite ve Tasarım.' In *Yaratıcı İstanbul*, edited by Z.Enlil and Y.Evren, p. 111-131. Istanbul: Istanbul Bilgi University Press.

- Fleming, T. (1999). *The Role of Creative Industries in Local and Regional Development*, Manchester: Government Office for Yorkshire and Humberside / Forum on Creative Industries (FOCI).
- Florida, R. (2002). *The Rise of the Creative Class*, New York: Basic Books.
- Florida, R. (2003, *Cities and the Creative Class*. City and Community, 2(1): p. 3-19.
- Kozaman, S. (2011). 'İstanbul'da Moda Sektörü: Üretimden Tasarıma.' In *Yaratıcı İstanbul*, edited by Z.Enlil and Y.Evren, p. 87-110. Istanbul: Istanbul Bilgi University Press.
- Landry, C. (2000). *The Creative City*, London: Comedia.
- Lorenzen, M. and L.Frederiksen. (2008). 'Why do Cultural Industries Cluster? Localization, Urbanization, Products and Projects.' In *Creative Cities, Cultural Clusters and Local Economic Development*, edited by P. Cooke ve L.Lazzeretti, p. 155-179. Massachusetts: Edward Elgar Publishing.
- Porter, M. (1995). 'The Competitive Advantage of the Inner City.' *Harward Business Review*, May-June: p. 55-71.
- Power, D. and A.J. Scott. (2004). *Cultural Industries and the Production of Culture*. New York: Routledge.
- Pratt, A.C. (2004). 'Mapping the Cultural Industries: Regionalization; the Example of South East England.' *In Cultural Industries and the Production of Culture*, edited by D. Power and A.J. Scott, p. 19-36. New York: Routledge.
- Scott, A.J. (2000), *The Cultural Economy of Cities*: Essays on the Geography of Image-Producing Industries, London: Sage.
- Scott, A.J. (2006). 'Creative Cities: Conceptual Issues and Policy Questions.' *Journal of Urban Affairs*, 28(1): p.1-17.
- Seckin, E. (2011). 'İstanbul'da Yapılı Çevrenin Biçimlenmesinde Mimarlık.' In *Yaratıcı İstanbul*, edited by Z.Enlil and Y.Evren, p.133-153. Istanbul: Istanbul Bilgi University Press.
- Smith, R. and K.Warfield. (2008). 'The Creative City: A Matter of Values' *In Creative Cities, Cultural Clusters and Local Economic Development*, edited by P. Cooke ve L.Lazzeretti, p. 287-312. Massachusetts: Edward Elgar Publishing.
- Uckan, O. (2011). 'Yaratıcı Kentler, Yazılım Sektörü ve Istanbul.' In *Yaratıcı İstanbul*, edited by Z.Enlil and Y.Evren, p. 31-55. Istanbul: Istanbul Bilgi University Press.
- Tore, E.O. (2010). *Istanbul Film Endüstrisi*. Istanbul: Istanbul Bilgi University Press.

About the authors
Zeynep Enlil (TR) is professor of urban planning and teaches at Yildiz Technical University. She was one of the research directors of a major Istanbul 2010 European Capital of Culture Agency project titled 'Istanbul 2010 Cultural Heritage and Cultural Economy Mapping and Compendium Project.'
zeynepenlil@gmail.com

Yigit Evren (TR) is a senior lecturer in regional planning and urban economics at Yildiz Technical University (YTU). He is also the co-editor of Megaron, the e-journal of YTU, Faculty of Architecture. Evren holds a PhD in Urban Planning from Cardiff University and writes about regional development, industrial clusters, relational geography and cultural industries
yigitevren@gmail.com

Esra Aysun

Abstract

As Europe is going under serious crisis of cuts in the state subsidies, the cultural scene in Turkey, Istanbul is attracting attention with its artistic and cultural landscape that is heavily shaped with the cultural investments of the private sector – sponsorship of corporations and investments of families of industrial conglomerates. This article aims to explore how an arts institution's cultural entrepreneurship in Istanbul could succeed in compliance with the support of its stakeholders. The study states that the Istanbul Bienniale needs to communicate to its constituencies its relevance to the city and society, with a focus on the social entrepreneurship.

The istanbul bienniale

Biennials have become an increasingly popular institutional structure for the staging of large-scale exhibitions causing *'the biennialization of the contemporary art world'* (Wu, 2003). Whereas Daniel Birnbaum, asserts that the idea of biennials have come to extinction as innovative art exhibitions are being suppressed by the glamour of art fairs (Erden, 2011), Obrist (2007) emphasizes this change is merely due to the relocation of geographies of the biennials, now flourishing in emerging economies, from Cuba to Korea, Senegal, Brazil, the United Arab Emirates and beyond as of the first decade of the 21st century.

The Istanbul Bienniale with its confinement in 1987, following the Habaña (1984) after the São Paulo (1951) Biennials, as one of the first of non-western Biennials, has been a leading force in the process of the culture of biennials replacing the conventional institutional art framework in the 1980's and 1990's by its high quality and engagement in major geo-political discussions. The Istanbul Bienniale, phrased in the Economist (2011, Sept 24) as *'poignant, relevant and intellectually engaging'* proudly announcing its being *'ranked amongst the most important European art events of the year along with the Venice Biennale'*, has concluded its 12th edition in 2011 with reports of a total of 110.000 visitors, with approximately 700 international press agents from 50 different countries and 4000 arts professionals and a total of 6000 international visitors in two months.

The Istanbul Bienniale is the second festival that sprang in 1987 from the International Istanbul Festival of the Istanbul Foundation for Culture and Arts (IKSV), founded by seventeen businessmen under the leadership of Dr. Nejat F. Eczacıbaşı of the Eczacıbaşı Family, a leading conglomerate in pharmaceutical industries, as 'an industrialist who planned an urban festival of arts, similar to those held annually in several European cities' (Yardımcı, 2009). As the art and cultural scene in Turkey function within an inadequate state, the Eczacıbaşı Family could be said to be either one of Wu's *intervening* companies (Wu, 2003) or Di Maggio's *Brahmin* families (Di Maggio, 1986). In spite of the praise the family has received, their name has also been targeted with accusations of being a monopolist in the local cultural scene for including the name of the city in their naming of two arts institutions, Istanbul Modern Museum (2004) as well as the IKSV both of which are being directed and sustained under their auspices.

It can be debated whether or not the Istanbul Bienniale happening as 'an event of the city, in the city, and about the city'[1] can be defined as among the best practice of Turkish private cultural entrepreneurism. In our analysis we will follow Hagoort (2007), treating the four fundaments of entrepreneurship; economical innovation; psychological intuition; the management related professional environment one must work at/self-entrepreneurship; and the biological - environment in which the organization must function.

---

[1] Görgün Taner, The General Director of the Foundation in his interview at Art Unlimited in September/October 2011.

The environment – the city and the state

The social, political and the economic context of the 1980's have had indispensable effects in the development of the Istanbul Bienniale. Looking at the first two editions in 1987 and 1989, which were entitled as *International Contemporary Art Exhibitions*, we see an isolated local artistic environment, where most were not interested in global arts developments in a peripheral country (Madra, 1996).

This scene though was reverted entirely with the opening of the *International Contemporary Art Exhibitions* to the international curators and hence to the global funds and networks as of the 4th edition; taking the name Istanbul Bienniale in 1995 in line with the rapid transformations in the city. Keyder stated in the late 90's that Istanbul was not becoming a global city, but experiencing the impact of globalization as an *'informal globalization'* because of the constraints imposed by the political sphere and the lack of coherent and unifying entrepreneurial vision at the local level (Keyder, 2010). The success of the city in the new century to follow though has created a *'divided city'* as in all global cities (Karaca, 2010). More and more the 'to be gentrified' districts of the city were crowned by the grand private investments of cultural institutions built by award winning architects. This, however, could hardly be claimed to be the result of mutual labor of the state and the private enterprises, as suggested by Wu in UK and USA. In the case of Turkey, the states' actions show more interest in ventures such as shopping malls and hotels. The state is also still working on defining its cultural policy and with its hesitation to ally with the local artistic scene, it seems to lend a hand to private investors leaving the public domain to the corporate hands (Aysun, 2011). Although the lease of public property to private cultural investors could be seen as evidence of such an alliance, dichotomy arises, as this partnership is not being supported by the necessary legal implementations or tax benefits for cultural institutions that are still regulated with restrictions in their activities of income generation.

Hence, the Istanbul Bienniale conveys 'entrepreneurship' and 'uniqueness' in the sense that it is the Bienniale of the city, which was not initiated by the city unlike its predecessors the Venice Biennial or Documenta, but initiated and sustained by a private foundation. The share of state support as well as that of the city to the Bienniale and to the rest of the festivals of IKSV has never been more than 10% in total, on an irregular basis, with the rest compensated by corporate sponsors for 75-80% of the total budget.

Emerging criticism

Despite of this success in realizing a worldwide acclaimed Bienniale without public support, however, the Istanbul Bienniale has been receiving much criticism, the majority of which initiated from the local arts scene. The Bienniale has been accused of abandoning traditional local artists and artworks produced before 1980's, because of the disinterest and ignorance of the foreign curators to the local arts scene; for being an 'ad-hoc show of carelessly collected and exhibited works'; for becoming a business deal for the sponsors and their star artists to show off and for getting funding from George Soros (Erzen, 2010).

From a sociological perspective, the Bienniale and the IKSV has most severely been criticized in a study by Yardımcı (2007) with her argument that IKSV is part of the *festivilized* urban life, where the festivals are unchallenging *'safe parades ranging from entertainment to soft-core politics'* because of their dependence on private funding.' Questioning the authenticity of the Istanbul Bienniale, Yardımcı also argues that Istanbul festivals *'fail to develop their own language'* but use canons of the aesthetic taste and criteria depicted by the cultural authorities of the international networks of global art markets instead of focusing on their own specificity (Yardımcı, 2007).

The entrepreneurial dimension

Kirby notes that entrepreneurs take initiative, assume autonomy and innovate taking risks only for *'they make things happen'* (Kirby, 2003). Indeed, this is what the Eczacıbaşı Group has done in creating IKSV and the Istanbul Bienniale. Under such circumstances, the intuition and innovation of the Eczacıbaşı's to found the Istanbul Bienniale have indeed created a respectable case of entrepreneurship, which carried the family and the company name to a level beyond any prior expectations. It started off as a philanthropic deed of creating a music festival like any other European counterpart. With its 40th anniversary today, it has become Turkey's most well-known and reputable arts institution, acting as an innovator realizing the first contemporary and international arts event in classical music, jazz, film, theatre and visual arts in the city.

In the American culture the free market economy offers the government a limited position. The self-reliance attitude of the philanthropic culture has made private entrepreneurship respectable (Chong, 2002). The constituencies of IKSV seem to value this more as an opportunity, and have led IKSV to be a power player and a monopoly in the scene. This rise as entrepreneurship of IKSV is regarded more commercial than social. Ironically, the Festivals of the IKSV in the focus of the Bienniale have been charged of being tools of the urban elites in their motivation to market the city, helping Istanbul to emerge as the showcase and gateway for Turkey's new era of integration into the world scene (Yardımcı, 2009).

Still, if IKSV's cultural entrepreneurship with private philanthropy is being taken as a model and a best-case scenario by other Biennials such as Athens in this era of economic crisis and termination of state funding, it should be Istanbul Bienniale's challenge to communicate this model to its local stakeholders.

Whether or not the cultural industry of the city will enjoy a share of Turkey's target to be one of the world's top 10 economies in 2023 - as Bülent Eczacıbaşı, the current chairman of the board of IKSV, hoped for in his speech at the opening ceremony of the 12th Istanbul Bienniale - is out of scope of this attempt to highlight IKSV's case of cultural entrepreneurism focusing on the Istanbul Bienniale. This search has proved that regarding the entrepreneurship of the Istanbul Bienniale, even though its necessity is unquestionable, the Istanbul Bienniale and the IKSV need to formulize a strategy to communicate to its constituencies their relevance to the city and society, with a focus on the social entrepreneurship.

References

- Aysun, Esra A. (2011). *Looking At The Independent Art Scene Of Istanbul As A Possible Case Study For The Future Positioning Of European Cultural Institutions* (paper presented at the AIMAC 11th International Conference on Arts and Cultural Management, Antwerp, Belgium, July 3-6, 2011.
- Chong, Derrick, (2002). *Arts Management*, Routledge.
- DiMaggio, Paul J (1986). *Non-Profit Enterprise in the Arts: Studies in Mission and Constraint*, New York: Oxford University Press.
- Erden, Osman (2011). *Türkiyede Güncel Sanat Alanını Şekillendiren Unsurlar* (unpublished PhD diss.), Istanbul Mimar Sinan University.
- Erzen, j. (2010). Art in Istanbul:Contemporary Spectacles and History Revisited, In: *Orienting Istanbul: Cultural Capital of Europe?*, edited by Deniz Göktürk,Levent Soysal, and İpek Türeli, (Oxfordshire: Routledge,), p. 216-233.
- Fleishman, J. L. (2007). *The Foundation: A Great American Secret: How Private Wealth is Changing the World* ,Public Affairs.
- Hagoort, G. (2007). *Cultural Entrepreneurship*, Utrecht University Utrecht School of the Arts Research Group Art and Economics.

- Hagoort, G. (2003). *Art Management Entrepreneurial Style*, Utrecht University Utrecht School of the Arts Research Group Art and Economics, Utrecht.
- Hanru, H. (2007). Not Only Possible, But Also Necessary: Optimism in the Age of Global War in: *10th International Bienniale Catalogue*, ed. İlkay Baliç Ayvaz, İstanbul Kültür ve Sanat Vakfı, Istanbul.
- Karaca, B. (2010). The Politics of Urban Art Events: Comparing Istanbul and Berlin. In: Orienting Istanbul: Cultural Capital of Europe?, edited by Deniz Göktürk,Levent Soysal, and İpek Türeli, Oxfordshire: Routledge, 2010, p. 234-250.
- Keyder, Ç. (2010). Istanbul Into the Twenty-First Century, In: *Orienting Istanbul: Cultural Capital of Europe?*, edited by Deniz Göktürk,Levent Soysal, and İpek Türeli, Oxfordshire: Routledge, p. 25-34.
- Keyder, Ç.r (1999). *The Setting, in Istanbul: Between Global and the Local*, ed. Çağlar Keyder. Rowman & Littlefield Publishers,Inc, p. 3-28.
- Kirby, D. A. (2003). *Entrepreneurship*, McGraw-Hill Education.
- Madra, B. (1996). *Post Peripheral Flux: A Decade of Contemporary Art in Istanbul* ,Istanbul: Literatür .
- Möntmann, N. (ed) (2005). *Art and Its Institutions*, Black Dog Publishing, London.
- Obrist, H.s U.: Futures, Cities, In: *Journal of Visual Culture* 6 2007, p. 359-364.
- Wu, C. (2009) Biennials Without Borders?, *New Left Review* 57. p. 107-115.
- Wu, C. (2003). *Privatising Culture, Corporate Art Intervention since the 1980s*, London
- Yardımcı, S.I (2007). *Festivilising Difference: Privatisation of Culture and Symbolic Exclusion in Istanbul*, European University Institute Robert Schuman Center for Advanced Studies, EUI RSCAS Mediterranean Programme Series 35

About the author
Esra A. Aysun (TR) is a cultural operator and a lecturer on arts management. She is the founding co-director of CUMA and is consultant for theatre DOT. She is the local Coordinator in Turkey for the Arts and Culture Program of the Open Society Foundation and a board member of IETM and the Cimetta Fund.
eaysun@c-u-m-a.org

Field configuring Events: How Culturepreneurs use space for the purpose of professionalisation in the design segment of Berlin

Bastian Lange

Abstract

The paper focuses on upcoming culturepreneurs (so-called cultural entrepreneurs) in the field of design and the analytical category of space as a socio-cognitive dimension in order to shed light on processes of professionalization. For policy makers and economic developers, it is of major importance to understand how high qualified graduates from design faculties are able to access markets. For academic researchers it is of great interest to understand the relationship between creative professions establishing and institutionalizing new markets and new their forms of spatial embeddedness within local creative industries. This article put its focus on the way how culturepreneurs work towards organizing micro-events and, in doing so, establish market as well as professional conditions by setting up and participating in different types of events as sites for playful experimentation and interaction.

The role of events in creative industries

This paper focuses on upcoming culturepreneurs (so-called cultural entrepreneurs) in the field of design and the analytical category of space as a socio-cognitive dimension in order to shed light on processes of professionalization. More than ever, organized events are of interest to management and economic geography scholars as *temporary social organizations* that encapsulate and shape the development of organizational fields (Lampel & Meyer, 2008). For this purpose, Meyer, Gaba, and Colwell (Meyer & Gaba et al., 2005: 467) have coined the term *field configuring events* (FCEs) to denote organized events as *places where business cards are exchanged, networks are constructed, reputations are advanced, deals are struck, and standards are set.*

Particularly in creative industries contexts, organized events have been studied as selection mechanisms and sites for the negotiation of values (Moeran & Strandgaard Pedersen, 2011).

Organized events play an important role in constituting creative markets (e.g. Caves, 2000) and the creation of symbolic and cultural values in these industries (Lampel & Meyer, 2008). At the backstage of the creative industries, organized events are important mechanisms for structuring activities, networks, meanings and resource flows. Film and music festivals, for instance, are not only a source of entertainment or a source of revenue for event organizers. They also perform economic functions for the film and music industries such as opening entry points for new or peripheral field actors or forming temporary *'ecologies of learning'* (Rüling & Strandgaard Pedersen, 2010). Trade fairs constitute *'tournaments of value'* (Appadurai, 1986) similar to award ceremonies. Presence at one of the four major art fairs worldwide, for instance, gives prestige to the galleries and artists that are selected (Thompson, 2011).

Events thus contain and represent a given field, but also feedback into the field. Events such as film festivals function as *'boundary organizations'* at the crossroads of art and commerce as they bring together artists with industry and media actors (Rüling/Strandgaard Pedersen, 2010). Usually embedded, sponsored, and utilized by cities, they are also placed at the intersection of local creative clusters and global project networks. In her analysis of industry fairs in the fashion industry, Skov (2006) speaks of *'intermediary fairs'* that conciliate a large set of globally dispersed actors far beyond mere export activities. Similarly, a music festival is not only a bridge between providers of aural goods and final consumers, but also connects these actor groups to selecting agents from the media (Paleo & Wijnberg, 2006). Many actors thus hold high stakes in events that somehow function as central nodes in an industry.

Methods of data collection

In order to understand the socio-spatial embedding of FCEs and their market-configuring role, Berlin's design market has been chosen as an

empirical reference case (Lange, 2007). The explorative approach focused on the role of informal micro-events that are organized by so-called young *('budding')* culturepreneurs. The aim is to gain access to their place-making processes, interactions, narrations and self-descriptions (Uzzi, 1996; Steyaert, 2007), that form the cornerstones of these events such as openings, closings, project presentations and irregular happenings.
Case studies have been selected (Silverman, 1986) and semi-standardized interview manuals have been used to describe the development of the Berlin-specific entrepreneurial approach, and to reveal how they defined their professional practices in relation to space (Hernes, 2003: 283-284).

Cultural codes, meanings of spaces and processes of evaluations, as well as devaluations have become the central hinges of recent socio-spatial analysis (Cook & Crouch et al., 2000). The focus of spatial analysis has shifted towards understanding the relationships governing cultural codes and enduring physical spaces, materialized spatial constructions and culturally coded identities (e.g. Faulconbridge, 2008; Glückler, 2006; Lange & Kalandides et al., 2008). Following Tor Hernes we shifted from the term *'context'* to that of 'space' as the central parameter for understanding the logics and social embeddedness of organization (Hernes, 2003, p. 277).

In order to analyze the field-configuring events as an expression of forming and accessing new markets, a combination of network (Johannisson, 1998) and milieu analysis (Matthiesen, 1998) is used. From the explorative approach the following criteria were developed in order to select study participants:

1 Work performance as a designer
2 Operation as an independent business-person for at least two years
3 The renting of workspace in Berlin

Case studies were selected by means of minimal and maximal contrast rules (Silverman, 1986). Individual case studies were also executed, targeted at generating themes, categories and narratives from sequences of semi-standardized interviews.

Results and perspectives

The empirical observations and case reconstruction demonstrate that a distinct place-making process frames the field as a site of social interaction. Although the spatial fields are pre-programmed by the organizers, the visitors start to interact with the spatial opportunities and thus create their own program.
The event is the opportunity to ensure who is relevant and who is currently on the site. It is thus – among other similar events – the only opportunity and occasion to claim the market as well as to shape the market by distinct products, practices and perspectives of what is state of the art. Field configuring events (FCEs) (Meyer & Gaba et al., 2005: p. 467) are a heuristic frame to understand these ephemeral socio-spatial contexts of emerging markets, where there is no pre- or externally evaluated set of production standards. Paradoxically, although these events are all held very playfully, many new entrepreneurs are seeking to distance themselves from usual habitual 'entrepreneurial' behaviors. Events are an occasion for positioning themselves as newcomers and as permanent mavericks, allowing them to be considered as innovators and founders of new trends and styles.

With interpretative methodologies, it was possible to show that young cultural entrepreneurs in this market attach more and more importance to informal milieu and network knowledge, in respect to standardized and codified forms of technical, management, business and organizational forms of knowledge. In contrast with formalized modes of knowledge, the ability to know how, where and when to interact is of the utmost importance. But these network and milieu forms of knowledge have a distinct, yet non-essentialist relation to space and place. Considering creativity as a decisive source for competitive advantage, it is crucial to shift the focus to spatially relevant practices in the field of symbolic production, because symbolically designed products must be assessed, enriched and upgraded first and foremost in social spaces.

The permanent creation of new genres, formats and products is connected with inventing narratives and social practices, as well as with strategies to place these products symbolically but also spatially in urban-based social places. Before being able to talk about, let alone sell and distribute products, it is necessary to invent a narration connected to the product, as well as to social practices so that clients might have the appropriate vocabulary to later talk about an immaterial good in the first place. Therefore, the encounter with the immaterial good, an imperative part of the process, has to happen on the basis of affective experiences. While focusing on the way in which products are introduced into the markets of creative industries, it is important to take into consideration those immaterial products. Meaning symbols, signs, sounds etc. not only have to be communicated in social networks, they should also initially be tested on the basis of their performative and atmospheric qualities. That is why products have to be placed in carefully and consciously arranged places – such as gallery openings, exhibitions, show cases, clubs and cool fairs, etc. - in order to allow performances to take place at all. Symbolic products therefore acquire social relevance. From this perspective, producing symbols is a social process that is stimulated, fostered, orchestrated or hampered by specific organizational as well as spatial contexts.

The category of space and spacing opens up the opportunity to analyze processes of product-based symbolical upgrading as well as re-evaluation in the field of creative industries. Forming space aims at achieving a necessary degree of professional competency with which they can present their symbolic products. These spaces provide an atmospheric-based story around the immaterial products. Professional scenes need club events, galleries, exhibitions, flexible fairs and staged office openings etc., that can be understood as temporary place-makings resulting from social formation on the urban stage. Scene-related clubbing practices not only have infiltrated the formation of professional identities as well as respective entrepreneurial strategies to access markets, they have even become a constitutive prerequisite to forming an entrepreneurial identity in the first place.

References

- Appadurai, A. (1986): Commodities and the politics of value. In: A. Appadurai (Hrsg.), *The Social Life of Things: Commodities in Cultural Perspective*. Cambridge, Cambridge University Press. p. 3-63.
- Caves, R. E. (2000). *Creative industries: contracts between art and commerce*. Cambridge, Mass.: Harvard University Press.
- Cook, I., Crouch, D., Naylor, S. & Ryan, J. (2000). *Cultural turns/Geographical turns*. Perspectives on Cultural Geography. Harlow, Prentice Hall.
- Faulconbridge, J. (2008). Managing the transnational law firm: a relational analysis of professional systems, embedded actors and time-space sensitive governance. In: *Economic Geography* 84, Vol. 2: p. 185-210.
- Glückler, J.s (2006). A relational assessment of international market entry in management consulting. In: Journal of *Economic Geography* 6: p. 369-393.
- Hernes, T. (2003). Organization as Evolution of Space. In: G Czarniawska/G. Sevon (Hrsg.), *Northern lights – Organization Theory in Scandinavia*. Copenhagen, Copenhagen Business School Press. p. 267-290.
- Hjorth, D. (2004). Creating space for play-invention – concepts of space and organizational entrepreneurship. In: *Entrepreneurship and regional development* 16, Vol. 5: p. 413-432.

- Hjorth, D. & Steyaert, C. (2004). *Narrative and discursive approaches in entrepreneurship: a second movements in entrepreneurship book*. Cheltenham, UK, Edward Elgar Publishing.
- Johannisson, B. (1998). Personal networks in emerging knowledge-based firms: spatial and functional patterns. In: *Entrepreneurship and regional development 10*, Vol. 4: p. 297-312.
- Lampel, J., Lant, T. & Shamsie, J. (2000). Balancing Act: Learning from Organizing Practices in Cultural Industries. In: *Organization science* 11, Vol. 3: p. 263-269.
- Lampel, J. & Meyer, A. D. (2008). Guest Editor´s Introduction: Field-Configuring Events as Structuring Mechanisms: How Conferences, Ceremonies, and Trade Shows Constitute New Technologies, Industries, and Markets. In: *Journal of management studies* 45, Vol. 6: p. 1025-1035.
- Lange, B. (2007). *Die Räume der Kreativszenen. Culturepreneurs und ihre Orte in Berlin*. Bielefeld: Transcript Verlag.
- Lange, B., Kalandides, A., Stöber, B., Mieg, Harald A. (2008). Berlin's Creative Industries: Governing Creativity? In: *Industry and Innovation 15* Vol. 5: p. 531-548.
- Maskell, P., Bathelt, H., Malmberg, Anders (2006). Building global knowledge pipelines: The role of temporary clusters. In: *European Planning Studies 14*, Vol. 8: p. 997-1014.
- Matthiesen, U. (1998). *Die Räume der Milieus. Neue Tendenzen in der sozial- und raumwissenschaftlichen Milieuforschung, in der Stadt- und Raumplanung*. Berlin, Edition Sigma.
- Meyer, A. D., Gaba, V. & Colwell, K. A. (2005). Organizing far from equilibrium: Nonlinear change in organizational fields. In: *Organization science 16*, Vol. 5: p. 456-473.
- Paleo, I. O. & Wijnberg, N. M. (2006). Classification of popular music festivals: A typology of festivals and an inquiry into their role in the construction of music genres. In: *International Journal of Arts Management* 8, Vol. 2: p. 50-61.
- Rüling, C.-C. & Strandgaard Pedersen, J. (2010). Film festival research from an organizational studies perspective. In: *Scandinavian journal of management* 26: p. 318-323.
- Silverman, David (1986). *Qualitative methodology and sociology: describing the social world*. Reprint.. ed. Aldershot: Gower.
- Skov, L. (2006). The role of trade fairs in the global fashion business. In: *Current Sociology* 54, Vol. 5: p. 764-783.• Steyaert, C. (2007). Life worlds-'Entrepreneuring' as a conceptual attractor? A review of process theories in 20 years of entrepreneurship studies. In: *Entrepreneurship & Regional Development: An International Journal* 19, Vol. 6: p. 453 – 477.
- Taylor, S. & Spicer, André (2007). Time for space: An interpretive review of research on organizational spaces. In: *International Journal of Management Reviews 9*, Vol. 4: p. 325-346.
- Thompson, D. (2011). Art fairs: The market is medium. In: Brian Moeran/Jasper Strandgaard Pedersen (Hrsg.), *Negotiating values in the creative industries: Fairs, festivals and other competitive events*. Cambridge, Cambridge University Press. p. 59-72.
- Uzzi, B. (1996). The sources and consequences of embeddedness for the economic performance of organizations: the network effect. In: *Amercian Sociological Review* 61: p. 674-698.

About the author

Bastian Lange (DE) is an urban and economic geographer and specialized within the creative industries, questions of governance and regional development. He has been Guest Professor at the Humboldt University in Berlin since 2011. Bastian Lange obtained his doctorate at the Johann-Wolfgang Goethe University, Frankfurt am Main, in 2006. He is a Fellow of the Georg Simmel Centre for Metropolitan Research at the Humboldt University in Berlin.

bastian.lange@geo.hu-berlin.de

Co-creation and Social Entrepreneurship: How to use creative entrepreneurship as the innovator in social contexts

Aukje Thomassen

Abstract

The potential for understanding social entrepreneurship through design is still underdeveloped. This chapter explores how design can enable social innovation, and specifically how creative entrepreneurship can enhance these innovations. We contend that creative entrepreneurship can provide solutions to collaborative international design and enable knowledge creation and innovation through tacit knowledge exchange. In recent publications design is seen as an enabler of user-centered innovation at a macro-economic level. There is a strong positive correlation between the use of design, national competitiveness and the potential of collective governance. This chapter will start with understanding innovation, and in particular social innovation, in the context of design. It will then unpack creative and social entrepreneurship through understanding the definition; what is needed to make it happen; and how it can be applied.

Introduction

Imagine a retirement village where elderly people walk their Aibo robot dog to get their daily exercise; enhance their cognition as they play chess via the Aibo's wifi with their friends and relatives remotely; or be monitored and reminded by the Aibo to take their daily medicine. Picture a neighborhood where people get to know each other by playing a game together using their mobile phones, and at the same time research can be done on how social cohesion and community engagement can be provoked. Design projects for special needs like these, implementing artificial intelligent systems in home environments or using games as a vehicle for research are examples of successful projects, and show that providing design solutions can improve the independence of living, health and cognition. And for this we need understand how design can help, support and enable social innovation.

Background: innovation and design

Design

For the purpose of this article the 'creative process' builds on Cziksentmihalyi's (1996) research in which he articulates it as a process that *'can enable change in a symbolic context, such as design, and this approach opens up understanding of the participatory aspects of design (and the designer) to an acceptance of the receiving field (field of application of design)'* (Thomassen & Preston 2010, p 46). Bilton (2007, p. 2) discusses how *'Creativity is not to be located in one state of mind, one room, one type of person, one individual. Rather it lies in the transition points between different ways of thinking (...) Creativity and business are not natural opponents - they have more in common than we may assume'.*

The definition of *'design as goal-oriented process to solve problems, meet needs, improve situations, or create something new or useful'* (Thomassen & Preston 2010, p. 46) is central to any design discussion in this article. The world is changing rapidly into a more complicated, competitive and challenging society, even for designers, new levels of creativity and problem solving are needed. Single problems, linear approaches and design craft skills are inadequate for facing the current paradigm shift (Tapscott 2006; Jenkins 2006). The new designer must be able to cope with adaptation, or *'sensemaking'* (Van Patter, 2007). This change is relatively new, in 2005, design agencies were changing their attitudes and strategies, however, the innovation for design education is currently synchronizing by implementing the entrepreneurial ingredients in their design curriculum. Design finds itself in a transition phase of becoming the agent for 'Social Transformation' (Van Patter, 2009).

Some research has been carried out on how design can be inclusive to society and its citizens, or what role creative entrepreneurship plays in enabling collective change. To respond to this designers need to apply a deep local human centered *'sensemaking'* (Jones, 2009), i.e. how can human centered design approaches transform social situations (Wiener, 1948). To understand this we need to go to the heart of design as a change agent which is innovation.

Design Innovation

Before innovation will be unpacked it is important to understand that this article will build on Schumpeter's definition of innovation *'the carrying out of new combinations'* (1971, p. 47). This definition is well aligned with the definition of design used for this article. As innovation is carrying out new combinations, design is achieving these by providing solutions. In combination with what Landry (2000) calls innovative creative thinking in an active and cultural climate, this can be the fuel for social-economic global dynamics. Research carried out by Kurzweil, (2005) and Salzman & Matathia (2007) show that three *'mega trends'* of global mobility, information technology, and communications are driving the innovation process (Thomassen & Rive, 2010). At the heart of this is the convergence of individuals, ideas, cultures and interactions; a so called global *'network society'* (Castells, 2000; Kurzweil, 2004; Salzman & Matathia, 2007). Following Schumpeter's approach on innovation we can understand how innovation can be seen as an important driver of education, economic development, and discovery, (Von Krogh, et al 2000). A new trend is that at the heart of the innovation process often design teams contribute novel solutions to user problems, which is aligned with the definition of design used in this article (Mau, Leonard, & Institute without Boundaries 2004; Suri & IDEO (Firm) 2005), it is *'distributed, plural, and collaborative'*, (Rive & Thomassen, 2011; Mau, et al 2004). Design has the potential, beyond *'delivering'* aesthetics to products and services, of creating social innovations that change the performance capacity of society through creative entrepreneurship (Drucker, 1985). In particular *'user centered'* design provides a context for social change; special needs, health, accessibility amongst others. Due to social and economic innovation, the potential of design, and its application, is getting more public attention (EU 2009). Effectively design can be seen as a driver and enabler of innovation, but further research is needed to sustain these innovations (UN, 2008).

VanPatter (2009) in his research essay describes what designers face is changing; no longer is a single designer needed for a simple problem. As society has become more complex, so have problems become more complex. And in that analogy it is important to understand that often problems are so complex that a designer needs at least a team to solve a problem, but moreover it needs an attitude change as well. Aesthetic refinement no longer is the solution. Designers are faced with applying more then craft focused solutions. Their entire skill set has become a more intrinsic part of the solution; understanding and adapting to complex situations, creating and envisioning alternatives, and the ability to create quantities of ideas and concepts have become the main ingredients (Thomassen, 2010).

Social innovation

Central to enabling design innovation is an understanding of how individuals can contribute to it; and in particular which attributes are pivotal to the ongoing development of design innovation. Schumpeter (1984) argued that innovation and change comes from entrepreneurs. Drucker (1993) explains in his work that the term *'entrepreneurship'* was introduced by Say (1803) to describe how an entrepreneur is to *'shift economic sources out of an area lower and into an area of higher productivity, and greater yield.'* (1993, p.21). This take on entrepreneurship has since been applied and theorized in several other fields, including creative, cultural and social entrepreneurship. For the purpose of this article, creative and cultural entrepreneurship will be investigated before social entrepreneurship is discussed.

Creative Entrepreneurship

According to Hagoort (2007) the foundations of creative entrepreneurship provide insights into the dynamics of the design and innovation. It is important to understand that creative entrepreneurship is different from cultural entrepreneurship. Cultural entrepreneurship refers to the process of leading a cultural organization from three perspectives:

1 To formulate a clear proactive cultural mission statement that offers direction,
2 to find a balance between cultural and economic values and
3 to maintain the cultural infrastructure surrounding the own organization (Hagoort, 2007).

In sum, the focus is on unifying cultural content and commercial possibilities as a basis for innovation.

Creative entrepreneurship on the other hand focuses on how creative and intellectual capital can be exploited. The trading good difference lies in the fact that a creative entrepreneur uses creative talent, attributes, skill and attitudes to capitalize, and how to apply these to developing innovation (Hagoort, 2006). Dealing with fluid systems requires creative skills, to help initiate discovery and exploitation of a system. In addition to this, Van Patter (2007) speaks of outbound and inbound skill sets, skills to participate and co-create with all the stakeholders within a defined and demarcated context, but also skills to be able to collaborate and to be a team player.

Social Entrepreneurship

Social entrepreneurship is crucial for social innovation with the potential to galvanize major changes across society through co-creation (Sanders et al 2003; Stappers et al 2006).

According to Bornstein (2007) *'it takes creative individuals with fixed determination and indomitable will to propel the innovation that society needs to tackle its toughest problems'* (2007, p. 3). He also indicates that a social change starts with an entrepreneurial author who has defined a problem and has a solution for it; who is able to organize systems that support the articulation of the solution; and who has the ability to act on that vision.

Light (2008) defines social entrepreneurship as *'an effort by an individual, group, network, organization, or alliance of organizations that seek sustainable, large scale change through pattern-breaking ideas in what governments, nonprofits and business do to address significant social problems'* (2008, p. 12). This requires efforts to solve intractable social problems through pattern breaking change. The following creative (social) entrepreneurial model outlines how change can be brought into a system.

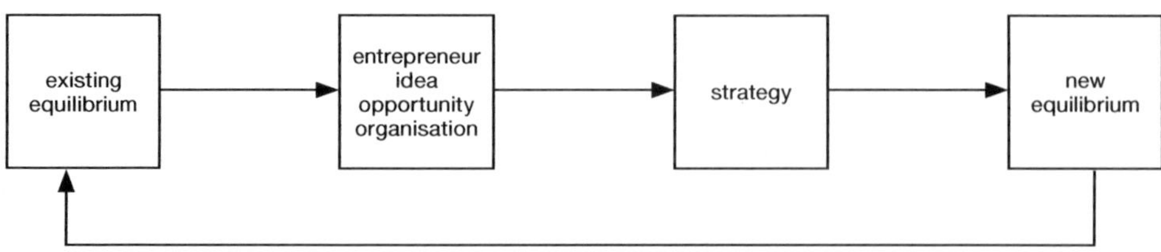

Figure 1. A first logic Chain of Social Entrepreneurship (Light 2008, p 54).

In this model Light (2008, p. 58 cited by Dietachmair 2009, p. 65) defines 8 steps:
- Step 1: Imagining a new equilibrium
- Step 2: Discovering an opportunity
- Step 3: Inventing the idea for change
- Step 4: Launching the idea into action
- Step 5 Scaling up for high impact
- Step 6: Diffusing the idea
- Step 7: Sustaining momentum
- Step 8: Navigating the changing social system

This model has been studied and applied to socio-cultural entrepreneurship in organizations by Dietachmair (2009). The model describes how to create change in a set context. It is important to understand that in order to create change from a current situation, initiatives need to be taken. This starts with creative thinking tasks of imagination, discovery and invention, followed by what Drucker (1983) calls an entrepreneurial spirit to launch and scale up the idea. Through upscaling, this activity will lead to diffusion, as it becomes active in other parts as well. When this settles we can speak of a sustained momentum. For a system to be in equilibrium, all its parts (subsystems) must be in equilibrium. If a system is in equilibrium, then its parts are in equilibrium. According to this Steady-State principle (Von Bertalanffy 1972), change can take place in small parts, as they clearly belong to a larger system. For the purpose of this article, this model will be applied to the case studies, discussed in section 4.0 below.

Co-creation

Collaboration with others is an intrinsic part of creative and social entrepreneurship. We see that in design as well, Mau already noted this in 2004 *'It is no longer avout one designer, one client, one solution, one place'* (2004, p. 17). Designers work together, either in teams of designers *'renaissance teams'* (Mau, 2004), or with other stakeholders in co-creation situations (VanPatter 2009). Current design projects that focus on social innovation are constructed on the concept of Co-Creation. Sanders and Simons (2009) define *'co-creation as any act of collective creativity that is experienced jointly by two or more people'*. Sanders and Simons explicitly distinguish co-creation from collaboration; it is referred to as *'a special case of collaboration where the intent is to create something that is not known in advance'* (p. 2). To stay within the context of design, and in particular design innovation, it is important to understand this difference. The lens for this article is on enabling social innovation through design; hence how to create social innovation using design that is particularly innovative, and therefore unknown before the creation process started. These are often communities that share a particular context, practice or objective, ie. businesses, stakeholders, (end) users. It is more common that stakeholders, end users or individuals are participating more intensly in developing experiences, and thereby wishing to express their creativity, as part of the design project. Leadbeater in 2007 discusses in his book *'WeThink: why mass creativity is the next big thing'* how the current consumers (inviduals) are becoming more prosumers (producers and consumers). They want be active *'players and participants'* and *'these are activities of mass participation rather than mass consumption.'* (Green, 2007, p. 9).

This phenomena of the experience economy is often driven by mechanisms through which individuals express citizenship, participate in democracy. Empowerment comes out of these networks and leads to political and democratic solutions for this same net generation. Castells (1996) Network Society differentiates the net and the self as two entities in a network structure, the organizational forms powered by network structures and the people who try to adapt and reaffirm to change caused by the net.

Especially for creating social value through co-creation, it is important to understand that the larger context and long term ideation is pivotal. Eero Saarinen refers to this as *Always design a thing by considering its next larger context — a chair in a room, a room in a house, a house in an environment, an environment in a city plan'* (cited by Sanders and Simons, 2009, p. 5).
The following model outlines the different elements in a co-creation process within the context of this article, ie. social innovations and experiences.

Co-creation of value	Objectives	Mindset	How people are seen	Deliverables
Use/Experience	- positive experiences - personalization - customization	- experience-driven - service orientation	- end-users - empowered customers	- Products and services that people need and want
Societal	- improve quality of life - sustainability	- human-centered - ecological	- partners - participants - owners	- transformation - ownership - learning

Table 1. Comparison of Three Types of Value Co-creation (Sanders and Simons 2009, p 3).

As research has indicated, individuals want to become more active participants in the developing of new innovative solutions for well-being, even if this takes time and requires long-term change. Ongoing support of change can be 'assured' by addressing the context, the co-creation modus of operandi and the participatory methods, and moreover understanding the current model of net-generation.

Concluding creative entrepreneurship and social innovation

Drucker (1985) discusses in his work that talented entrepreneurial people are able to transform ideas into successful business for society through a sense of initiative; bold, business oriented mind; visions and product specific strategies; and export performance via global markets. It is important to understand that design innovation, creative and social entrepreneurship are growing rapidly. Partly because the state and churches no longer exclusively drive society, people are becoming more active in applying change and organizations are set up due to technological enhancement on an international and global scale. Bornstein (2007, p. 7) sums it up by saying *'more people today have the freedom, time, wealth, health, exposure, social mobility, and confidence to address social problems in bold ways'.* Which brings us to understanding why the field of design is particularly applicable to enable change: Partly because the net-generation is seeking agency and designers are responding to that by developing 'social media'; partly because of the development and acceptance of different network structures; and partly because design and creativity are providing more open entry. These dynamics have led to new requirements for designers;

a   they need to understand innovation as a specific instrument of entrepreneurship,

b   they have to become a heroic entrepreneur, combining strategy with intuition,

c   be able to adapt to their context of activity sense of initiative, imagineers,

d   and basically having to learn to adapt to any new situation which enables transformation of ideas into successful business for society.

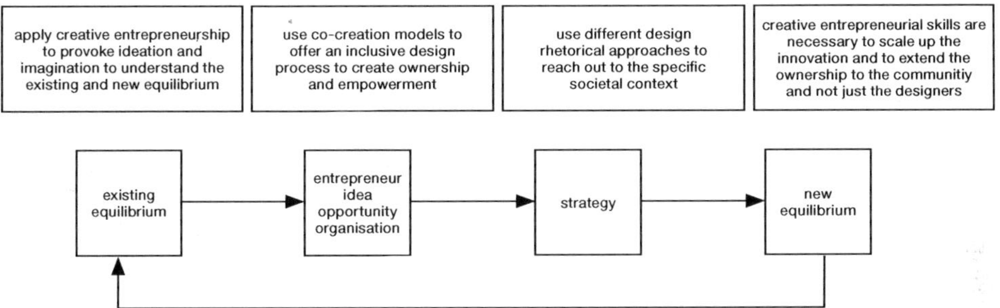

Figure 2. Social entrepreneurship model applied to creative entrepreneurship and co-creation.

It is important to understand how new these changes are, and how little has been reported on combing creative and social entrepreneurship for the benefit of design innovation and well-being. A solution for ongoing development is applying creative entrepreneurship to the chain of social entrepreneurship model. According to this model we need to develop an equilibrium imagination of the future, where designers are trained to deliver ideation through imagination. If models such as co-creation and play are used to create leverage and agency, strategies for change can be developed. Part of reaching out is knowing how to reach out, and again design offers novel and engaging ways of reaching out. In attempt to answer how to use design entrepreneurship as the innovator in social contexts, it is important to understand the dynamics and differences between creative and social entrepreneurship. This research suggests that a combination of both types of entrepreneurship, along with co-creation as the modus of operandi for developing design innovation, are a good point of departure for any design enabling social innovation process. Heroic approaches, creative thinking and an aim for achieving new combinations within design seem to be the recipe for initiating social change and well-being.

References

- Bilton, C. (2007). *Management and creativity: from creative industries to creative management.* USA: Blackwell Publishing.
- Bornstein, D. (2007) *How to change the world.* Oxford: Oxford Press.
- Bødker, S. (1996). Creating conditions for participation: Conflicts and resources in systems design, In: *Human Computer Interaction, 11*(3), pp. 215-236.
- Bryan, L. L., & Joyce, C. I. (2007). *Mobilizing minds: creating wealth from talent in the 21st-century organization.* New York: McGraw-Hill.
- Castells, M. (2000). *The rise of the network society* (2nd ed.). Malden, MA: Blackwell Publishers.
- Csikszentmihalyi, M. (1996). *Creativity: Flow and the Psychology of Discovery and Invention.* New York: Harper Perennial.
- Dos Santos Duisenberg (Ed) (2008). *Creative Economy Report 2008.* United Nations UNCTAD, Geneva.

- Drucker, P.F. (1985). *Innovation and Entrepreneurship*. Oxford: Butterworthy-Heinemann.
- European Commission (2005). *Future of Creative Industries. Implications for Research Policy European Commission*, London: European Commission.
- European Union (2009). *Design as a driver of user-centred innovation*. Commission Staff Working Document. European Union.
- Green (2007) *Democratizing the future*. The Netherlands: Koninklijke Philips Electronics N.V. .
- Hagoort, G. ed. (2007). *Read This First, Growth and Development of Creative SMEs*. Research group of Arts and Economics, Utrecht, The Netherlands: University of Applied Arts.
- Hagoort, G. (2007). *Cultural Entrepreneurship: On the freedom to create art and the freedom of enterprise*. Inaugural Lecture June 6 2007, University of Utrecht, The Netherlands.
- Hamel, G. (2007). The future of management. Boston, Mass.: Harvard Business School Press.
- Huizinga, J. (1998). *Homo Ludens: A Study of the Play-Element in Culture*, Routledge.
- Jenkins, H. (2006). *Convergence Culture: Where Old and New Media Collide*. New York University Press.
- Kim H, Nakamura C, and Zeng-Treitler, Q. (2009) Assessment of Pictographs Developed Through a Participatory Design Process Using an Online Survey Tool. In: *J Med Internet Res;11*(1):e5.
- Kooyman, R. (Ed) (2009). *Creative Industries; Colourful Fabric in Multiple Dimensions*. Research group of Arts and Economics, The Netherlands: Utrecht University of Applied Arts and Eburon Press.
- Kurzweil, R. and Grossman, T. (2004). *Fantastic voyage: live long enough to live forever*. [Emmaus, Pa.]: Rodale : Distributed to the trade by Holtzbrinck Publishers.
- Landry, C. (2000). *The Creative City*. London: Earthscan 2000.
- Leadbeater (2007). *We-think: The Power of Mass Creativity*, retrieved from: www.wethinkthebook.net .
- Mau, B., Leonard, J., & Institute without Boundaries. (2004). *Massive change*. London: Phaidon.
- PriceWaterhouseCoopers. (2008). *Managing the risks and rewards of collaboration*. Retrieved from http://www.pwc.com/gx/en/technology/technology-executive-connections/index.jhtml [Accessed 03/01/2010].
- Sanders, L., & Vanpatter, GK. (2003). Science in the Making. In: *NextD Journal: ReReThinking Design5*(1).
- Rive, P. & Thomassen, A. (2011) International Collaboration and Design Innovation in Virtual Worlds: lessons from Second Life. In: *Computer-Mediated Communication across Cultures: International Interactions in Online Environments*, edited by K. St.Amant, East Carolina University and S. Kelsey, Louisiana State University, IGI Global (US)
- Sanders, L. and simons, G. (2009) *A Social Vision for Value Co-creation in Design*. Retrieved from: http://www.osbr.ca/ojs/index.php/osbr/article/view/1012/973 [Accessed 01/03/2010].
- Salzman, M. L., & Matathia, I. (2007). *Next now: trends for the future*. New York: Palgrave Macmillan.
- Say, JP., (1803). *A Treatise on Political Economy* (1st edition). Philadelphia: Lippincott, Grambo & Co.
- Schon, D. (1983). *The Reflective Practitioner. How Professionals Think in Action*, Temple Smith, London.
- Schumpeter, J. (1975). *Capitalism, Socialism, and Democracy*. New York: Harper.
- Suri, J. F., & Ideo (Firm). (2005). *Thoughtless acts?: observations on intuitive design* (1st ed.). San Francisco: Chronicle Books.
- Tapscott, D. & Williams, A. D. (2006). *Wikinomics : how mass collaboration changes everything*. New York: Portfolio.
- Thomassen, A. (2007). Design of the netgeneration: Streaming the flow of design and science in the educational practice of the creative industry. In: *Special Edition of Cybernetics and Design of Kybernetes Journal, Volume 36* (9/10), pp. 1529 - 1542.
- Thomassen, A. (2009) Social Innovation through employing Design Actualization, In: Kooyman, R. (Ed) (2009). *Creative Industries; Colourful Fabric in Multiple Dimensions*. Research group of Arts and Economics, The Netherlands: Utrecht University of Applied Arts and Eburon Press, the Netherlands.
- Thomassen, A. (2010). *Designing Social Innovation; the redefinition of design as a transformative force, from Keynote of Creative Grounds Conference*. Utrecht School of the Arts, The Netherlands, on 18th March 2010.

- Thomassen, A. & Easterly, D. (2009). A Pedagogical Framework for Designing Urban Games to Promote Sustainability. In: *Proceedings of the 13th Computer-Human Interaction Netherlands Conference* June 11 2009, Leiden (The Netherlands), available at http://www.chi-conferentie.nl/2009/06/website/wp-content/uploads/2009/07/proceedings_chi_nederland_2009.pdf.
- Thomassen, A. & Mulder, I. (2008) Aard van het Beestje, (Healthcare and the AIBO robotdog). In: *Technologie en Langdurige Zorg of the researchgroup Technology and Healthcare.*
- Thomassen, A. & Preston, J. (2010) 'Writing' through design, an active practice, *Journal of Writing in Creative Practice,* Goldsmiths, University of London, UK.
- Thomassen, A. & Rive, P. (2010) How to enable knowledge exchange in Second Life in Design Education? *Journal issue of Learning, Media and Technology: Learning in Virtual Worlds.*
- Tunstall, E. (2008) *US Design Policy,* retrieved from: http://www.designpolicy.org/.
- Vanpatter, G.K. (2007). Rethinking Wicked Porblems (Part 2): Unpacking Paradigms, Bridging Universes (Part 2), in: *NextDesign Leadership Institute Journal.*
- VanPatter, G.K. (2009). *Design 1.0, 2.0, 3.0, 4.0 - Understanding Futures that Have Already Arrived!.*
- Von krogh, G., Nonaka, I. & Ichijo, K. (2000). *Enabling knowledge creation : how to unlock the mystery of tacit knowledge and release the power of innovation.* Oxford ; New York: Oxford University Press.
- Wiener, N. (1948). *Cybernetics or Control and Communication in the Animal and the Machine,* Cambridge, MA, MIT Press.

About the author

Aukje Thomassen (NZ) is Associate Professor and Head of Research at the School of Art & Design, Faculty of Design & Creative Technologies at the Auckland University of Technology AUT. Her research focuses on Social Innovation (creative entrepreneurship and co-creation) through Design Research (Philosophy, Didactics and Methodologies) and thereby studying Knowledge Creation in the Creative Industries (especially in the area of Game Design/Interaction Design) within a theoretical framework of Cybernetics.
aukje.thomassen@aut.ac.nz

Artists' interventions for innovation
Typologies of projects, results and intermediaries

Sofie van den Borne, Joost Heinsius, Lucie Huiskens

Abstract

To remain competitive, European business must strengthen its creativity and innovativeness. One of the most promising ways to connect innovation to creativity is the combination of artists and business. This article will focus on the analysis of different types of matching artists and business and the different types of artistic interventions that follow from this matching.
This analysis is part of the EU-funded project 'Training Artists for Innovation' (TAFI), that collects and defines the experiences of five participating organizations from Denmark, Finland, Sweden, Spain and the Netherlands. In the end the project will result in a framework for qualifications artists need to work in business, but will also develop recommendations on how to improve the conditions for this kind of work through intermediaries and training. The paper will concentrate on the first phase of the project and present several typologies of intermediaries and artistic interventions. In the end these results will show how artists can improve their entrepreneurship when developing this market, and it will show how artist can contribute to innovation within business.

Introduction

'If Europe wants to remain competitive in this changing global environment, it needs to put in place the right conditions for creativity and innovation to flourish in a new entrepreneurial culture' as it states in the European Commission Green Paper (2010).
One of the most promising ways to connect innovation to creativity is the combination of artists and business. To successfully develop this promising trend further, there are three obstacles to conquer. Within business the possibilities of working with the arts, as a way of intervening, are not very well known, and often seen as hazardous or uncharted territory. In addition, there are only a few intermediary platforms in Europe with a solid body of experience in this field. And thirdly, there are not that many artists who already have the skills to work in business and organizations solving their problems.

At present, one can identify a gap between the need for creativity in business and the way artists and creatives can deliver this creativity to external enterprises. To bridge this gap, the project *'Training Artists for Innovation'* (TAFI) has been developed, a EU-funded cooperation project between organizations from the Netherlands, Sweden, Finland, Denmark and Spain. This project analyses the needs of business entrepreneurs, the experience of existing intermediaries, the experience of existing training of artists for creative interventions, and the experience of artists delivering creative interventions.

To develop a qualification & skills framework it is important to know the different possibilities of matching arts and business. According to Berthoin Antal (2009), *'the interaction with the art form can be more or less active, and more or less entertaining, provocative, and educational.'* She states that *'In such meetings with the arts, members of organizations can become aware of the distinctive features of their language, perspectives, and practices, and have the opportunity to generate variations in ways of seeing and doing things from which to choose in the future.'*
The basic question we have to look at is the possible correlation between interventions and the qualifications needed. Do different types of interventions also require different skills and qualifications for artists?

Typologies of intermediary platforms matching arts and business

Matching artists with business questions is often been done by intermediary platforms. These intermediaries are the link between the business organization and the artist, matching artists with business questions and sometimes also guide the artist and the business during the process of an artistic intervention. There is a large range of types of matching which of course has an impact on the activities of the artists and on the competencies they need. These intermediary platforms pursue different goals. The goal can be for example to provide artists with new market possibilities, to train artists or, at the other end of the scope, to earn money using artists as a 'tool' for creative consultancy. These diverse goals have consequences for the relationship between the artist and the business organization, and for the business model of the intermediary platform.

The process of intervention can be divided into several phases: acquisition, definition, research, execution, evaluation. The artist and the intermediary platform can have a role in all phases, but do not necessarily have a role in each phase. At the start of a project, the intermediary can e.g. have the role of originator, the main contractor or can just serve as a pass-through. The intermediary can select an artist based on the initial question of the organization, and then leave it up to the artist to define and develop the project in order to answer the request. Another option for the intermediary is to develop the idea for the artistic intervention, and select an artist who can execute that idea. In the examples we studied, the bigger the role of the intermediary platform at the start of the project, the later the artist enters the project. Of course the level of control the intermediary platform has in later phases influences the relationship of the artist with the business organization, but also the relationship between the intermediary platform and the artist. And consequently, it influences the competencies needed to act successfully.

Different business models

Intermediaries can have different business models, depending on their goals in matching arts and business and on the goals of financing bodies.

a   If the intermediary has the role of consultant using artists as part of its 'toolbox', the work of the artist is part of the consultancy assignment, and will be incorporated in the fee for the job, and thus the income depends on the commissions it gets from companies and business organizations.
b   Other intermediaries are co-financed by employers-organizations who find it important to introduce more creativity into the workplace.
c   A third possibility is when the intermediary's goal is to educate artists and to provide them with new markets. The income of the intermediary platform will in this case often depend on funding bodies and their specific goals.

The goal of the intermediary platform in the project and the way it is funded, does have consequences for the possible roles of the artists in these projects. The way intermediary platforms interpret their role in the process of acquiring, defining and executing the project, and the way the intermediaries organize their business model, have a large impact on the way these projects are carried out. These roles can influence the type of intervention and subsequently also the competencies artists need for successful interventions.

Typologies of artistic interventions

Besides different types of intermediaries and of matching arts and business, there is also a large range of types of artistic interventions. Because the typology of the intervention has consequences for the competencies artists need, and subsequently for the training model, it is important to take a look at the different types of interventions. For the typology of the intervention, three questions are important. To what can the intervention contribute (1), how is the process of the intervention organized (2), and what degree of intensity characterizes the intervention (3)?

About the first question some research has been done in the past. Schiuma (2009) for example, takes a managerial approach to the effects of artistic interventions. He states that *'the involvement in arts and the adoption of Arts-Based Initiatives (ABIs) within organizations are not just new trends, but rather relevant management approaches to be integrated with the more traditional and rational-based management models and tools.' According to Schiuma, ABIs can 'provide processes, models and tools for a new management approach within organizations.'*

Another typology of artistic interventions is the model of Lotte Darsø (2004). This model is based on the notion that business can learn from the arts, and that learning can be invoked somewhere on the axes of 'ambiguous-well defined' and 'art as role model – art in action'.

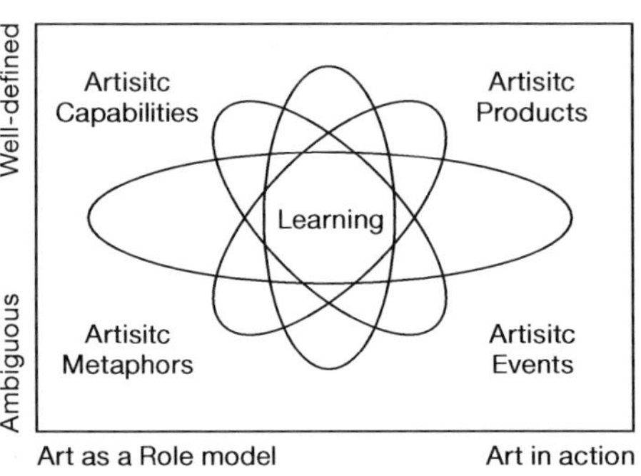

Figure 1. Model for artistic interventions. (Darsø, 2004).

In another study, Darsø and Kerr (2008) found four approaches to Arts-in-Business, art for decoration, for entertainment, as instruments for teambuilding, communication training, leadership development, problem solving, innovation processes and to integrate the arts in a strategic process of transformation, involving personal development and leadership, culture and identity, creativity and innovation, as well as customer relations and marketing.

In the Arts & Business Report (2004), the distinction is made between two modes of impact that artistic interventions can have in organizations: a technical mode with the transfer of skills and knowledge, and an inspirational mode when artists introduce a different role model and new ways of thinking and doing. However, Berthoin (2009) states that 'it is not always possible to distinguish clearly between the technical and the inspirational mode of learning.' To answer question two - how is the process of the intervention organized? -, the intervention can be open, with open outcomes and an open process, or can be the opposite, with defined questions and a defined process. Interventions with an open character are often projects which are touching on authenticity, values and attitudes of people. On the opposite side are interventions that have a defined question and process. These interventions are for example projects by trainer actors to improve e.g. presentation skills en enlarge the self-esteem of employees (figure 2).

It is obvious that there is a very wide range of possible interventions if you look at the three axes we describe: the area of intervention, the way the intervention is organised and the intensity (length, number of people, and number of sessions).

Conclusion

As suggested, there is an increasing number of these artistic interventions happening within business organizations. It is our understanding that artistic interventions have a lot to offer, and by now there are ample testimonials to prove their effect. We also see an increase in intermediaries necessary to organize these artistic interventions on a larger scale.
But it is also clear that these types of interventions and the way they are organized and carried out need additional attention. The large variety of possible interventions and ways of

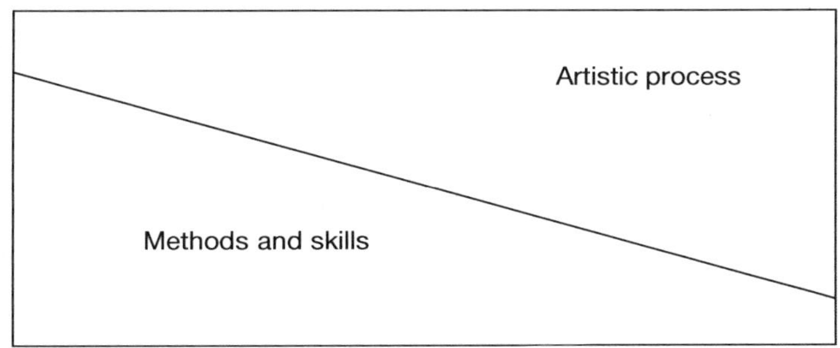

Figure 2. types of interventions.

matching arts and businesses has still to be described yet, let alone fully understood in terms of competencies needed. Additional insights are needed in order to understand what it is exactly that artists have to learn, in order to be successful in this line of work. Within the project Training Artists for Innovation (TAF) an attempt is made for matching arts and businesses. By describing the possibilities and the competencies artists need to be successful interveners, artists can prepare themselves in order to be able to provide an additional value to business organizations.

References

- Arts & Business Report,. (2004). *Art works. Why business needs the arts.* Arts & Business, London.
- Berthoin Antal, A. (2009). *Research Framework for Evaluating the Effects of Artistic Interventions in Organizations,* TILLT Europe project.
- Buswick, T, Creamer, A. & Pinard, M. (2004). *(Re)Educating for Leadership: How the arts can improve Business.*
- Darsø, L. & Kerr, C. (2008). 'Introduction, Re-conceiving the artful in management development and education.' eContent Management Pty Ltd. In: *Journal of Management & Organization* 2008, 14.
- Darsø, L. (2004). *Artful Creation. Learning-Tales of Arts-In-Business.* Samfundslitteratur.
- European Commission. (2010). *Unlocking the potential of cultural and creative industries.* Green Paper, Brussels, 2010 , 2.
- Schiuma, G. (2009). *The Value of Arts-Based Initiatives. Mapping Arts-Based Initiatives.* London: Arts & Business.

About the authors

Sofie van den Borne (NL) works as researcher at Cultuur-Ondernemen. She attained her Master Arts Policy and Management in 2010 with a thesis on career development in the arts.

sofie_van_den_borne@hotmail.com

Joost Heinsius (NL) is a consultant and publisher on managing volunteer-professional relationships. He is Manager Knowledge & Innovation at Cultuur-Ondernemen (Culture-Entrepreneurship).

jheinsius@cultuur-ondernemen.nl

Lucie Huiskens (NL) is an independent consultant for the creative sector. She is Project Manager of KIS (Artists, Innovation & Strategy), a course for artists who want to work with business on innovation and change issues at Cultuur-Ondernemen, Amsterdam.

lhuiskens@kunstenaarsenco.nl

Economies of Interaction
Frances Joseph

Abstract

This case study discusses a pilot project engaged with the development of an interactive screen exhibition program in Auckland, New Zealand. The project is considered in relation to emergent local government strategies and national arts council policies and the implicit tensions that exist between cultural and creative industries frameworks in the context of creative technologies, disciplinary histories and innovation strategies.
In New Zealand, The Edge - Auckland's leading performing arts centre - and CoLab - a creative technologies research centre at the Auckland University of Technology (AUT) - have initiated a collaborative project. This initiative - Digital Art Live (DAL) - has led to the development of an interactive screen exhibition. This program engaged both public and private entities, artists, creative content and technical developers, staff and students from three universities and community organizations.

The Edge

In 2010 The Edge Council reallocated some funds earmarked for buying traditional artworks for the theatre foyer, to the purchase of interactive screen technology. At a meeting between CoLab and The Edge staff in mid 2010, the potential of both organizations to work together and establish a technology platform and a dynamic exhibition program of interactive works was recognised. A yearlong pilot program was established to research, develop, test and evaluate strategies for engagement, content generation, capability building, funding and program organization for the interactive screen environment. The screen was installed in January 2011 with a test program shown in February and the official opening in April. A part time curator, Nolwenn Hugain-Lacire, was appointed. An ongoing program of original interactive works running for six weeks and some shorter special showings to coincide with cultural events such as the Indian Festival of Diwali saw nine exhibitions presented in 2011. In addition the CoLab Interaction Lab at AUT was configured to provide a space for workshops and testing and a technical support system.

The program

The Edge management decided the format and location of the interactive screen. Sited on a wall in the foyer beside the ASB Theatre, the screen itself consists of 12 Samsung thin flat screens organized into a large composite screen. The overall size of the wall is 4100mm x 1737mm. While the multiple screen set-up presents certain challenges for artists, it has other advantages including the clarity and definition of image, and the opportunity to produce single or multiple screen works. The size and hanging level of the screen is similar to a large painting and the grid format of the screen itself echoes the grid in the history of painting. While a number of the DAL exhibitors have been visual artists, the project is engaging creative practitioners from a number of different fields across the cultural and creative industries, including spatial designers, animators, special effects artists, communication and games designers, filmmakers, computer programmers and engineers. The opportunity to develop an ongoing interactive media showcase outside of a gallery venue enables creative practitioners from different disciplinary backgrounds and sectors to draw from a diversity of media, references and discursive frameworks to enable a range of experimental approaches and support broader inquiry into the ontology and teleology of interactive media.

Frameworks

Location has been a distinguishing factor in the theorization of interactive screens. Outdoor urban screens located in public environments have been characterized in terms of connections between digital media, architecture, and urban space (Mobile Publics, 2008). This discourse emphasizes communication, recognizing the political importance of urban screens for experimentation and community expression to build relations between people and places through technologically enabled forms of engagement. A second arena is associated with interactive art, sited in gallery spaces. While embracing technological innovation, the focus of work produced in this context is towards meaning and insight as the result of the interaction (Polaine, 2004). This artistic paradigm has tended to support an approach to interaction as a technique to enable or trigger insight into the content of a work of art, rather than as an experiential mode in itself.

Another significant domain is interactive gaming in domestic environments, with systems like Nintendo Wii and X Box Kinect among the most widely adopted forms of interactive digital devices. Entertainment and exercise are key drivers in this market. Gestural interaction in games systems tends to be operationally oriented, replacing the mouse as 'control' system with the 'intuitive' nature of these human interfaces regarded as a significant development. Narrative and play are central features of interactive entertainment technologies. A fourth perspective has emerged from the area of marketing, where interactivity is recognised as a way of actively engaging consumers. This approach *enables engagement further down the marketing funnel'* (Michelis and Send, undated, unpaged). This *'economy of engagement'* recognises attention that leads to engagement will more likely result in purchase.

Interactivity and the performing arts

The theatrical act of performing has traditionally been concerned with representation through action. While theatre, dance, and performance art are still regarded by many people as *'relics of live-ness in a media-saturated world'* (Saltz, 2008, unpaged) that challenge the virtuality or disembodiedness of digital media, the use of computer technologies in the performing arts are well established. Saltz suggests that this

has led to a reconsideration of the way these art forms are conceived by *'collapsing the neat ontological divide that once separated (or seemed to separate) the live performing arts from reproductive media such as film and video'* (ibid). There are a growing number of examples of creative works where the relationship between audience and performer has been challenged through the use of computers in the performing arts (Saltz, 2008; Gianacchi, 2004; Jacucci, 2004). The theatrical dimension of virtual reality – and the virtual reality of theatre - are not just created through the artifice of the set or the performer in costume or the avatar, but through the immersion or psychological engagement of an audience member in the situation, the drama or the game etc. It is this *'paradoxical relationship with the real'* (Gianacchi, 2004, p.123) that is fictional as well as physical, which links theatre and digitally mediated reality.

Sustainment

The teleological and ontological distinctions that characterize these approaches to interactivity underpin some of the difficulties we have faced in developing a singular economic strategy for sustaining the DAL project. The underlying issues of purpose and nature can be considered in relation to emerging policy frameworks for the creative and the cultural industries.

The relationship between the economics of arts culture and the creative industries is not well understood (Holden 2007). Within emergent 'new-media' domains these relationships are more complex in that digital technologies not only enable new forms of creative practice but also provide new distribution channels, opportunities to connect with audiences and even new business models.

The discussion paper Do My Arts Look Good On This? Media Arts and Digital Platforms sought feedback on how its *'various funding programs, capability-building initiatives and advocacy activities should support New Zealand media artists over the next five years*

(2012–2017),' and how it might *'best support the New Zealand arts sector to take advantage of digital technologies and platforms,'* (p. 4). The distinction made between 'media arts', as artworks that have been created with the use of new technologies and 'digital platforms', as media to engage with audiences, to promote, discuss, document and distribute work, recognizes CNZ's mandate to support the cultural industries in terms of creative production, critique and dissemination.

A second discussion document released by the Auckland Council is the Draft Auckland Plan (2011). This policy distinguishes the Creative and the Cultural Industries in Auckland in two separate chapters. Chapter Three addresses Auckland's Arts Culture Heritage and Lifestyle, while Chapter Four addresses Auckland's Economy, recognizing *'a number of enabling capabilities, important for improving economic performance across multiple sectors'* including *'digital content.'* In this report the value of the creative arts are acknowledged (in Chapter Three) in terms of their cultural and social value. Strategies for maximizing government funding for the region through institutional collaborations are emphasized. Sectors including Film, Gaming, Advertising, Television and Publishing are recognized (in Chapter Four) in terms of their economic contribution as part of Auckland's Creative Industries sector.
These distinctions between state funded cultural industries and economically focused creative industries correspond to the first and third models of Potts and Cunningham's theory of the dynamic value of the creative industries (2008). Potts and Cunningham recognize that a welfare-like, subsidy based policy is evident in a model of the cultural industries (model 1) as a *'merit good'* sector *'that produces cultural commodities that are welfare enhancing but that are only economically viable with a transfer of resources from the rest of the economy'* (p. 2). Another of their models (model 3, the growth model) positions the creative industries as drivers of economic growth, requiring investment and development policies.

With its diverse group of public and private stakeholders; various forms of creative engagement and dissemination; and emerging community of interactive practitioners; the DAL project can be positioned across these local policy frameworks, with their divisions between cultural and creative industry models and associated economic frameworks. While these policies recognize the value of 'media arts' as a form of creative practice; 'digital platforms' as distribution and communication systems to support artists and arts organizations; and 'digital content' as an economic commodity, they overlook the significance and value of this cross disciplinary creative technologies arena as a critical part of the innovation system. Potts and Cunningham's characterization of the innovation model (model 4) where the creative industries are part of 'a higher-order system that operates on the economic system' (p.10) is relevant here. The creative industries, in this model, generate and coordinate change in the knowledge base of the economy. They have crucial, rather than marginal, policy significance. This theory recognizes the dynamic value of the creative industries in the development and application of new knowledge.

Conclusion

In relation to the DAL project and its ongoing sustainability, we have worked pragmatically and successfully with model 1 strategies. We are working with a number of cultural organizations and industry bodies to develop new interactive works for exhibition in festivals and events. We are in discussion with sponsors from the IT sector and engaging with companies involved with digital content production and distribution to explore branding and indirect marketing opportunities. Qualifying the dynamic value of this experimental program of interactive inquiry in terms of its contribution to the innovation agenda will also support the development of a wider and richer discourse about the value and sustainability of such initiatives.

REFERENCES

- *Aotearoa Digital Artists* (ADA), retrieved from: http://www.aotearoadigitalarts.org.nz/.
- Auckland Council. (2011). *Draft Auckland Plan.* Retrieved from: http://www.aucklandcouncil.govt.nz/EN/AboutCouncil/PlansPoliciesPublications/theaucklandplan/draftaucklandplan/Pages/home.aspx .
- Creative New Zealand, (2001). *Do My Arts Look Good On This? Media Arts and Digital Platforms.* Wellington, Ministry of Culture and Heritage. Retrieved from: http://www.creativenz.govt.nz/en/about-creative-nz/corporate-and-strategy-documents/do-my-arts-look-good-on-this-media-arts-and-digital-platforms .
- Holden, J. (2007). *Publicly Funded Culture and the Cultural Industries.* London, Arts Council England. Retrieved from: http://www.demos.co.uk/publications/publiclyfundedcultureandthecreativeindustries.
- Giannachi, G. (2004). *Virtual Theatres.* London, Routledge.
- Jacucci, G. (2004). *Interaction as Performance.* Oulu, University of Oulu.
- Michelis, D. and Send, H. (Undated). *Engaging Passers By with Interactive Screens – A Marketing Perspective.* Lecture Notes in Informatics. Mobile Publics Conference Program. (2008). Federation Square Multimedia and International Urban Screens Association, Melbourne. Retrieved from: http://subs.emis.de/LNI/Proceedings?Proceedings154/gi-proc-154.
- Polaine, A. (2004). *Lowbrow, High Art: Why Big Fine Art Doesn't Understand Interactivity.* Conference, Banff new Media Institute. Retrieved from: http://www.polaine.com/playpen/wp-content/images/apolaine_whybigfineart_refresh_paper.pdf .
- Potts, J. and Cunningham, S. (2008). *Four models of the creative industries,* International Journal of Cultural Policy, Volume 14, Issue 3, p233-247.
- Saltz, D. (2008). *Digital Literary Studies: Performance and Interaction.* Edited by Susan Schreibman and Ray Siemens. A Companion to Digital Literary Studies. Oxford, Blackwell.
- Struppek, M. (2006). *Urban Screens – The Potential of Public Screens for Interaction.* Intelligent Agent, Vol. 16/2 . Retrieved from: http://www.intelligentagent.com/archive/Vol6_No2_interactive_city_struppek.htm.

About the author

Frances Joseph (NZ) Frances Joseph is co-director of CoLab, Creative Technologies Research Centre and director of the Textile and Design Laboratory at the Auckland University of Technology, New Zealand. Since 1992 Frances has been involved in the strategic development and realisation of cultural and creative projects involving multidisciplinary teams. She joined AUT as head of Postgraduate Studies in Art and Design in 1997 and worked in this role until 2005. Her current research is concerned with innovation through creative technologies, with a focus on areas of interaction design and aesthetics, e-textiles, design research methodology, creative entrepreneurship and the design and management of interdisciplinary projects.

frances.joseph@aut.ac.nz

Feasibility of a 'Fair Music' Business Model for both Creators and Consumers

Burak Özgen

Abstract

'Fair Music Campaign' aims to establish fair rules in music business. It strives for the protection of artistic freedom, well balanced contracts and fair remuneration for musicians, as well as a fair distribution of opportunities for smaller producers worldwide. Fair music adopts the idea of the Fair Trade Organisations and applies it to cultural world for fairness in music industry. It supports the diversity of global repertoire, increases the entrepreneurial activities of creators and offers a unique option for consumers. Based on the surveys and studies conducted under the campaign, this article first indicates various possibilities and challenges arisen from the progress of new media in music business. The statutory and contractual provisions are discussed.

Introduction

The market for physical sales of recorded music is declining; nevertheless, it is still a major part of total business volume. Physical sales still account for the majority of industry revenues, with nearly 70% of global trade revenue (IMPALA), compared to 27% from digital sales (IFPI) and 5% from performance rights revenues. Two of the growing markets are live performance and online distribution.

There is a potential market of self-promoting artists, small or medium size independent labels, small or medium size concert promoters and agencies that would need the support of a marketing initiatives like fair music and that are willing to fulfil the necessary standards. New technological developments have resulted in far reaching structural changes in the music sector, leading to the opening up of new distribution channels and possibilities. This change also has an impact on cultural works. The effects of technological improvements bring challenges: dealing with piracy, directing the payment-flow towards the creators and deliberations on who decides about access for producers and consumers to music and culture.

There are no existing balanced or social standards for the contractual situation in the music business, apart from unions' contracts that only concern certain parts of the music business, for instance the field of live performances. Few rules in national laws actually dissuade music companies to change their excessive practices in most cases. There are several vendors who offer alternatives to conventional relationships between musicians and labels or distributors. However, neither the potential of new markets is fully explored, nor the rights of artists better secured than before when they try to reach their audiences.

Copyright and contract law related aspects of musicians' earnings

The relations of musicians, as performers of music, with their record labels, online music services and live venues depend on the rights exercised by those entities. While a right to remuneration as regards the broadcasting and communication to the public of their recorded performances[1] are subject to certain tariffs administered by collecting societies, the exclusive rights[2] are directly used by themselves through contracts, whose provisions in most cases transfer those rights as a whole to record companies.

Freedom of contract is a principle adopted by most jurisdictions around the world. In that respect, commercial parties can contract on almost anything that provides for far more or

---

[1] Rome Convention, 1961, Article 12 'Secondary uses of phonograms'; WPPT, 1996, Article 15 'Right for broadcasting and communication to the public'.

[2] Rights of reproduction, distribution, rental and making available.

far less protection than is actually stipulated in law, unless the statutory rules refer to public policy restrictions or to excessively unequal contractual terms and/or bargaining power. In many countries, collective bargaining is allowed and even privileged in determining certain contractual relations (mostly in labour markets). In many countries, collecting societies perform a similar function in order to strike a better deal on behalf of a group of rightholders against media conglomerates or dominant commercial users. Furthermore, in some countries, rightholders are provided with specific copyright contract laws circumscribing the freedom of contracting parties on certain issues that would otherwise enable a total buy-out of musicians' rights (Hilty, 2004).

In this respect, the underlying legal background of these relations covers three areas:

a   the rights conferred on artists and producers of phonograms,

b   existence of compulsory or mandatory licensing schemes for some of those rights and

c   the authority of national laws to retain some guarantee provisions for musicians that cannot be overruled by way of contracts.

The main reasons causing market frustration are restrictive recoupment provisions, nontransparent deduction structures and imbalance in bargaining powers, forcing (not famous/well-known) artists to accept unfair contractual terms. The rights of authors and performers vary according to jurisdictions, although international treaties and regional laws are intended to create a certain level of harmonisation. Establishing frameworks protecting the weakest party against unfair practices in contractual relations, in this sense, becomes particularly important to reduce the frustration in the market both for the artists who create the musical works and the public that spends money to enjoy them.

The relation between Fair Trade and music industry

In today's globalized and digitalized world, music could find a global audience and could produce revenues for its creators independent from set distribution channels and the conventional music business. The *'Fair Music Campaign'* wants to bridge the gap and offer a trusted label for both artists and audiences to match their needs: thus emphasizing musical diversity, recognition and remuneration. It believes that people would pay for music they love, knowing that its creators get a fair share from their payment.

The *'theory of disproportionate exchange'* (Nohlen, 1993) explains an action, where goods are not traded according to the amount of work and the prices on the world market do not correspond to the value of work. According to EFTA,[3] Fair Trade is a trading partnership, based on dialogue, transparency and respect that seeks greater equity in international trade. It contributes to sustainable development by offering better trading conditions to, and securing the rights of, marginalized producers and workers – especially in the South. Fair trade organizations (backed by consumers) are engaged actively in supporting producers, awareness raising and campaigning for changes of the rules and practices of conventional international trade.

To do that, principles such as payment of a fair price, selection of producers, pre-financing, transparent and long-term commercial relations, direct purchase from producers, an additional fair trade premium for social projects and control mechanisms to ensure the credibility are being implemented by Fair Trade Organisation (Naka, 2010). The assessment of the situation in the music business, and also the potential buyers of fair music, have made it clear that an agency for certification of *'fair music'*,

---

[3] European Fair Trade Association - Joining fair trade forces, retrieved from: http://www.european-fair-trade-association.org/efta/Doc/What.pdf.

structured after the model of fair trade, could be an important marketing tool for the development of the industry and could help it to regain a better image. The music industry is suffering severely from the slump in revenues from sales of recorded music, the result of which also affects musicians' income.

Consequently, the idea of Fair Music, similar to Fair Trade, aims to strengthen the position of musicians; creating a new marketing model for labels, retailers, promoters and venues, encouraging customers to buy music legally; a trademark for customers who want to support musicians; enhancing cultural diversity in the age of globalization; creating access to world markets for musicians from economically underprivileged countries; safeguarding artistic freedom and possibilities for innovation; helping artists and rights holders in getting a fair share; assisting labels, online services and other marketers in their relationship with consumers; and helping the whole music industry to improve its public image.

The structure and business model of Fair Music

When and if it is implemented, the most crucial aspects of the fair music project are having a credible structure and building a sustainable business model.

The project has already foreseen the establishment of two separate bodies. The first is the Fair Music organisation to set the standards and conduct the operations by licensing and marketing the fair music label. The second body is the Fair Music Agency, which awards fair music certification to those companies that meet the fair music standards, following the requirements of ISO Guide 65. In this way, the agency could act independently and impartially without any political motivation and the organization could focus on the business aspects of the initiative by directly dealing with industry players for developing fairer standards and for marketing the initiative more extensively.

Several different sources of income could be envisaged to run the project in a sustainable way and to benefit the artists, companies and the listeners. Licence fees (i.e. fee as a percentage of the retail price for these items) for offering and distributing fair-music-branded items, or a membership fee charged to the companies after they are certified with Fair Music label, could formulate the financial side of licensee relations of the organization. A reasonable revenue model from the standardisation process itself could also be considered, insofar as it does not create an unbearable burden for, especially, small and medium sized music companies.

Funding via non-profit organizations, donations, subsidies and public funding could always be considered as an important source of income as well. Attracting corporate social responsibility spending for this purpose, or promotion of the initiative through product development such as combination with Fairtrade products, or co-branded products such as music players, instruments, software or merchandise can generate extra income.

Development of fair music as a brand could, in this way, become a unique selling point for distributors, while attracting consumers with cultural and social responsibility to make their music related spending on this direction. This could raise an awareness to pay for music and to support creation of arts.

In the short term, Fair Music will solely focus on its main standards in recorded music, live performance and online music services. In the near future, however, additional standards in the music sector could be incorporated so to realise the main objective to bring justice to music business.

Once this core business is established, the initiative could be expanded towards a unified label for cultural goods and services, which are produced under fair conditions. The fair music principles of adequate recognition, just remuneration and cultural diversity could serve as a leitmotiv in the development of new, creative and innovative services.

REFERENCES

- AEPO-ARTIS. (2009). Study: *Performers' Rights in European Legislation: Situation and Elements for Improvement*, Dec. 2009, p. 45.
- Arnold, P. (1997) *Performers' Rights* (2nd ed.) Sweet and Maxwell .
- Darling, K. (2011). *Copyright and New Media: A Law and Economics Approach to Restricting Unknown-Use Licenses.* Retrieved on 30.07.2011 from http://www.tilburguniversity.edu/research/institutes-and-research-groups/tilec/pdfs/events/20-21june2011/paper-Darling.pdf.
- European Commission. (2008). Staff Working Document: *Impact Assessment On The Legal And Economic Situation Of Performers And Record Producers In The European Union* 23.04.2008, Brussels.
- Goldstein, P. (2001). *International Copyright-Principle, Law, and Practice*, Oxford University Press.
- Hilty, R. & Peukert, A. (2004) . E*quitable Remuneration in Copyright Law: The Amended German Copyright Act As A Trap For The Entertainment Industry In The U.S.?*, 22 Cardozo Arts & Entertainment Law Journal.
- Horx, M., Huber , J., Steinle , A., & Wenzel, E. (2007). *Zukunft machen - Wie Sie von Trends zu Business-Innovationen kommen.* Campus Verlag, Frankfurt am Main.
- *IFPI Digital Music Report* (2010). Retrieved from: http://www.ifpi.org/content/library/DMR2010.pdf, 30.07.2011.
- *IMPALA European Music in Numbers.* Retrieved from: http://www.impalamusic.org/info_03_indfact.php , 30.07.2011.
- Jenner, P. & Brown, M. (2006). *Beyond The Soundbytes.* London: Music Tank Report.
- Kretschmer, M. (2006). *Music artists' earnings and digitisation: a review of empirical data from Britain and Germany.* Retrieved from: http://eprints.bournemouth.ac.uk/3704/1/Birkbeck_06_04_final.pdf. , 30.07.2011.
- Lupo, A.V. & Radcliffe, M.F. (eds.) (2001). *Music on the Internet: Understanding the New Rights & Solving New Problems – Volume I.* New York: Practising Law Institute.
- Nohlen, D. & Nuscheler, F. (1993). *Handbuch der Dritten Welt:, Grundprobleme-Theorien-Strategie,* Bonn. J.H.W. Dietz.
- *Study On The Conditions Applicable To Contracts Relating To Intellectual Property In The European Union (2002).* Amsterdam: Institute voor Informatie Recht.
- *The Economy Of Culture In Europe.* (2006) KEA European Affairs Study for the European Commission.
- *The Social Situation Of Musical Performers In Africa, Asia And Latin America.* (2001). International Labor Organization (ILO) – International Federation of Musicians (FIM) Study .

About the author

Burak Özgen (BE) works as an independent consultant in Brussels. He advises international music companies, trade organizations, NGOs and local governments on copyright, European affairs and culture related matters. He is also a member of the Fair Music standards setting expert group and a PhD researcher at the Ghent University.

burak.ozgen@eurokent.eu

Evaluating Innovation Policies in the Creative Industries: Assessment of the Flemish media sector

Heritiana Ranaivoson, Sven Lindmark, Karen Donders, Pieter Ballon

Abstract

The paper provides a framework to assess the impact of innovation policy in the creative industries. It is applied to an ex-ante assessment of various set-ups for innovation policy in the Flemish media sector, and relies on a novel conceptualization of innovation and a mix of qualitative and quantitative approaches.

Introduction

While most stakeholders agree on the importance of innovation in the media secto r, there is a lack of consensus on how to best promote it, in particular in a context of technological convergence (Donders et al., 2010). Public intervention to promote innovation may be needed when innovation generates positive externalities (Hauknes and Nordgren, 1999), all the more so in the media sector, considering the public good characteristics of media and its contribution to pluralism (Murdock, 2007; Cunningham, 2009). Hence, adapted tools to analyse the impact of media innovation policy are needed.

A framework is needed to assess the impact of innovation policies in the creative industries. We want to combine the numerous, generic studies on impact assessment (IA) and innovation policy with a conceptualisation of innovation in the creative industries. For any IA, it is vital to clarify the arguments that justify the intervention; and the expected logic that connects immediate short-term effects, with indirect longer-terms effects and, with objectives and the underlying policy needs.

A lack of clearly stated problems and objectives

Public intervention is required when markets and other non-public processes cannot solve existing *problems*. Then, *objectives* must be specified, aiming at solving the problems (PRO INO Europe, 2009).

In Belgium, there are two separate audiovisual markets, *i.e.* the Flemish and the Walloon ones. As in many European markets, broadcasting in Flanders is catered for through a dual, public-private, system (Michalis, 2009). The Flemish public broadcaster VRT accounts for 40% of the market (EAO, 2009). Private competitors have criticized it for being too dominant and distorting the market (Van den Bulck and Moe, 2010). It is therefore not surprising that, during the renegotiation of the management contract of VRT in Spring 2011, the private stakeholders argued for reforming or even abolishing VRT-Medialab, the innovation unit related to VRT (Donders, 2010; Lieten, 2010).

VRT Medialab aside, the regional government has relied on a number of other funding mechanisms to promote innovation in the media sector, notably the funding of media related projects in IBBT (the Interdisciplinary Center for Broadband Technology: an inter-university institution focusing on research into media related projects) and through IWT (the Government Agency for Innovation by Science and Technology) (Donders et al., 2011).

The main *problems* include the lack of acceptance of VRT-Medialab. Other initiatives are perceived as too inflexible, implying problems of organization and timing, in particular for SMEs. Such problems are, however, not clearly spelled out at the policy level, and neither are the *objectives*: it remains unclear what exactly the Flemish government wants from innovation for media. This is in itself a weakness of the current policy (Donders et al., 2011).

Inputs: the enhancing and inhibiting factors

The next step of the IA outlined five scenarios for innovation policy in the Flèmish broadcasting sector and analysed the inputs through the level of funding for each scenario, how it was split and which were the key distinguishing features of the scenarios in terms of organization of innovation. Our IA assumes a similar level of public funding across the scenarios, equalling the amount that VRT-medialab.

1 In Scenario 1 (a Flemish Innovation Lab – **FL IL**) VRT-Medialab is completely separated from VRT. It is obliged to cooperate with the entire Flemish media sector. Resulting innovation projects would revolve around a commonly defined innovation programme with government intervention kept minimal.

2 Scenario 2 (**IBBT**) allocates more funding to the existing IBBT structure. The IBBT research groups would then need to attract the additional funding on a project basis and team up with external partners to engage in collaborative R&D efforts aiming for market-oriented solutions for jointly defined problems.

3 In Scenario 3 (**IBBT-IL**), the accumulated knowledge and competencies of VRT-Medialab would be consolidated and integrated into a full-fledged media innovation lab within the IBBT. Like the other research groups within IBBT, it would have to attract funding on a project basis.

4 Scenario 4 (**IWT**) strengthens existing media funding mechanisms within IWT. These are project-driven and foresee short-term collaborative efforts between companies and research centers.

5 Scenario 5 (**IBBT-IWT-IL**) combines the two previous ones, assuming an increase of the budget devoted to projects within IBBT and IWT alike plus some additional innovation funding of VRT. Moreover, a new entity would be created, which would work at setting-up projects with partners to engage in media innovation.

Our analysis showed that, in terms of the organization of innovation, all scenarios, except Scenario 1 (**FL IL**), would depart strongly from the current situation. All scenarios would also rely more on private funding, in particular Scenario 3 (**IBBT-IL**) and Scenario 4 (**IWT**).
The analysis brings forward a few salient *Enhancing and Inhibiting Factors* across all scenarios. First, Scenario 1 (**FL IL**) and to a lesser extent Scenarios 3 (**IBBT-IL**) and 5 (**IBBT-IWT-IL**) would allow for better retention of the knowledge that has been built within VRT-Medialab. On the other hand, Scenarios 2 (**IBBT**) and 4 (**IWT**) would not necessitate the time-consuming introduction of a new framework for organising innovation.

Scenario 5 (**IBBT-IWT-IL**) combines some strengthsof the other scenarios while mitigating some of their drawbacks. Thus, like Scenarios 2 (**IBBT**) and 3 (**IBBT-IL**), it allows the media competencies within, and the media company networks around, IBBT to be strengthened. But thanks to the mediating structure, it is less likely to trigger opposition from the private sector due to IBBT's orientation towards research and allows for having more strategic orientation of innovation.

Outputs: different options for different types of innovation

The direct results of policy implementation are outputs, here the type of innovation favoured by the policy option. *Outputs* are analyzed using a typology of innovation based on two dimensions. The first dimension concerns the novelty and maturity of the innovation. Following the knowledge funnel (Martin, 2009), we make a distinction between phases of innovation. In the first phase (hunch) a broad, multi-faceted, topic is under scrutiny, which requires fundamental research. In the second phase (heuristics) one starts transposing research into development. In the third phase (algorithm) concrete, replicable new processes, products or business models are developed and valorised. The early phases are crucial in order to open up innovative opportunities (Holmén et al., 2007) and to sustain long-term innovation dynamics. These early phases are known to be more subject to private sector underinvestment, and may therefore warrant public intervention, notably for broadcasting (Cunningham, 2011).

The second dimension concerns the type of innovation, and revolves around the standard distinction between product and process innovation (e.g. Schmookler, 1966; Cave & Frinking (2007). For media, product innovation relates to content and the way it is accessed by customers, while process innovation to the production of media content, from creation (e.g. a new camera) to consumption (e.g. possibility to choose which camera is followed during a sport event), the latter being at the intersection of product and process innovation (Donders et al., 2011). In terms of degree of novelty, Scenario 1 (**FL IL**) is likely to promote innovations with a medium-term horizon. This would also be the case for Scenarios 2 (**IBBT**) and 3 (**IBBT-IL**) but due to the university connections of the IBBT research centers, they are also likely to generate more long-term research. Scenario 4 (**IWT**) would, following current IWT schemes, favor projects that are close to commercialisation. Finally Scenario 5 (**IBBT-IWT-IL**) would likely promote a combination of short-term and medium-term innovation.

Two innovation outputs remained similar across the scenarios: (1) none of them would promote content innovation to any significant extent (television channels compete directly through content and are therefore unlikely to collaborate on content innovation) and (2) all scenarios would promote process innovations including media consumption.

Outcomes and impacts

Outcomes and impacts are respectively middle and long-term changes that arise from the policy implementation. *Outcomes* should relate to the objectives of the intervention while impacts are generally broader. *Outcomes* were analyzed in terms of effects on Collaboration and spillover effects. Impacts proved difficult to assess *ex ante* due to a lack of data.

Five *spillover effects* (see e.g. Buisseret et al., 1995; Georghiou 1998) were considered. The triggering effect is the additional private spending towards R&D and innovation that each scenario is likely to generate. As some funding mechanisms imply that private partners contribute to the funding of innovation, any public spending on innovation through such mechanisms can trigger some private spending. Reach corresponds to the number and type of companies that can benefit from the generated innovation. Actually, one aim of innovation policy is to include as many companies as possible and in particular SMEs. Consistency reflects the extent to which each scenario allows to better align the existing schemes and organizations. Outcomes were also mapped with respect to the extent of *Collaboration*, where the main finding was that all scenarios increase Collaboration.

Conclusion and policy recommendations

Building on the innovation conceptualization and state-of-the-art IA practice, the research outlines a framework for an ex-ante IA, which could help with analyzing policy problems, setting targets, facilitating debates, and reaching consensus among stakeholders.

The framework was used to analyse five scenarios for how to organise public media innovation support. Of these, Scenarios 1, 2 and 4 were considered less attractive, due to a number of drawbacks. Given the strong Triggering Effects and Reach favored by Scenarios 3 and 5, and a number of serious remaining issues, we propose a combination of those scenarios including a 'light-weight', valorization coordination entity within IBBT.

References

- Buisseret, T., Hugh C. & and Georghiou, L. (1995). 'What difference does it make? Additionality in the public support of R&D in large firms'. *International Journal of Technology Management* 10: p. 587-600.
- Cave, J. & Frinking, E. (2007). *Public Procurement for R&D.* Coventry: University of Warwick.
- Cunningham, Stuart D. (2009). *Reinventing television: the work of the 'innovation' unit.* Oxon: Routledge.
- Donders, K. (C.s). (2011) . *Naar een Ecosysteem-Model voor Onderzoek en Innovatie rond Audiovisuele Consumptie in Vlaanderen. Deliverable 2.* Desirable and feasible scenarios for collaborative innovation in the Flemish media sector, Brussel / Gent: IBBT-SMIT, VUB / MICT, UGent.
- Donders, K. (2010). *Under Pressure? An Analysis of the Impact of European State Aid Policy on Public Service Broadcasting. Marginalisation or Revival as Public Service Media?.* PhD Thesis. Brussels: Vrije Universiteit Brussel.
- EAO (European Audiovisual Observatory). (2009). *Yearbook 2008. Film, Television and Video in Europe.* Strasbourg: EAO.
- Georghiou, L. (1998). *Issues in the Evaluation of Innovation and Technology Policy.* Evaluation 4: p. 37-51.
- Hauknes, J. & Nordgren, L. (1999). *Economic Rationales of Government Involvement in Innovation and the Supply of Innovation-Related Service.* STEP Working Paper. Oslo: Step Group.
- Holmén, M., Magnusson M., & McKelvey, M. (2007). What are Innovative Opportunities?. *Industry & Innovation* p. 14: p. 27-45.
- Lieten, I. (2010). *Visienota media: de VRT als uitdager en partner in het Vlaamse medialandschap.* Brussels: Vlaamse Regering.
- Martin, R. L. (2009). *The design of business: why design thinking is the next competitive advantage.* Boston: Harvard Business Press.
- Michalis M. (2007). *Governing European communications : from unification to coordination.* Lanham: Lexington Books.
- Murdock, G. (2007). Public Broadcasting and Democratic Culture: Consumers, Citizens, and Communards. *In A Companion to Television,* edited by Janet Wasko, p. 174-198. Malden: Blackwell.
- Van Den Bulck, H. & Moe, H. (2010). *Public Service Media Governance after the Crisis: Comparing Assessment Practices in Flanders and Norway.* Paper presented at the RIPE@(2010): Public Service Media After the Recession conference. London, United Kingdom, 18-20 September (2010). Retrieved from: http://ripeat.org/(2010)/public-service-media-governance-after-the-crisis-comparing-assessment-practices-in-flanders-and-norway/.
- Schmookler, J. (1966). *Invention and Economic Growth.* Cambridge, Harvard University Press.

About the authors

Karen Donders (BE) lectures European Media Policy and European Information Society at the Vrije Universiteit Brussel. She is a postdoctoral fellow with the Flemish Research Foundation (FWO) and Senior Researcher at IBBT-SMIT (Center for Studies on Media Information and Telecommunication).

Pieter Ballon (BE) lectures Media Economics at the Vrije Universiteit Brussel. He is the head of the Market Innovation and Sector Transitions Unit in IBBT-SMIT, Vrije Universiteit Brussel.

Heritiana Ranaivoson (BE) and **Sven Lindmark (BE)** are Senior Researchers at IBBT-SMIT, Vrije Universiteit Brussel.

hranaivo@vub.ac.be (corresponding author)

Cultural authenticity in product design for cultural message expression

Tsen-Yao Chang , Che-Ting Wen

Abstract

This article discusses how products can be representative of culture. Categories by which to classify *'cultural authenticity'* in the development of products are developed. Moreover, the study explores how cultural products create an impression of authenticity on customers and identifies the factors affecting such authenticity. In designing cultural products, developing an understanding of a culture is an important step. Achieving a balance between the needs of the market and cultural authenticity is obligatory.

Cultural products: the question of cultural authenticity

Enhancing tourism by promoting customer interest in Taiwan's local culture, particularly through the production of cultural products, is a current trend. Cultural products are popular instruments representing a local culture. Such products serve as instruments that translate messages, narrate memories and historical events, and establish emotional connections with customers. However, the expression of cultural authenticity has changed to reflect popular views and to cater to the needs of the market. When authentic artifacts are altered by market preferences, they can be transformed into new products that may be branded as *'fake'*.

The Modern-day Interpretation of Souvenir: Cultural Product

Culture is defined in various ways. Broadly, culture is the way people express themselves, not only verbally, but also in their manner of clothing, lifestyle, beliefs, and practices (Crocombe, 1983). Culture is an anthropological term referring to the fundamental values, beliefs, and codes of practice that identify a community. The customs of a society, the self-image of its members, and the things that differentiate it from other societies constitute its culture (Fincham & Rhodes, 1994).
Shopping is probably one of the easiest means

of experiencing the uniqueness of native tourism (Hsieh & Chang, 2006). Souvenirs inspire tourists to contrast trips with their everyday experiences, to expand their world-view, to differentiate themselves from others, and to experience a more authentic cultural life (Littrell, 1990). Therefore, what is cultural product? Although we cannot deny that all products are cultural, we should note that not all products are a cultural product. A cultural product is one that presents a cultural identity.
Identifying cultural products as *those that are recognizably local and original* is a first step.

However, how can a cultural product be distinguished from a souvenir? Throsby (2003) suggested the following important criteria when identifying cultural products: *aesthetic properties, spiritual significance, symbolic meanings, historic importance, artistic trends, authenticity, integrity, and uniqueness* (Lee et al., 2009). *'Cultural product'* might as well be defined as the modern-day interpretation of souvenir, which not only offers cultural identity, but is also characterized by normal product functions, and is thus designed to appeal to modern-day taste. Figure 1 illustrates the relationships among souvenirs, cultural products, and normal products.

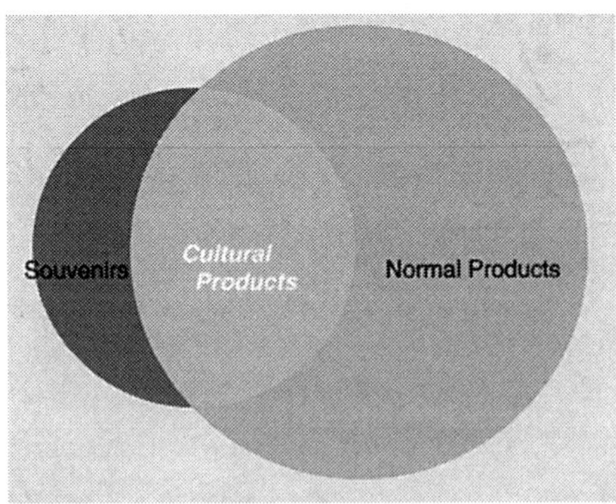

Figure 1. Relationships among souvenirs, cultural products, and normal products.

Authenticity in Cultural Products
The use of local features in design as a strategy to create product identity in the global market

has enabled designers to realize the importance of associating products with cultural features. This association enhances product value (Lin, 2007), that is, cultural products are consciously designed with the function of cultural identity. However, the decision to pursue cultural tourism is often made with incomplete knowledge of the potential adverse effects or the requirements for successful product development (Mckercher,B. et al., 2004). This condition has resulted in a negative portrayal of authenticity, in that events invariably seek to commodify various markets and appropriate them for commercial purposes in temporally discrete spaces (Getz, 2008). Thus, designers have to determine how culture is driven and how authenticity exists in cultural products, since cultural products are expected to be able to satisfy the market.

Methodology

Research Structure
The current research used the grounded theory to analyze how governments build the conception and image of a cultural product, and to discover the core value of a cultural product through the analysis of art- and design-related magazines published by the government. These tasks were undertaken to determine whether the core value can be identified by general customers. The present work con-

structed an analyzable scale based on semantic differential method, using the keywords generalized from the first part of experiment. This scale yielded four different quadrants. These quadrants were used to construct the level of cultural authenticity. In the final stage of the experiment, keywords were identified through the implementation of card sorting. Card sorting aimed to determine the factors affecting respondent's perception of cultural authenticity. The keywords associated with cultural products were then compared with the different perspectives presented by the government to general customers to arrive at a comprehensive conclusion and to formulate suggestions (see Figure 2).

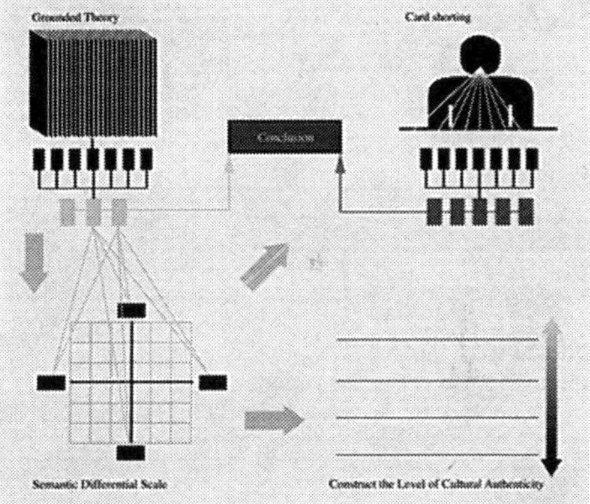

Figure 2. Research structure.

Theme	Cultural product
Variation of study	Keyword of cultural product
Text	Fountain of Creativity magazine, Design magazine
Article sampling	Article on cultural products or brands of cultural product
Image sampling	A total of 56 images of cultural products were recognized in the 'Fountain of Creativity' and 'Design' magazines. Products that repeatedly appeared and numerous products made by the same brand were excluded. As a result, 20 images were recognized as image samples.
Time area	Based on the government policy 'Challenge 2008 National Development Plan: Cultural and Creative Industry development plan,' the present study selected the years 2009 and 2010 to examine the results of the government policy.

Table 1. Study and sampling area.

Area of Study and Sampling

The present work uses the *'Fountain of Creativity'* magazine, published by the General Association of Chinese Culture, and the 'Design' Magazine, published by the Taiwan Design Center, as reference materials. Table 1 presents the study and sampling area.

Results and discussion

The present study generalizes open coding. A total of 13 keywords comprise the axial coding. Eight keywords were then obtained from the pictures. Based on the 13 keywords from the text and the 8 keywords from the picture, axial coding was established as the core value of cultural products: cultural content, emotional response, and value recreation (Figure 4).

In a cruciform scale, four quadrants were constructed: high cultural content with high emotional response, high cultural content with low emotional response, low cultural content with high emotional response, and low cultural content with low emotional response. These keywords were generated through coding from magazines.

However, one of the keywords, *'value recreation'*, was hard for the respondents to recognize. Respondents were subsequently asked to describe the cultural products that they thought had high cultural content and elicited high emotional response from them. They were also asked to categorize the description using short and simple keywords. The factors that were found to influence cognition of cultural content and manifestation of emotional response were the following: cultural image, personal experience, appearance, tactile impression, and function (Figure 5).

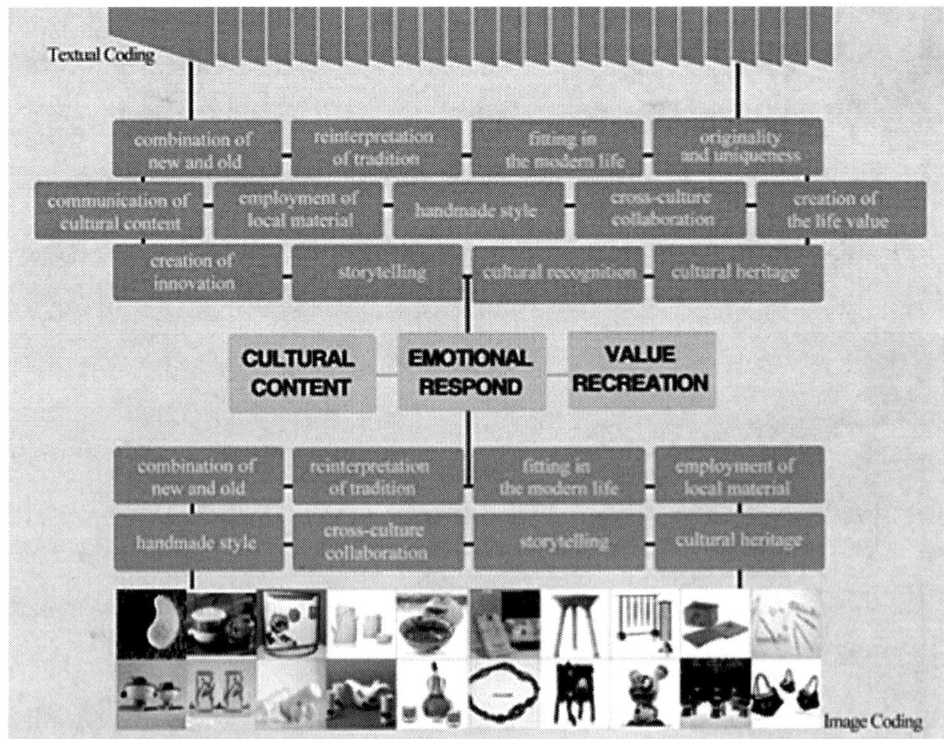

Figure 4. The Coding Process.

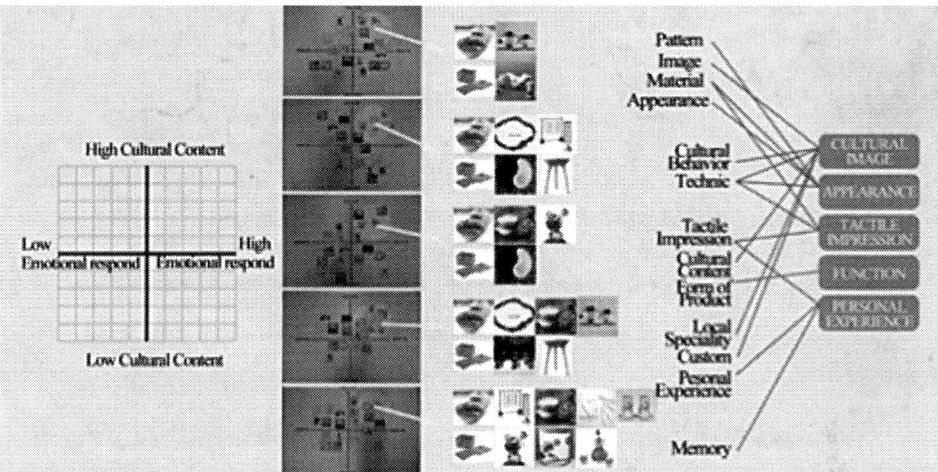

Figure 5. Semantic differential scale and card sorting process.

The manner by which designers and the government build the perception of general customers on cultural products should be analyzed if authenticity in cultural products is to be discussed. Through the analysis of the magazines published by the government, three core values of cultural products are identified: cultural content, emotional response, and value recreation. Cultural content and emotional response not only reflect the first impression of general customers, but also serve as a medium to communicate cultural messages. Therefore, cultural authenticity is based on the utility of how a cultural message can be communicated.

The authenticity of cultural products is classified according to the following:

1 high cultural content with high emotional response;
2 low cultural content with high emotional response;
3 high cultural content with low emotional response; and
4 low cultural content with low emotional response.

The utility of 1 and 4 is obvious. However, the reason why cultural authenticity is stronger in 2 than in 3 is difficult to comprehend because without an emotional response from customers, a product, even if it has high cultural content, is hardly capable of effectively sending a cultural message (To see the presentation on the level of cultural authenticity, please refer to Figure 5).

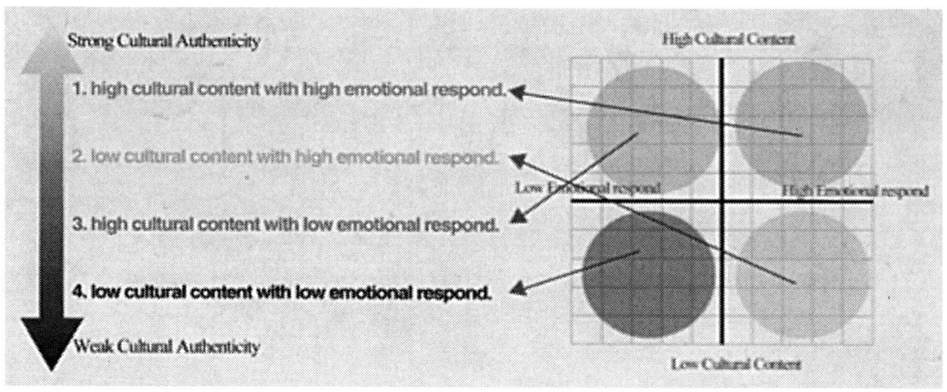

Figure 6. Level of cultural authenticity.

Conclusion

The perceptions that the government attempted to build were compared with how general customers conceptualized cultural products. We conclude that, first, personal experience is vital, and second, a cultural product is still a product.

First, the cognition of cultural content and emotional response relates to personal memories and experiences. How respondents experience cultural authenticity primarily depends on how well they can recognize and understand the culture. Therefore, in designing cultural products, keen observation and understanding of a culture is fundamental. Moreover, utilizing the right culture for the right target market is equally necessary. Regardless of how deeply designers understand a culture, and how appropriate the employed cultures were, the cognition of authenticity remains difficult to perceive if customers cannot recognize the culture. Thus, regarding how to communicate and with whom designers want to communicate, customers are the important factors affecting cultural authenticity.

For customers, a cultural product is still only a product. In designing a cultural product, the basic needs of customers, such as in terms of appearance, tacit impression, and function, should be satisfied, not sacrificed, by emphasizing the core value of the cultural product. The quality of design can affect cognition of cultural authenticity by customers. Aesthetics and creativity may be a gray area for the cognition of cultural authenticity, but designers should still work on this aspect. However, this condition does not imply that higher quality results in a stronger cognition of authenticity. Thus, we realize that over-designing and over-emphasizing creativity can possibly be a barrier to the perception of cultural authenticity.

Although differentiating authenticity may be difficult to perceive for customers from the global market, it is still vital. For instance, Chinese characters tattooed on foreigners can mistakenly represent authenticity. Two possibilities exist if such products are mistaken as authentic overseas. First, when local people cannot recognize the authenticity of a cultural product, their perception of culture becomes confused. Second, the original culture could gradually be replaced by the culture that is mistaken as authentic overseas.
Designing a cultural product entails the best balance between the needs of the market and cultural authenticity. Designers should consistently advocate cultural creativity, instead of solely focusing on the needs of the market.

References

- Asplet, M. & Cooper, M. (2000). Cultural designs in New Zealand souvenir clothing: the question of authenticity, *Tourism Management, 21*, p. 307-312.
- Crocombe, R. (1983). *The south pacixc: An introduction.* Auckland: Longman Paul.
- Fincham, R. and Rhodes, P. S., (1994). *The individual work and organisation: behavioural studies for business and management.* Oxford University Press, Oxford.
- Getz, D. (2008). Event tourism: Definition, evolution, and research. *Tourism Management, 29*, p. 403-428.
- Hofstede, G. (2001). *Culture's consequences: comparing values, behaviors, institutions, and organizations across nations.* Sage Publications, Thousand Oaks.
- Hsieh, A. & Chang, J. (2006). Shopping and tourist night markets in Taiwan. Tourism Management, 27(1), p. 138-145.
- Lin, R.T. (2007). Transforming Taiwan aboriginal cultural features into modern product design: A case study of cross-culture product design model, In: *International Journal of Design, 1*(2), p. 45-53.
- Littrell, M. A. (1990). Symbolic significance of textiles crafts for tourists. *Annals of Tourism Research, 17*, p. 228-245.
- Mckercher, B.,Ho, P.S.Y. & Du Cros, H. (2004). Attributes of popular cultural attractions in Hong Kong. *Annals of Tourism Research, Vol.31*, No.2, pp.393-407.
- Throsby, D. (2003). Determining the value of cultural goods: how much (or how little) does contingent valuation tell us? *Journal of Cultural Economics, 27*, p. 275-285.

About the authors

Tsen-Yao Chang (TW) is currently Assistant Professor in the Department of Industrial and Commercial Design at National Taiwan University of Science and Technology (NTUST), Taiwan. Dr. Chang recent research interests have focused on cultural and creative industries project.
changty@mail.ntust.edu.tw

Che-Ting Wen (TW) is a MA student and a research assistant of Dr. Chang in NTUST, Taiwan.
dustin_le_robot@livemail.tw

Entrepreneurial graduates and their contribution to the creative and cultural economies

Paul Coyle

Abstract

Even today in the UK it is acknowledged that it is difficult to capture the full extent of activity in the creative sector, in comparison to other parts of the economy, given for example that the small scale of activity undertaken by many creative businesses is not recorded by UK government standard business surveys. The subjects enterprise and entrepreneurship have grown as a focus for national policy across the UK.

The role of the university education and the contribution towards innovation is discussed here. The author supports the concept of *'the Entrepreneurial University'*. He states that entrepreneurship can be learned. Yet it should be noted that students may exhibit *'entrepreneurial behaviours'* without recognizing such terminology. He puts forward a plea for entrepreneurial creative graduates.

The creative industries: definitions and measurements

A variety of published reports have cited the important role of the creative industries in terms of economic and cultural impacts in the UK, EU and worldwide. However, there are a number of key questions associated with the definitions of the term 'creative industries' and measurements of their contribution to economic prosperity.

In the UK, the creative industries were first defined by the Government's Department for Culture, Media and Sport in November 1998 (DCMS, 1998). The document defined a number of creative sectors (advertising, antiques, architecture, crafts, design, fashion, film, leisure software, music, performing arts, publishing, software, and TV & radio). Roodhouse notes that *'These sub-sectors would not necessarily recognize themselves as creative industries, for example architecture has much more in common with construction than it does with the arts and antiques trade'* (Roodhouse, p. 1); the point being that the 'creative industries' is a policy construct.

A second mapping document was published and maintained the original definition of the creative industries given in 1998 as: *'...those industries which have their origin in individual creativity, skill and talent which have a potential for job and wealth creation through the generation and exploitation of intellectual property'* (DCMS, 2001, p. 5).

The 2001 document also maintained the thirteen creative sectors that had been determined in 1998 but recognised *'close economic relationships with other sectors such as tourism, hospitality, museums and galleries, heritage and sport'* (DCMS, 2001, p. 5).

Jarvis et al. noted in 2008 at the Regional Studies Association Annual International Conference in Prague that *'much creative industries literature and commentary find itself struggling for clarity as a result of the implicit acceptance of creative industries as a coherent single sector.'* (Jarvis et al, 2008, p. 1). Clews reports that the National Endowment for Science, Technology and the Arts evolved a *'refined model of the creative industries focusing on how commercial value is created. The model organises the creative industries based on four characteristics: creative service providers, creative content producers, creative experience providers and creative originals producers'* (Clews, p. 20).

A decade on from the DCMS reports, the challenge of defining the creative industries remains. Consequently, Local Government Improvement and Development acknowledges the continuing difficulties of developing definitions and in particular the problem of the conflation of the terms *'cultural'* and *'creative'* since the term *'creative industries'* is then taken to value culture solely from an economic perspective (LG Improvement and Development, 2009).

Measuring Performance and Sector Segmentation

The problem of measuring the performance of the Creative Industries was acknowledged by the DCMS at the outset of its work. *'Although there has been some improvement in the provision of official statistics, the complex nature of the creative industries makes 'scientific' definition difficult, so there are still difficulties in producing robust data'* (DCMS, 2001, p. 5). Even today in the UK it is acknowledged that it is difficult to capture the full extent of activity in the creative sector, in comparison to other parts of the economy, given for example that the small scale of activity undertaken by many creative businesses is not recorded by UK government standard business surveys. Local Government Improvement and Development advises that much of the data on the Creative Industries can only be regarded as indicative.

The European Commission in its Green paper noted that *'At European level, the framework for cultural statistics set up in 2000 identified eight domains (artistic and monumental heritage, archives, libraries, books and press, visual arts, architecture, performing arts, audio and audiovisual media/ multimedia) and six functions (preservation, creation, production, dissemination, trade/sales and education) that constitute the 'cultural sector' from a statistical point of view.'* Work is currently ongoing to update this framework and define the scope of CCIs' (European Commission, 2010, p.5).

A key question is whether the data that is available is the right data that could help to understand the Creative Industries and the key factors that influence their economic performance. Clews notes that *'In policy terms the number of business start-ups has become the measure of economic health and a proxy for entrepreneurship (as indicated in surveys such as the Global Entrepreneurship Monitor). However there is also the issue of entrepreneurship beyond start-up, in terms of sustained growth and accessing larger markets'* (Clews, p. 23). The evidence based on employment and skills in the creative industries is, however, considered to be improving and Reid et al report the increasing availability of more longitudinal data. This data shows skills shortages, for example, in broadcast engineering, management and business skills have remained problematic for some years (Reid et al., p. 25).

Post 2008, the recession has been a major threat to growth in particular sectors of the creative industries. UK advertising suffered the highest rate of business failure (Reid et al, p. 20) but high-tech services like software have been less affected (Reid et al, p. 22). UK and EU studies have found that small to medium sized enterprises are a significant proportion of the creative industries. *'Enterprises consisting of one to two people represent the overwhelming majority of the companies of the sector and encompass this new type of 'entrepreneurial individuals' or 'entrepreneurial cultural workers'* (European Commission, 2010, p. 11). And as Reid et al. note *'The creative industries are particularly vulnerable to economic downturns, partly because the disproportionately large number of very small businesses in the sector mean the sector finds it harder to absorb exogenous financial shocks'* (Redid et al, p. 20).

The Role of the Entrepreneurial University

Clews (2007) notes that as enterprise and entrepreneurship have grown as a focus for national policy across the UK, so *'policymakers have urged education at all levels to address the entrepreneurial capacity of learners through enhancing the learning environment, developing the curriculum and building stronger links with industry'* (Clews, p. 13). Thorp believes that *'If entrepreneurial thinking can be introduced and integrated into the dialogue on the campuses of our great universities, these institutions can emerge as true engines of innovation'* (Thorp, p. 21).

Gibbs et al (2009) note a considerable international literature addressing '*the entrepreneurial university*'. They argue for increased engagement of universities with their stakeholders. They advocate the role of a university within its region e.g. in supplying graduates, articulating regional needs to central government, undertaking research, brokering international connections and attracting investment. They see the university as potentially being the hub in a regional and international network, engaging in what Etzkowitz and Leysdorff (2000) describe as the '*triple helix of university-industry-government-relations*'. The European Commission has also highlighted the need for actions that will help '*to improve the physical and social environment in which creative workers and related institutions, such as art and design schools or museums, can effectively operate in clusters*' (European Commission, p. 10).

Clark reflects on the challenges for universities of responding to these policy initiatives. He examined five universities in Europe that attempted in the 1980s and early 1990s to become more enterprising, 'even aggressively entrepreneurial' (Clark, p. Xiv). Clark and Thorp both identify the importance of skilled university leaders who over time can build entrepreneurial organizational cultures. Thorp describes such a culture as one that '*thrives in a climate that celebrates creativity, innovation and excellence*' (Thorp, p. 86).

Clark noted that the creation of an organizational culture is a lengthy process and that in Europe '*the 'professorial' university of forty years ago had been partially replaced by the 'participatory university' of the post-1968 period, which had now partially given way to the 'managerial university'*' (Clark, p. 58). Gibbs, Knapper and Piccinin (2009) describe '*a perceived shift of organisational culture over time from, collegial to bureaucratic to corporate and finally to a fourth entrepreneurial culture characterised by a focus on competence and an orientation to the outside world, involving continuous learning in a turbulent context*' (Gibbs et al, p. 6).

Thorp cautions that '*Injecting an entrepreneurial point of view into an academic environment is easier said than done*' (Thorp, p. 151). Clark and Thorpe argue for clarity in mission and objectives if a university is going to be successful. Clark concludes that specialized universities in Europe and America have been more easily able to adopt '*entrepreneurial postures*' (Clark, p. 135).

Developing entrepreneurial graduates

The University for the Creative Arts (UCA)
UCA is a specialist, creative arts university based on five campuses in the South East of England and was created in 2005 with the merger of two former art and design institutions that can trace their histories back to 1866. The university offers a wide range of undergraduate and postgraduate art, architecture, design and media courses. It aims to produce graduates who have relevant knowledge and high-level skills suited to the needs of the Creative Industries.
Students develop a wide range of knowledge and skills (in drawing, design, making and the application of technology), which are underpinned by theoretical and contextual studies, combined with the development of 'graduate skills' (e.g. teamwork, communication, initiative and leadership). The combination of subject-based knowledge and graduate skills is geared towards future employment & entrepreneurship.

Entrepreneurism and the Curriculum

Thorp reports that *'Many entrepreneurs contend that 'entrepreneurs are born and not made' and that entrepreneurship is not teachable.'* (Thorp, p. 118). However, experience at UCA confirms the findings of Clews and Thorp that entrepreneurship can be learned. Yet it should be noted that students may exhibit *'entrepreneurial behaviours'* without recognizing such terminology. Kellet found that 'The term *'creative entrepreneur'* is not readily understood or accepted by artists, freelancers or even creative business owners' (Kellet, p. 38). Clews also notes *'students still have mixed views on entrepreneurship. They express discomfort with many popular stereotypes that focus attention on a very narrow view of entrepreneurship'* (Clews, p. 14).

UCA academics make substantial use of project work to help students to develop their entrepreneurial knowledge and skills. These projects can involve *'live briefs'* set by industry partners such as major retailers, design agencies, charities and local government. Students also enter national competitions such as the annual, prestigious Design & Art Direction Awards in which they often win top prizes. Clews study found that *'Forty per cent of deliverers state that entrepreneurial skills are embedded in just a few projects undertaken by students, while a similar number (38%) believe that entrepreneurial skills are embedded in most projects'* (Clews, p. 15).

UCA's Graduate Employment and Entrepreneurship Strategy aims to address Clews' recommendation that the project-based approach to developing entrepreneurship needs to be supplemented by more explicit elements of the curriculum. Kellet agrees that *'There is a growing need to clearly define new and emergent pedagogical processes used in Creative Enterprise Education, as a means of teaching the creative discipline student the business skills and successful routes to market strategy'* (2006, p. 38).

The UK's National Centre for Entrepreneurship in Education, formerly called the National Council for Graduate Entrepreneurship, developed in 2010 a benchmarking template of 8 potential key outcomes from entrepreneurship education:

1 Key entrepreneurial behaviors, skills and attitudes have been developed
2 Students clearly empathize with, understand and 'feel' the life world of the entrepreneur
3 Key entrepreneurial values have been inculcated
4 Motivation towards a career in entrepreneurship has been built and students clearly understand the comparative benefits
5 Students understand the process (stages) of setting up an organization, the associated tasks and learning needs
6 Students have the key generic competencies associated with entrepreneurship (generic how to's)
7 Students have a grasp of key business how to's associated with the start up process
8 Students understand the nature of the relationships they need to develop with key stakeholders and are familiarized with them

Thorp reports key areas of entrepreneurship study as opportunity identification, strategy, marketing, execution and finance and he identifies the challenge of developing financial literacy in ways which will engage students. Yorke et al. concluded that there is no single, ideal prescription for embedding employability in the curriculum and identified 39 aspects of employability, including 10 personal qualities (e.g. self confidence and adaptability), 12 core skills (e.g. creativity and global awareness) and 13 process skills (e.g. commercial awareness and ethical sensitivity). A study by the Hogeschool voor de Kunsten Utrecht identified a number of factors as important to the success of creative businesses, including access to finance and markets, intellectual property, innovation and collaboration; these may, therefore, be topics to be addressed in the undergraduate and postgraduate curriculum (Kooyman, 2010).

Entrepreneurial Academics

Clark sees an ideal two-way collaboration between Universities and business: *'The university learns from outside firms as the companies learn from the university'* (Clark, p.138). Clews identifies the ways in which these external collaborations not only contribute to curriculum development but also *'the development of effective continuing professional development for creative industries practitioners and higher education teachers'* (Clews, p. 15). UCA recognizes that the experience, knowledge and skills of its academics are crucial factors in whether students will be able to develop as entrepreneurs. Ideally, academics should be able to role model entrepreneurial abilities to students. Approximately 30% of the academic staff at UCA work part-time and of these the majority work in the Creative Industries and/or have their own creative businesses. All full-time academics either undertake research and/or liaise with the Creative Industries. A significant feature of the impact of research on teaching at UCA are the connections that academics' research enables them to make for students to a 'real world' experience, the Creative Industries and the potential for future employment (Coyle, 2009).

Therefore, the majority of UCA academics, whether part-time or full-time, have access to industry networks, facilitate visits by student to creative businesses, secure projects for students to work on and negotiate work placements and internships. Academics also maintain connections to UCA's alumni who are working in the Creative Industries. Kellet notes the important role alumni can play in peer-to-peer learning with students gaining valuable knowledge about the Creative Industries 'by listening to the next generation who are only a few steps further on in their journey' (Kellet, p. 38)

Entrepreneurial Creative Graduates

Creative Graduates Creative Futures is a major longitudinal study that tracked the career patterns of more than 3,500 UK graduates in art, design, and media subjects examining their careers paths up to six years after graduation. The study found that graduates work in sectors that match their course of study and not unsurprisingly given what is known about the composition of the Creative Industries, they are self-employed and/or working freelance as sole traders or in micro businesses. *'At the time of the survey, 23 per cent of respondents were self-employed of undertaking freelance work and 18 per cent were running a business, and this was seen as a serious ambition for the future with 40 per cent of all graduates expressing an interest in running a business as their careers progressed'* (Ball et al, p. 5).

When asked whether their course had prepared them well for the world of work just over half the graduates agreed. Respondents suggested that their courses could have given them an *'improved understanding of client needs, training in IT/software, business skills and the practicalities of working freelance'* (Ball et al, p. 9). The graduates considered that their entrepreneurial skills were not well developed and yet they also did not rate these skills as being important for career development. This finding may need further examination in the light of students understanding of the terminology. The overall study gives clear indications to universities about the areas of the curriculum that need to be developed, so as to better prepare graduates for employment and setting up their own businesses.

References

- Ball, L., Pollard, E. & Stanley, N. (2010). *Creative Graduates Creative Futures*. Retrieved from http://www.employment-studies.co.uk/pubs/report.php?id=471, July 2011.
- Clark, B.,R. (2007). *Creating Entrepreneurial Universities – Organisational Pathways of Transformation.* Emerald Group Publishing Limited.
- Clews, D. (2007). *Creating Entrepreneurship.* National Endowment for Science, Technology and the Arts. Retrieved September 2011 from http://www.adm.heacademy.ac.uk/projects/adm-hea-projects/creating-entrepreneurship-entrepreneurship-education-for-the-creative-industries.
- Coyle, P. (2009). *Achieving a Balance Between Teaching, Learning and Research in Art and Design,* paper presented at the Cumulus Conference, Melbourne, November.
- DCMS. (1998). *Creative Industries Mapping Document.* Retrieved from http://webarchive.nationalarchives.gov.uk/+/http://www.culture.gov.uk/reference_library/publications/4740.aspx, September 2011.
- DCMS. (2001). *Creative Industries Mapping Document.* Retrieved from http://webarchive.nationalarchives.gov.uk/+/http://www.culture.gov.uk/reference_library/publications/4632.aspx, September 2011.
- Etzkowitz, H. & Leydesdorff, L. (2000). *The dynamics of innovation: from National System and 'Mode 2' to a Triple Helix of university-industry-government-relations.* Research Policy, 29, p. 109-123.
- European Commission. (2010). *Unlocking the potential of cultural and creative industries.* Green Paper, Brussels .
- European Commission. (2010). *European Competitiveness Report.* Brussels.
- Gibb, A. (2010). *Towards the Entrepreneurial University.* National Council for Graduate Entrepreneurship.
- Gibb, A., Haskins, G., et al. (2009). *Leading the Entrepreneurial University: Meeting the entrepreneurial development needs of higher education institutions.* National Council for Graduate Entrepreneurship. Retrieved from http://www.ncge.org.uk/publication/leading_the_entrepreneurial_university.pdf, July 2011.
- Gibbs, G., Knapper, C. & Piccinin, S. (2009). *Departmental Leadership of Teaching in Research Intensive Environments.* Leadership Foundation for Higher Education.
- Kellet, S. (2006). *Emergent Practices in Entrepreneurship Education for Creatives.* Retrieved from http://www.adm.heacademy.ac.uk/projects/adm-hea-projects/emerging-practices-in-entrepreneurship-education-for-creatives, November 2011.
- Kooyman, R. (Ed) (2010). *The Entrepreneurial Dimension of the Cultural and Creative Industries.* Hogeschool voor de Kunsten Utrecht HKU, Utrecht.
- LG Improvement and Development. (2009). *What are the creative industries?* Retrieved from http://www.idea.gov.uk/idk/core/page.do?pageId=11136366, September 2011.
- Jarvis, D., Lambie, H. & Berkeley, N. (2008). *Creative Industries and Urban Regeneration.* Retrieved from http://www.regional-studies-assoc.ac.uk/events/2008/may-prague/papers/Jarvis.pdf, September 2011.
- Reid, B., Albert, A. & Hopkins, L. (2010). *A Creative Block? The Future of the UK Creative Industries.* The Work Foundation.
- Roodhouse, S. (2008). *Defining the Creative Industries : Simon Roodhouse gauges the government's creative industries.* Retrieved from http://www.simonroodhouse.com/defining_creative_ind_IQ.htm, September 2011.
- Thorp, H. & Goldstein, B. (2010). *Engines of Innovation - The Entrepreneurial University in the Twenty-First Century.* The University of North Carolina Press.
- Yorke, M. & Knight, P. (2006). *Embedding Employability in the Curriculum.* The Higher Education Academy.

About the author

Paul Coyle (UK) is a Pro Vice-Chancellor for teaching and learning and Executive Dean at the UK University of Creative Arts. He holds the title of Professor of Leadership and Management and has presented papers at international conferences on the themes of creativity, culture, entrepreneurship and the connections between teaching & research.
PCoyle@ucreative.ac.uk

Towards Gross National Happiness: A needs-based perspective on creative entrepreneurship

Pernille Askerud

Abstract

Throughout the world, deep-seated structural changes in the global economy are forcing even smaller and peripheral economies to engage proactively with these new economic trends, largely through support for knowledge or information-based business development. The emergence of the creative economy, as a dominant strategy for economic development, has occurred in tandem with the shift in focus from production to finance as motors for the economy. This represents a new political agenda and a fundamentally different approach to culture and education that has yet to be properly reflected within institutional forms.

The changes in education and occupation stimulated by the introduction of new technology are part of these changes. Importantly, the emergence of the creative economy does not only imply a shift from one kind of products to another, but a qualitative change in how production/businesses are organized and in the way we live and understand ourselves. The change is a reflection of the fact that education is extended to almost all strata of society, thanks in part to the global drive for *Education for All*[1] and the resulting expectation by many of these new graduates to be engaged in paid employment. Many countries are addressing the need to instill a more entrepreneurial mind-set among their youth to enable them to participate in new economic trends. The case of Bhutan is an interesting example in this respect.

A new (industrial) revolution

Whether or not the notion of the creative economy refers to economic activities that differ sufficiently from the mainstream economy, to warrant the application of specific economic policies, is not the key issue here (Dos Santos Duisenberg, 2010). Our statement is that the way business generates money is sufficiently different today from the industrial production of last century. It requires people/workers/employees to possess very different skills and knowledge to succeed in these activities. *Creativity* and *ideas* have become keywords to the understanding of this transformational process; though it is far from clear what it means in reality.

For the creative economy, the raw material is human talent: the talent to have new and original ideas and to turn those ideas into economic capital and saleable products. In all industries creative products become more important as they pass along the value chain. The management of creativity puts a premium on entrepreneurial, just-in-time, temporary and ad-hoc working. It is driven more by education than by technology. Investments in education, research and thinking increase creativity's value and effectiveness, as surely as do investments in other capital assets increase theirs' (Howkins, 2001).

The creative economy differs perhaps most significantly from the mainstream economy by its structure, which has led to the emergence of a small number of very large, often multi-national businesses and a wealth of very small businesses or clusters of businesses, and by the break-down of the firm division of specializations so characteristic of assembly line production. Mid-size businesses that used to dominate the economy are disappearing.

---

[1] Education For All (EFA) is a global movement started in 1990 led by UNESCO, aimed at meeting the learning needs of all children, youth and adults. At the World Education Forum (Dakar, 2000), 164 governments pledged to achieve EFA and identified six goals to be met by 2015. Governments, development agencies, civil society and the private sector are working together to reach the EFA goals. For more information please see: www.unesco.org/new/index.php?id=18646&L

The consequences in employment patterns are most obvious in the shift from blue-collar to white-collar jobs (Florida, 2001). In addition, the success of small businesses necessitates an understanding of business economics and management by many more people than the manufacturing industry model. The skills needed to do well in a very large business and a very small business are not necessarily identical and considerations related to both must be taken into account when planning institutional support, training and education. A particular challenge for policy-making in this respect is the different, indeed often conflicting, interests of large companies and small businesses.
ICT has facilitated and been the source of many of these changes. Driven by technological development, the relative importance of copyright-based industries became significant because these industries do not only entail a whole new range of products linked to a new and more consumption-driven lifestyle, but also embody the possibility of penetrating an increasingly global and easily-accessible market. In this context, the creative industries evolved to encompass a wide range of very different sub-sectors.[2]

Creativity and business

Over the last 20 years, the number of people worldwide who have gone through school and higher education has risen enormously and the number of young adults expecting to find paid jobs within traditional white collar job-categories has similarly increased. Depending on the country, the demand for paid employment may be more or less difficult to meet. In many developing countries, the need to create and sustain a vast number of new jobs and opportunities for income-generation is a difficult challenge. The ability to address that situation is perhaps the most pressing issue facing educators and decision-makers today.
To address these challenges, the idea of 'entrepreneurship' has emerged as the driver of successful business development and economic growth. Hence the cultivation of entrepreneurial skills is seen as a priority and a key to ensure more sustainable development through the empowerment of young people and local communities. In the process, the entire concept of entrepreneurship is changing as a wide range of training institutions and ad-hoc courses have addressed the need for appropriate training in different contexts throughout the world, and have contributed to a much wider interpretation of the term, also including social and cultural or creative entrepreneurs. Other broad-based concepts e.g. *creativity, innovation,* and *design* have become popular as a way of defining and grasping the nature and characteristics of these challenges.

Although done so reluctantly by some parties, it is generally agreed that accommodating to this situation cannot be left to the regulation of free market forces alone. The State must step in to guide the development, thereby balancing the interests of economic and social development. The terminology may have lost some of its liberal and political connotations in the embrace of a national strategy but bowing to the free market agenda is still an underlying theme which stipulates goals and priorities.
The implications for institutions aimed at supporting competence building and enhancing the competitiveness of business in different countries/regions are numerous enough to warrant speaking about the need for deep-reaching institutional reform. The major challenges for these institutions include the massive income differentials associated with the new economy, as well as those of inclusion and exclusion from the benefits of the creative economy.

[2] E.g. core cultural industries such as publishing and performing arts, crafts, fashion, graphic design, and new creative industries such as biotechnology and databases, but also non-dedicated support industries such as the production of instruments and equipment, and ICTs.

Increasingly, it is understood that while not everyone will become business owners, entrepreneurial competencies support a culture of resourcefulness and encourage the identification of new models for income-generation and social engineering that are particularly suited to a specific situation. These competencies are needed not only to ensure the success of individual economic prosperity but perhaps more importantly as a vital tool in enabling participation and the negotiation of the pervasive change process (Home Affairs Bureau, 2005).

In this context, the need to come up with concrete ideas about specific training needs and the practical institutional support mechanisms related to creative entrepreneurship remains a challenge.

Centre and periphery

Creative or cultural industries are often seen as an important driver for cultural diversity and the development of these a win-win proposition for economic development in many local communities.

> *'Cultural industries .. are knowledge and labor-intensive, create employment and wealth, nurture creativity - the 'raw material' they are made from -, and foster innovation in production and commercialization processes. At the same time, cultural industries are central in promoting and maintaining cultural diversity and in ensuring democratic access to culture.' (UNESCO, 2004)*

The creative industries have particularly thrived in urban centers and in more affluent environments. Development of the cultural/creative industry sector is also increasingly adopted as a strategy for local economic growth in poorer regions. According to this strategy, local economies must engage in the global knowledge-based economies by stimulating a culture of entrepreneurship and the development of new products and markets. In very poor and rural contexts these efforts are often, though not always, focused on the development of crafts-based industries. The introduction of commercial production often presents a host of problems as economic concepts and experience with the mechanisms of business are often negligible and totally foreign to the way of thinking in place. This is where entrepreneurship courses are often employed.

The introduction of new technology and working procedures is an aspect of this development. Very often, the knowledge and skills and the attitude (spirit) needed to support the integration of these innovations are lacking; they are neither taught in schools nor included in the training offered to professionals working in the cultural industries. Clashing with proven traditional practice and knowledge, new products therefore tend to exist in a space where traditional notions of quality no longer applies, presenting a serious challenge to quality, innovation, as well as to notions of authenticity and the preservation of cultural diversity. The result is that the idea of quality is often linked exclusively to traditional products while new products are viewed as being of lesser quality - also as a result of the drive to produce more competitive products. While it is absolutely necessary to preserve the knowledge and respect for traditional practice as an element of the creative capital, the fostering of creative and critical skills needed to innovate procedures and design for new products and adaptations of existing products are equally important. In this context, however, the notion of design is almost totally absent - and where the concept is known it is primarily as fashion design, which is perceived as a purely aesthetic notion, closely related to modern mass media and consumer culture.

In addition to the traditional competencies strengthened in projects focusing on entrepreneurship development, the introduction of analytical tools used in *'design thinking as a field of technical research'* (Buchanan, 1998) may offer training elements that would make the entrepreneurship programs more sensitive to the cultural context and therefore more effective. Tools are needed that will facilitate the development of appropriate solutions bridging the gaps between traditional practice and knowledge, new media and technology, and the market.

A note of caution is needed: design education programs have already been introduced, for example in India with almost the opposite result of what is needed.[3] In the European context, design has long chiefly referred to a tool or methodology to plan and control the creative process, in order to ensure the quality and replicability of individual products in a dialogue with the market and its demands. This concept has proven so useful that design thinking has entered almost every area of the value chain and has become an indicator of quality in itself.

So how do we define design and design competence in a context that transcends the European cultural experience? By being conscious of the cultural context, and of the cultural meanings implicit in imported models and by using the integrative design skills that support the integration of insight and knowledge from different spheres (e.g. cultural traditions, industrial design, engineering, and marketing) into a workable solution to a problem. These skills may be applied to potentially any matter and are therefore also a powerful tool/skill in the negotiation of change regarding conditions, materials, norms, etc.

A needs-based approach to entrepreneurship training

As technology and new media is revolutionizing the way we work and live, so creativity, entrepreneurship and design have emerged as key concepts in the establishment of education and training programs needed to meet the demand for design-led entrepreneurship and methodologies for driving social development and sustainable change in businesses, organizations and communities (Chick, 2011).

The kind of knowledge we are talking about here is not just to be understood as an add-on training module. To effectively support the transition to a very different economic system, these competencies must be integrated in the education system as a new discipline of practical reasoning and argumentation that is particularly suited to cultivate trouble-shooting skills and address cross-sectoral issues. In order to do so, the development of new training curricula must be based on accurate information on the actual competencies and needs in a given context or situation.

The case of bhutan

Bhutan, a small Himalayan kingdom, may eventually provide a model for this kind of needs-based approach. Over the last few years, the Royal Government has initiated programs aimed at transforming the country's economy from a feudal, agrarian subsistence economy to a self-sufficient market-oriented economy that offers gainful employment to the majority of the Bhutanese population. The success of this major challenge is absolutely dependent on the integration of a different work ethic and associated vales and attitudes. This is where the need for a broad-based approach to entrepreneurship development comes in.

---

[3] The dependence on imported models for design education may, on the other hand, also simply be adopted as an efficient way to capitalize on cheap labor by imitating Western designs for the export market, as design schools in China have done in recent years.

Considering that only very few students enter technical and vocational training, it is particularly important to emphasize that entrepreneurship promotion is not only an issue for these students but also highly relevant and important for other graduates whose futures depend on successful private sector development in Bhutan. Economics are of course an important topic for graduates hoping to get into business and administration studies at university level, but an understanding of basic economics and entrepreneurship is also important for other students if they are to have the best chances of achieving gainful employment. It is a way of thinking that needs to be inculcated at an early stage of life. Many students find the subject difficult and irrelevant. The challenges involved in changing the perception of business and work amongst youth in Bhutan are complex and wide ranging. However, it is certain that it includes both the need to address these issues through mass media in a sustained campaign as well as curriculum reform and teacher training.
A great number of entrepreneurship training courses are being implemented both by different Government institutions (MOEA's regional offices, Bhutan Chamber Commerce and Industry (BCCI), etc.) and by individual projects and private institutes and foundations. However, all this activity is as yet un-connected and ad-hoc and is to a great extent dependent on outside funding.
While a number of new private training institutions have emerged in recent years, it is doubtful that these have qualified teachers in the area of entrepreneurship training. For the more traditional train-ing institutes such as the Zorig Chusum and the Vocational Traditional Institutes, it is safe to say that none of the teachers have this kind of capacity and no courses are currently be offered (MOLHR, 2010).

In Bhutan, as in general development contexts, entrepreneurship tends to denote a more holistic ap-proach and to represent the embodiment of an approach or attitude to education and work rather than just an approach to business development. For example, this is expressed in the emphasis on entrepreneurship as essentially a human resource issue. New trends in entrepreneurship, notably the concept and practice of social entrepreneurship, which embodies innovative approaches to so-cial development including income-generation and employment, but also an overriding concern for socially responsible business development, resonate particularly well with the Bhutanese develop-ment goal of Gross National Happiness (GNH)(Adler, 2009).

Conclusion

Many countries are addressing the need to instill a more entrepreneurial mind-set among their youth to enable them to participate in new economic trends. The case of Bhutan is interesting be-cause it is comparatively easy to see that, in order for this newly-born democracy to develop, there is a need to ensure that the young Bhutanese integrate an entirely new set of skills, and to see that they must review existing values and attitudes related to work and money. The State must support and guide this process carefully, with particular consideration of how to balance social values with the new economic direction.
Fundamentally, this is not so different from the situation in many other countries. Creative industries will dominate but a more diversified picture of these activities will emerge in time. To succeed in the creative economy we all need to find new ways to teach the young what they need to know. In doing so, we need to consider knowledge from different spheres, new ideas, and to preserve ethical values and traditions. This is in itself a creative process that produces value.

Over the years we have learned that the application of western models to developing countries is fraught with difficulties, and we are slowly recognizing that it only works if models are not copied but used for the elaboration of similar activities with proper reference to local knowledge and cultural values.

Maybe this could also teach us that a higher degree of contextualization of training and education opportunities within, for example, the EU may not only address the needs of the periphery better but also help to unleash cultural resources for the development of creative industries that may otherwise remain hidden?

References

- Adler Braun, A. (2009). *Gross National Happiness in Bhutan: A Living Example of an Alternative Approach to Progress.* Retrieved from: http://www.grossnationalhappiness.com/OtherArticles/GNHPaperbyAlejandro.pdf, September 24, 2009.
- Chick, A. A. (2011). *Design for Sustainable Change.* New York.
- Dos Santos Duisenberg, E. (2010). *Creative Economy Report 2010. A feasible Development Option.* Geneva: UNCTAD
- Florida, R. (2002). *The Rise of the Creative Class.* New York: Basic Books.
- Gohse, R. (1998). Design, Development, Culture and Cultural Legacies in Asia. In V. M. Buchanan, *The idea of Design.* MIT Press.
- Home Affairs Bureau. (2005). *A Study on Creative Index.* Homg Kong: Hong Kong Special Adm. Region Government
- Howkins, J. (2001). *The Creative Economy. How People Make Money from Ideas.* Penguin.
- MOLHR, (2010). *Entrepreneurship Development for Economic Growth, Poverty Reduction and Community Vitalization in Bhutan.* MOLHR (unpublished report Dec. 2010).
- UNESCO. (2004). *25 Questions on Culture, Trade and Globalization.* Paris: UNESCO.

About the author

Pernille Askerud (DK) is Senior Expert for Creative industries, BDS and Entrepreneurship Development at UNIDO Private Sector Development Unit. She is International Senior Expert Strategic Planning for Development. She was lead consultant for UNESCO Bangkok's program on cultural industries in Asia-Pacific, and main editor of the Bhutanese Baseline Report on Cultural Industries (2009).

pernille@askerud.org

Swing Bridges and Soft Skills: Internship Models Bridge the Gap into Industry

Nancy de Freitas

Abstract

Contemporary educational context for artists and designers entering the creative and cultural industries are discussed. It explains the need for transitional experiences that bridge the gap between academy and industry, compares different internship models and suggests key competency areas for effective bridging experiences into the creative and cultural industries. A bridging model in the present context is defined as a framework for flexible introduction for artists or designers to industry conditions. It opens the way for novices to test themselves in situations where they have to relearn how to be the creative practitioners they think they are.

Three types of bridging model are identified, but hybrids of any two or all three are possible. Each model is described along with examples of their application in specific educational institutions that use them. Regardless of the depth and quality of internship and industry partnerships, the successful transition from an academic way of thinking to an entrepreneurial one is in the eyes of the author not achieved by institutional structures. The successful core of an internship bridging experience is found in the quality of active leadership, monitoring and management of these projects and people.

Introduction

New millennium developments across a broad range of universities worldwide have seen many institutions overtly turning their attention towards industry sectors for reasons of research relevance, social and economic significance and beneficial partnerships.

For professional art education to maintain and improve its contribution to the creative and cultural sectors, the quality of its programs and pedagogical approaches must be examined with a view to improving the quality of graduates emerging into professional roles in the sector. The approaches taken to nurturing and expanding imaginative capability, resilience, inventive approaches, focused thinking and a wider raft of soft skills, such as communication and interpersonal skills and critical and material thinking, will increasingly be conducted in partnerships, in turn based on sustainable working relationships.

Among others, university art and design programs are increasingly focused on developing vital industry partnerships. Art and design schools and departments actively seek to partner with local and international arts, design and cultural organizations, creative sector businesses and local government organizations. They offer the collaborative support they need to ensure their students will be capable and confident at bridging the gap from academia into entrepreneurial, professional positions. Employers are seeking new graduates with skills that enhance their domain knowledge and professional expertise, such as common sense, familiarity with the basics of economic, business and commercial practice, social confidence in dealing with people, a positive approach to difficulties and a flexible attitude in defining solutions.

Moreover, the creative sector in general places high value on face-to-face interaction and networking opportunities that can only be fostered in new graduates through real life experiences in the sector.

The non arts-based working pattern of many artists and designers is an important factor contributing to reduced entrepreneurial strength in the creative and cultural sectors. Important studies of artists' career patterns and their economic prosperity or otherwise, have been reported by Alper and Wassall (2000, 2006), Abbing (2002), Rengers (2002), Towse (2006) and Throsby & Zednik (2011). Throsby and Zednik's analysis of survey data suggests that economic factors do force professional artists into non-arts labor markets, but that significant numbers are able to find work and apply their creative skills in other areas.

Although the effects, positive or negative, of this distributed working pattern are not well understood, it does indicate that professional artists and designers about to enter the sector need preparation for coping with career changes, job instability and long-term financial survival.

The bridging model concept

A bridging model in the present context is defined as a framework for flexible introduction for artists or designers to industry conditions. It opens the way for novices to test themselves in situations where they have to relearn how to be the creative practitioners they think they are. The process is a gradual one as the ground shifts below them, a process to which Brown (2011, p. xi) refers in his *'theory of learning to become'*. We have identified three different types of bridging models.

A The Internship Model

Internship is a generic term used to refer to bridging models for enabling design in a *'real world'* context. The purpose of an internship is to facilitate the linking of practical and theoretical domain knowledge acquired in the university with live tactical action and application.

The internship model can exist in many different forms in universities and across the creative and cultural sectors. Industry partners, individual research students or academic supervisors may propose and negotiate these internship projects, the research design and the goals. The nature of the proposed internship experience, the type of project work and the form of student reporting varies significantly. Institutional expectations also vary depending on the industry environment and on university expectations such as the length of time that a student is expected to invest and the number of credit points assigned to the internship. The intensity and value of internship periods is also highly variable. High-quality experiences are of great benefit all round, but mediocre or difficult experiences are common and when this happens, monitoring and intervention play an important role in reviving the process or mediating a crisis.

B The industry oriented project model

A common bridging model is the industry-oriented project model. The industry partner, the academic partner or the student conceives a defined project with clear aims, objectives and a time limit. With conditions set, resources available and approvals granted, the work can proceed. Industry projects, because they are clearly defined, goal oriented and more narrowly focused, are less exposed to unexpected turns, which makes them easier for a student to manage. This can be a good thing but it can also limit the student's experience of the kinds of unexpected contingencies that offer rich learning and growth experiences in the creative industries. This model is commonly available as an alternative option when an appropriate internship is not available to students or when the project concept necessitates an independent or entrepreneurial route.

C Living lab model

The living lab or design factory model is a hybrid of an industry-oriented project model and internship model. The living lab concept is predicated on long-term institutional commitments between university and industry partners. The best living lab models are truly collaborative partnerships with a high level of mutual confidence, which, according to Goonetilleke et al (2008) is an emergent form of partnership that entails a more collaborative and deep-seated involvement where both organizations work as one to gain benefits to meet their respective organizational goals.

The Swinburne University of Technology *Design Factory* is a Living Lab developed in collaboration with Aalto University in Finland. In this new Swinburne model, a core objective is to build research capacity and contribute to knowledge transfer for the industry sector and the University. With this model, the activity is often relocated within the university or school administrative structure and often within the physical campus as well. The design lab model subtly shifts the locus of control and influence back into the academic sphere. While this may offer better opportunities to manage the internship environment and create collaborative teams, the environment may be less influenced by the hard imperatives and multi-disciplinary interactions of an industry environment.

The experiential value of a living lab internship can be as variable as the more isolated solo internship experience in industry. The maturity of the industry/university partnership is also an important determining factor. In their case study analysis of an exemplar university and industry partnership between Queensland University of Technology and the Brisbane Airport Corporation, Goonetilleke et al (2008) contend that there are three partnership phases in the development of a living laboratory model: the initial experimentation phase, the engagement phase, and the regeneration phase (Goonetilleke et al., 2008)

Skill and capability

Development of skills and capabilities is an important feature of transitional models. In the academic environment a challenge is to develop the best learning experiences and opportunities that enable students to gain skills and build confidence for inventing, designing and producing in a professional context characterized by these defining features. Innovative thinking produces new knowledge and new knowledge shared across disciplinary or industry domains requires transdisciplinary and intercultural understanding, all of which is enhanced by networked structures and networking processes. Hearn and Bridgestock (2011) contend that there are four imperatives in a creative economy: domain specific creativity; innovation; transdisciplinarity and networks. The challenge is to identify and develop relevant capabilities required to drive the four key features of the creative economy.

The social and technological environment into which university graduates are currently emerging is described as one in which they will all need to be *'creatives'* in order to survive (Cunningham, 2005, 2006; Florida, 2002; Florida & Goodnight, 2005). It is an environment that expects more than simple problem solving based on accessing available information. The cultural and creative industries will increasingly require individuals who are adept at rapid co-creative response in challenging situations where there is a lack of information, a high level of uncertainty and a need for new networks of relationships to be created. In this context, the transitional learning experiences available to art and design students prior to graduation can be just as valuable as all the disciplinary skills they have previously acquired. The capabilities they will need to thrive in this environment may at first be easy to identify but are more difficult to cultivate. Professional and industry contexts vary, but some capabilities or aptitudes appear to be universally desirable. Each one is briefly considered below.

There is a category of multiple capabilities that relate to the processing of the content of proposals, design concepts, reports and strategic plans. The ability required here is one of filtering or sifting through information and picking up relevant content that will bring information and data across the entrepreneurial gap to a viable outcome. Here experiences that provide opportunities to engage in this process of filtering information are valuable. Developing these capabilities must involve dialogue at regular or cyclic points of decision-making and there is particular value in interaction across parallel teams arriving at different conclusions on critical content.

Optimism is a capability grounded in a positive outlook. It is the technique that will turn an accident or a stroke of luck into something definitive. Optimism in the form of questions and further enquiry is a linguistic tool for changing course. What other application might work? What happens next if we change this part? What if we went this way instead? While creativity may be an essential component of entrepreneurial activity, novel ideas are just thin air until they have been shaped and honed into an applied or material form. In an internship, the economic or social consequences of the student's actions are cushioned by mentoring or host support, which offers a perfect opportunity for moving decisively to an implementation stage. This is the active, playful action of creativity that Kane (2004) believes is important for productivity in commerce and industry in the future.

Patience and persistence are also key features of successful entrepreneurial activity. They are two sides of one coin. Patience, waiting for the right moment and persistence, pushing through barriers regardless of minor setbacks are both critical to successful new ventures. Persistence is also the 'practice' factor that ensures the best chance of excellence or competence. Developing these capabilities in an internship is directly related to the quality of support available at difficult stages.

A conclusion with forward momentum: what needs to be done?

Regardless of the depth and quality of internship and industry partnerships, the successful transition from an academic way of thinking to an entrepreneurial one is not achieved by institutional structures. New synthesis and entrepreneurial thinking take place through authentic interactions with people and ideas.
The successful core of an internship bridging experience is found in the quality of active leadership, monitoring and management of these projects and people. The transition from an academic art and design environment into the professional, competitive, market or audience driven reality of the cultural and creative industries is more dependent on the mediating positions that steer, supervise or mentor individual students, than on the formal structure of the institutional model. It is, therefore, important for institutions setting up these partnership models to pay particular attention to the human resources within the overall scheme.

The internship as a pedagogical bridging model does not operate in isolation of institutional structures and resources. Successful bridging will occur when the support, supervisory and/or mentoring processes are strong. It is hardly possible to compare student work and experiences across different internship models because each experience or project is unique and individual students approach the internship environment with diverse skills. However, perceptions of personal growth in relation to professional expertise and social capability can be measured and this would be a valuable international survey to implement across a range of design domains.

Jaaniste and Haseman (2009) have identified other key areas that need to be better understood through scoping studies and research in order to bridge the research and innovation gap between the University sector and the creative industry sectors. They suggest that we need to look at the way in which practice-led research activity produces knowledge gains and in particular we need to study the exchange of this knowledge between university and industry sectors. There is scope for research here.

Recent envisioning reports and green papers all around the world are testament to the global interest in building cultural and creative industries, and in developing strategies for the evolution of strong creative communities and cities. Design thinking development policies have been proliferating and a great deal of material designed to guide decision-making and funding for entrepreneurial and innovation agendas.

The education sector has been slower to respond. On a final note, it is worth ending this chapter with the most difficult issue. Hearn and Bridgestock (2011) identified four imperatives in a creative economy: domain specific creativity; innovation; transdisciplinarity and networks. Of these, the most difficult to embed in practice is transdisciplinarity, which is oriented outward, away from disciplinary methods, towards the significant issues and challenges of the world.

In this respect, it is a socially focused concept. Although the notion of transdisciplinarity began with the philosophical writings of Kuhn (1962) and Jantsch (1972), there is currently renewed interest in its significance as a conceptual underpinning for the complex design problems of our potentially unsustainable, globalised world. Nicolescu (2002) argues that a transdisciplinary, outward-looking focus in solving problems is one that attaches importance to all relationships and human contexts.

It will be the responsibility of academic and industry mentors, working in partnership, to ensure this perspective is ingrained in the professional demeanor of future designers. There must be a focus on mediating the experiences of students in internships and other transitional models and opening up the project horizons as a strategic ploy to enable tactical transdisciplinary action.

References

- Abbing, H. (2002). Why are artists poor? The exceptional economy of the arts. Amsterdam: Amsterdam University Press.
- Alper, N.O. & Wassall, G.H. (2000). More than once in a blue moon: Multiple jobholdings by American artists (Research Rep. No. 40). Washington, DC: National Endowment for the Arts.
- Alper, N.O. & Wassall, G.H. (2006). Artists' careers and their labor markets. In V.A. Ginsburgh & D. Throsby (Eds.), Handbook of the economics of art and culture (Vol. 1, p. 813–864). Amsterdam: Elsevier/North Holland.
- Brown, J. (2011). Education in the Creative Economy. Foreword. In Araya, D. & Peters, M. (Eds.) Education in the creative economy: Knowledge and learning in the age of innovation. New York: Peter Lang.
- CCI Annual Report (2010). Centre of Excellence for Creative Industries and Innovation Annual Report 2010. Australian Research council and Queensland University of Technology.
- Cunningham, S. (2005). Creative Enterprises. In John Hartley (Ed.), Creative Industries (p. 282-298). Malden, MA: Blackwell.
- Cunningham, S. (2006). What price a creative economy? Platform papers #9. Sydney: Currency House.
- Danish Enterprise and Construction Authority (2010). The Vision of the Design2020 Committee. The Danish Enterprise and Construction Authority. <http://www.ebst.dk/publikationer/ER/The_Vision_of_the_Danish_Design_2020_Committee/index.htm>.
- Florida, R. (2002). The rise of the creative class: and how it's transforming work, leisure, community, and everyday life. New York: Basic Books.
- Florida, R. and Goodnight J. (2005). Managing for Creativity. Harvard Business Review 83(7/8), p. 124-131.
- Goonetilleke, A., Betts, M. and Goodwin, S. (2008). Living laboratories to support collaboration, Proceedings of the CIB International Conference on Building Education and Research: Building Resilience, 11th - 15th February 2008, Heritance, Kandalama, Sri Lanka. CD Rom publication.

- Hearn, G. & Bridgstock, R. (2011). Education for the Creative Economy: Innovation, Transdisciplinarity and Networks. In Araya, D. & Peters, M. (Eds.) Education in the creative economy: Knowledge and learning in the age of innovation. New York: Peter Lang.
- Jaaniste, L. & Haseman, B. (2009). Practice-led research and the innovation agenda: beyond the postgraduate research degree in the arts, design and media. Proceedings of ACUADS 2009 Conference: Interventions in the Public Domain, Queensland College of Art, Griffith University, Brisbane, Queensland.
- Jantsch, E. (1972). Towards Interdisciplinarity and transdisciplinarity in education and innovation. In CERI (Ed.), Interdisciplinarity: Problems of Teaching and Research in Universities (pp. 97-121). Paris: OECD.
- Kane, P. (2004). The Play Ethic. A Manifesto for a Different Way of Living. London: Macmillan.
- Kuhn, T.S. (1962). The Structure of Scientific Revolutions. Chicago: University of Chicago Press.
- Nicolescu, B. (2002). Manifesto of Transdisciplinarity. Translation: Karen-Claire Voss. Albany, NY: SUNY Press.
- Philanthropy New Zealand (2007). Giving New Zealand. Philanthropic Funding 2006. Report prepared by Business and Economic Research Limited (BERL) for Philanthropy New Zealand, Wellington.
- Rengers, M. (2002). Economic lives of artists: Studies into careers and the labour market in the cultural sector. Utrecht: Interuniversity Center for Social Science Theory and Methodology, Utrecht University.
- State Government of Victoria (2010). Report: Victorian Design Action Plan. Department of Innovation, Industry and Regional Development.
- Swinburne University of Technology (2011). Report: Victoria's Design Research Infrastructure: How to Create Global Impact for Victoria through a World-Class Design Sector. Swinburne University of Technology, Faculty of Design.
- Throsby, D. & Zednik, A. (2011). Multiple job-holding and artistic careers: some empirical evidence, Cultural Trends, 20:1, p. 9-24.
- Towse, R. (2006). Human capital and artists' labour markets. In V.A. Ginsburgh & D. Throsby (Eds.), Handbook of the economics of art and culture, (Vol. 1, p. 865–894). Amsterdam: Elsevier/North Holland.

About the author

Nancy de Freitas (NZ) is Associate Professor, Postgraduate Studies and Program Leader, Master of Arts Management, Faculty of Design and Creative Technologies works at the School of Art and Design, Auckland University of Technology (AUT) University, New Zealand. She is Editor-in-Chief of *Studies in Material Thinking*.

nancy.defreitas@aut.ac.nz

Responding to industry requests for design knowledge

Reflections on a private educational initiative from Turkey: 'Favori Gold Design Academy'

Ayse Coşkun Orlandi, Serkan Bayraktaroğlu

Abstract

Jewellery in Turkey, beyond its material existence has shown importance as emotional, symbolic, socio-cultural signifier. Reinforced by strong gold consumption traditions, the jewellery production in Turkey keeps a strong bond to its multi cultural historical craft traditions. The Turkish jewellery sector has gained acceleration globally within the past twenty years as a supplier. Like many other countries, the Turkish jewellery industry gets rooted in craft tradition. With the arrival of the CAD/CAM technologies within the production process, the tradition encounters a more hybrid structure shifting between the workshop and the factory. This complex structure, which is based on both craftsman tradition and automated mass production, requires new abilities and educational background for designers who are expected to foster innovation and creativity.

At the moment the jewellery design education in Turkey is neither capable of affording the real requests of the emerging industry, nor capable of re-defining a new design language in the contemporary context. This gap seems to limit entrepreneurial behaviour and innovation potential of SMEs in jewellery business, which represents the majority of the jewellery production in Turkey.

Creative industries, innovation and entrepreneurship in Turkey

The term 'creative industries' was first adopted by the British government in 1997 when they launched the new 'creative economy' (Galloway, 2006; Matheson, 2006). Since then creative industries have been at the centre of many development policies of the EU. The last Creative Economy Report presents the map of creative economies and points out the 'jewellery' industry under the 'design' section as a part of 'functional creation' (UNCTAD & UNDP, 2010). Creative industries are expected to foster social and cultural development along with economic development. The Creative Economy Report underlines how jewellery could be a perfect match between tradition and high value-added activity as a creative industry (UNCTAD and UNDP 2010).

Cultural and Creative industries have been discussed in Turkey since 2007 (CCI, 2007), especially with the influence of the 'European Capital of Culture' organization in Istanbul in 2010. Even though there had been appreciation by local governments via some support from development agencies for creative industries, it is hardly possible to mention a coherent governmental policy focused on the creative industries and their future in Turkey.

Many development agencies and associations provide entrepreneurship education and financial support for entrepreneurs in Turkey. Despite such a supportive environment, however, entrepreneurial behavior is increasing very slowly. Lack of national policies on creative industries and insufficient support for entrepreneurship results in a paradox within the jewellery industry in Turkey. There is a mixture of craft based skills and contemporary design understanding.

Contemporary overview of Turkey's jewellery industry

As reported by the World Gold Council, Turkey is considered as the second country after Italy for the global export of golden jewellery (Akman, 2006). Throughout the centuries, East Asia, the Indian sub-continent and the Middle East accounted for high volumes of gold demand. India, Greater China (China and Hong Kong), US, Turkey and Saudi Arabia represented over half of world gold demand. A different set of socio-economic and cultural incentives drives each market, creating a diverse range of factors influencing demand. Rapid demographic and other socio-economic changes in many of the key consuming nations are also likely to produce new patterns of demand in the foreseeable future (WGC, 2011).

Turkey ranks as the third country after Italy and India for the production of golden jewellery and the fourth country for the consumption of golden jewellery in the global markets. As the world's fourth biggest market for gold jewellery, it's the third largest manufacturing centre and second biggest exporter (Akman, 2006). Almost all of the gold fabricated in Turkey is utilized in jewellery production. The average firm size of the industry is a micro-scale workshop (4-5 employees per workshop), which represents the characteristics of the production scale. The number of people employed only within the micro-scale workshops is estimated to be around 50,000. With an annual capacity of fabricating 400 tons of gold and employing approximately 250,000 workers, the structure of Turkey's Jewellery Sector is well reflected through these SMEs.

Throughout the industrialization period, goldsmithing has undergone great shifts. The shift from a micro-scale *atelier* to a factory has conveyed a great challenge bringing in a corporate approach through product ranges. The industry constituted a new image and a territory for a new way of consumption. Today large scale corporations are the signifiers of branded products, branded retail stores and design (Coşkun Orlandi, 2009).

Brief historical background

Reinforced by strong gold consumption traditions, jewellery production in Turkey keeps a strong bond to its multi-cultural historical craft traditions. The Turkish jewellery sector has gained acceleration as a supplier at a global scale within the past twenty years. The main factor of this success is linked to the metal-smithing traditions of past civilizations that are geographically placed in Turkey and around. Goldsmithing was a major work in almost every civilization in this area. Almost every civilization that existed within the geographical territory of Turkey today has left an important heritage of goldsmithing.
As the raw material itself is a trade asset for the industry, the jewellery industry has a particular

character of production process and a particular production atmosphere. The workshop owner is the entrepreneur as well as the master. The tacit knowledge process is a continuous system dating back to the Renaissance tradition which set out the traditional characteristics of the quality of production.

Turkey's internal consumption pattern demonstrates rather a severe pragmatic approach in parallel to the Middle Eastern socio-economic consumption values. A jewellery item is an investment asset; with anonymous design, less workmanship, high-purity of the precious metal; whereas contemporary global consumption trends impose an individual possession and look, mixed semi precious materials and outstanding design and branding. One of the major resources behind the growth is declared to be the craftsmanship found in Turkey today, which owned a diverse skilful tradition as stated above. The sector is facing a strong challenge on product design, design management processes and brand creation due to its dominant supplier position in world markets.

Jewellery education: systems and structure

Knowledge transfer in jewellery production can occur in two ways. The first one is the traditional tacit knowledge system, dating back to the Ottoman guild systems. The tacit knowledge transfer is basically a master-apprentice system that is seen as the most efficient way to inherit a mastership. The system today faces severe problems and is considered to be a threat for traditional workmanship.
As an equivalent to this system we see vocational high schools to educate goldsmiths, which are criticized as insufficient in both practice and theory. One of the major problems of this educational structure is that the duration of the education is too short, and that it doesn't give enough time for apprenticeship. There is no creative curriculum to foster innovation and design at this level of formal vocational education.

The second group of educational institutions are the vocational schools of higher education which tend to focus more on design. Yet these institutions are still far from being sufficient in terms of the curriculum, the teaching environment and professional experience. Only in the last few years have there been some attempts to build an undergraduate level university education focusing only on jewellery design. Yet these attempts have not been supported by faculties of art and design. Some new initiatives try to change the educational patterns. An example is the case of Favori Gold Academy.

Founded in 1992 in Istanbul, Favori is one of Turkey`s large scale corporate manufacturers, importers and exporters of fine gold jewellery. Favori as an enterprise is a prominent example of a jewellery business model reflecting the industrialization period of Turkey's jewellery sector. The owner is an entrepreneur himself, having an educational background in agricultural engineering with a PhD degree and a career in business administration.

The academy was established in 2005 as a social responsibility project as an initiative under the brand Favori. Favori Gold Academy aims to be a scientific, rational, interchanging, perfectionist educational institution.. It focuses on design, production and sales with established certificate programs under design and retail departments and supported universities' jewellery design departments. The institution not only publishes books on jewellery design but has also organised several conferences on the topic. Since its establishment, approximately 100 participants have graduated. Throughout the establishment process, the structure of the academy has been based on academic collaboration, blending professional experience with academic and artistic knowledge.

Conclusions and discussions

Turkey plays an important role in golden jewellery production and consumption in global scale. However, it has not gained sustainable competitive advantage due to lack of design input as a driving force for innovation. There are no national policies about creative industries and insufficient supports for entrepreneurship; the environment needed to enrich innovation through design is not available.

Creative industries theory has a special emphasis on innovation, creative networks, communication and teamwork. Matheson (2006) discusses the importance of design education with its influence in entrepreneurship in creative industries, and points out the necessity for a change in design education in order to meet the creative practitioners profile demanded by creative industries theory. A recent study on the entrepreneurial characteristics of Turkey shows that SME entrepreneurs in Turkey see the inability to attract and retain reliable employees as their second most serious problem (Benzing, Chu & Kara ,2009). Besides this inability to attract such employees, authors mention the importance of better matching student skills with a special emphasis on professional technical curricula. They address restructuring vocational schools to fill this gap.

Since its establishment, Favori Gold Academy presents a unique case providing a hybrid education formed specifically for designer needs of the industry. The outcomes of a recently executed case study on Favori Gold Design Academy showed the potential of an educational model, fostering design based innovation and entrepreneurship behaviour in the creative industries. Favori Gold Academy supports a hybrid educational model, standing between traditional tacit knowledge systems and contemporary design education.

References

- Anonymous. (2005). *2004'te Türkiye'de Kuyumculuk*. İstanbul: İstanbul Altın Rafinerisi Hizmet Yayınları
- Armatlı Köroğlu, B., A. Uğurlar and T. Ö. Eceral, (2009). The Story of a Jewellery Cluster in Istanbul Metropolitan Area: Grand Bazaar. *Gazi University Journal of Science 22*, no. 4 (2009): 383-394.
- Benzing, C., Chu, H.M., & Kara, O. (2009). 'Entrepreneurs in Turkey: A Factor Analysis of Motivations, Success Factors, and Problems.' *Journal of Small Business Management 47*(1) (January): 58-91. doi:10.1111/j.1540-627X.2008.00262.x. Retrieved from: http://doi.wiley.com/10.1111/j.1540-627X.2008.00262.x., October 29, 2011.
- Carcano, L. & Lojacono, G. (2002). *A Comparison Between Two European Design Models in the Jewellery Business*. Milan: SDA Bocconi.
- CCI. (2007). Symposium: *Creative Cities and Industries in the 21st Century*, organized by UNCTAD and Yildiz Technical University – Istanbul. Retrieved from: http://www.unctad.org/, October 29, 2011.
- Favori (2011). *Favori Altın Akademisi*. Retrieved from: http://www.favorialtinakademisi.com.tr/, October 29, 2011.
- Galloway, S. (2006). Deconstructing the concept of 'Creative Industries. *Cultural Industries: The British Experience* (May). Retrieved from: http://eprints.gla.ac.uk/5243/, November 5, 2011
- Garnham, Nicholas. (2005). From cultural to creative industries. *International Journal of Cultural Policy 11* (1) (March): p. 15-29.
- Green, T. (2007). *The Ages of Gold*. London: GFMS
- İrepoğlu, G. (2000). 'Osmanlı Mücevheri' *P Dergisi 17*: 100-112
- KOSGEB. (2010). *2010 Annual Report*. Ankara. Retrieved from: http://www.kosgeb.gov.tr/pages/ui/Baskanligimiz.aspx?ref=23, November 5, 2011.
- Köseoğlu, C. (1980). *Topkapı Sarayı İmparatorluk Hazinesi*. İstanbul: Ak Yayınları Kültür ve Sanat Kitapları.
- Kuşoğlu, M. Z. (1994). *Kuyumculuk, Dünden Bugüne İstanbul Ansiklopedisi (Cilt 5)*, İstanbul: Türkiye Ekonomik ve Toplumsal Tarih Vakfı, p. 144.
- Matheson, Billy. (2006). 'A culture of creativity: design education and the creative industries.' *Journal of Management Development 25*(1): 55-64. doi:10.1108/02621710610637963. Retrieved from: http://www.emeraldinsight.com/10.1108/02621710610637963, November 5, 2011.
- Meriçboyu, Y. A. (2001). *Antikçağ'da Anadolu Takıları*, İstanbul: Akbank Yayınları. 12.
- UNCTAD & UNPD. (2010). *Creative Economy Report : Creative Economy a Feasible Development Option*. New York. Retrieved from: http://www.unctad.org/en/docs/ditctab20103_en.pdf., November 5, 2011.
- WGC. (2011). Demand and Supply. *World Gold Council*. Retrieved from: http://www.gold.org/investment/why_how_and_where/why_invest/demand_and_supply, November 5, 2011.

About the authors

Ayşe E. Coşkun Orlandi (TR). She received her BA as Industrial Product Designer in 1997 at Marmara University (Istanbul). In 1998 received a Master in Design degree at Domus Academy, Milan, Italy. In 2003 received an MA at Marmara University (Istanbul). In 2009 she has got her PhD at Mimar Sinan Fine Arts University (Istanbul). She has been lecturing, researching, publishing in the field of industrial product design since 2000. She is currently working as Asst. Prof. at Kadir Has University, Istanbul, Turkey. *acoskunorlandi@khas.edu.tr*

Serkan Bayraktaroglu (TR). Born in Sakarya, Turkey in 1982 got his undergraduate degree in 2003 in the field of Industrial Engineering. He had his graduation from Industrial Design and Manufacturing master program (2008) that is offered by a consortium of T.U. Dortmund and University of Twente. His master thesis, 'Management of communication in complex product development' was written in cooperation with Product Development Institute of T.U. Munich and AUDI A.G. He is a PhD student in Istanbul Technical University – and works as a lecturer at Kadir Has University, Turkey. *serkan.bayraktaroglu@khas.edu.tr*

The shift from scarcity to abundance in CCI's: a matter of perception?

Gerardo Neugovsen

Abstract

When discussing cultural entrepreneurship and cultural management a number of questions arise. Are we living a fundamental moment of change, or are we observing a transition process between the Industrial Age and the Knowledge Era? Which underlying assumptions are being modified because of this transition in regard to the economic and productive value of culture, knowledge, creativity and innovation? And how does the educational world that is busy forming entrepreneurs for the Cultural and Creative Industries has to be prepared for the new challenges?

This article explores the relevance on the economic and productive (re)valuation of the concepts of culture, innovation, creativity and knowledge under the transition between the Industrial Age and the Knowledge Era. The concepts are confronted with a practical case, implemented at the Chilean 'Valparaiso University' recently.

Cultural and Creative Industries (CCI); the metamorphosis of the ugly duckling

Cultural and creative activity is emerging from the dark zone to which it was once confined, being associated with the image of the 'starved artist' or the always low-waged cultural manager. Both actors share the scene with the CCI-Entrepreneur, who adds innovative dimensions and transcends the existing concept of Arts Administration, opening the doors to new productive dynamics. At a very quick pace this sector - which was usually ignored by the traditional economy - has transformed itself like an 'Ugly Duckling'; generating more than 7% of the world's GDP (Dos Santos, 2010) and being good for more than 2,3% of Europe's employment (EC, 2006). The growing rate of the sector is superior compared to the average economy (EC, 2006) and the exports represent 854.000 million dollars (Dos Santos, 2010). This may indicate a change in the perception of the economic and productive value of culture, creativity, innovation and knowledge. Is it that suddenly those bohemian, always chronically bankrupt artists and cultural managers have understood how to make money, or has the general perception regarding the economic and productive value of culture and creativity changed in our society?

Scarcity versus abundance: the shift between industrial and knowledge era

The reason for the positive change regarding the economic and productive value of culture, creativity, innovation and knowledge may be related to the transitional process we as humans are experiencing moving from the Industrial Age towards the Knowledge Era. This brings a major change in the perception of how wealth and prosperity can be built, as Peter Drucker forecasted back in the sixties under the concept of *'Knowledge Economy'* (Drucker, 1969). Cumulating scarce tangible assets is not the only way to create wealth anymore, as it is supposed under the rules of the present economic model. Intangible assets – which are the raw materials of the CCI's – are now becoming a very relevant source for sustainable development. As Castells points out (Castells, 1996), this transition means that the source of productivity at the present stage of capitalism *lies in the technology of knowledge generation, information processing and symbol communication'*.

Moving from one Era to the other modifies one of the fundamental principles of capitalist economy: the administration of scarce resources. The very definition of economy, as postulated in 1935 by the British economist Lionel Robbins states that: *'Economics is a science which studies human behavior as a relationship between ends and scarce means which have alternative uses.'* (Robbins, 1935). But, in the Knowledge Era scarcity of means seems not to be the ruling pattern anymore. As Weller (Weller, 2011) states: *'The economic model which has underpinned many content based industries has been based on an assumption of scarcity. With a digital, open, networked approach we are witnessing a shift to abundance of content, and subsequently new economic models are being developed which have this as an assumption.'* In contrast to the still ruling obsession for cumulating scarce material assets as ground for economic and social wealth, the Knowledge Era focuses more on intangible assets.

According to the economist Baruch Lev (Lev, 2001) some characteristics of intangible assets are:

- They are abundant and tend to be inexhaustible.
- Deployment is possible at the same time in multiple users.
- Intangible assets increase returns instead of diminishing them, since the marginal costs tend to be close to zero.
- They have strong network effects and form the core of important networks.

The consequences for the CCI sector are relevant since new ways of interacting, funding, producing, distributing and commercializing goods and services are created based on other principles than the known under the Industrial Era. Some evident particularities are:

- Private ownership makes way for collective ownership (Shareware, freeware, community-based design, Open Source Programs, crowdsourcing, net-collaboration, copyleft, Creative Commons and similar);
- Financial capital accumulation and concentration makes place for crowdfunding, knowledge-sharing and -distribution and networking;
- Training and educational processes are not attached to physical classrooms anymore;
- New business-models arise based on abundance criteria instead of scarcity (for example: long-tail (Anderson, 2006); Interactive advertising model (Rodger & Thorson, 2000), enterprises with multiple benefits (not only profit maximization).
- New jobs, professions and professional fields arise, demanding new competencies and knowledge.

In order to deal with those changes, new forms of business-models and related competencies are needed at the CCI-Entrepreneurs. Therefore major changes should be made from an educational point of view. As Klamer states, the main drive for the cultural managers is related to the (cultural and creative) content: 'Everything else, including the economics, is subsidiary.' (Klamer, 2006). For a CCI-entrepreneur, 'economics' acquires a new meaning related to the satisfaction of fundamental human needs (Max Neef et al, 1991). If those changes are to be reflected in the educational world, it is necessary to review the underlying assumptions connected with the economic and productive value of culture, knowledge, innovation and creativity. Since educating CCI-Entrepreneurs is a relatively new activity the questions are: Are the related colleges adequately preparing future graduates for the new challenges? And more specifically: what are the underlying assumptions that rule most of the educational proposals until now?

Mental models and the (under)valuation of culture and creativity

Cognitive scientists study mental models and schemas in order to understand how humans know, perceive, make decisions and build behavior. Mental models strongly influence the way in which humans interact with the surrounding world. According to March: *'They are the ligaments of social life, establishing links among individuals and groups across generations and geographic distances [...] They give context for understanding history and for locating oneself in it. This happens through myths, symbols, rituals and stories'* (March and Simon, 1958). They are an essential component at educative and forming processes. Mental-models and underlying assumptions influence the way in which entrepreneurs design their business-models. This can be defined as a description of *'the rationale of how an organization creates, delivers and captures value'* (Osterwalder, Pigneur, 2010). This is because business- and mental-models are intimately related. As Hamel describe: *'A business-model is a 'thing'. The mental-model is a set of beliefs about the 'thing''* (Hamel, 2000). The assumption that culture, creativity, innovation and knowledge have little economic and productive value may be connected with certain historical and cultural facts. Being aware of those assumptions is relevant for the teaching environment.

All of the facts mentioned above may influence our mental models resulting in the underlying assumption that culture, creativity, innovation and knowledge has 'social' value and are relevant for general development and progress. But it has none or little productive or economic value. Therefore, it should be of no surprise why in Western world those elements were not included into the list of productive and wealth developing activities till now. Consistently, the educational system ruled by Behaviorism limits the development of creativity and innovation in students, educating people that stay far away from the independent, entrepreneurial and innovative person the Knowledge Era demands. As Sir Ken Robinson postulates (Robinson, 2006) *'The educative system kills creativity'*.

The valparaíso experience: competencies-profile of the future graduates

Between August and November 2011 a reconceptualization of the contents of the curricula and review teaching methods has been executed at the Valparaíso University (UV), one of the most prominent educational institutions at the Republic of Chile. The educative teams belonged to the Faculties of Theater, Music, Film, Tourism and Culture Management as well as the Public Administration Faculty. Members of the educative teams were invited to reflect about the above-mentioned issues in relationship to their own educative practice. The point of departure was two questions: a) are we properly preparing future graduates for the 21st Century's challenges? And b) if there is a market for exchanging cultural goods and services, what kind of human needs are satisfied?

Participants acknowledged the unconscious influence on their underlying assumptions of the above mentioned 'layers' of historical and cultural facts and recognized a lack of awareness of the human needs that are satisfied by culture. They were pleased with the possibility of reflection on those subjects from a renewed conceptual framework. Except for the Tourism and Culture Management (TCM) Faculty, most of the participants had never thought of culture as a productive and/or economic valuable sector, nor about the entrepreneurial competencies of the graduates. Even the Dean of the TCM Faculty acknowledged the difficulties they had when integrating the 'cultural' dimension of the College with the more pragmatic (and commercial) aspects of tourism. The notion of 'industry' was generally resisted until it was put in a context of social and economic relevance. When debating the 'entrepreneurial spirit' which should be spread all over the contents, most of the participants agreed with the image of an entrepreneur as somebody that can take creative human actions. It implies an ability to build valuable proposals from practically nothing. There is a persistent search for opportunity, regardless of resources or lack thereof. This requires a vision, passion and commitment to lead others in the pursuit of that vision, but also requires the willingness to take calculated risks (Timmons, 1989).

Most of the participants recognized their difficulty of introducing changes that can lead to the development of these competencies. Beside the generic entrepreneurial competencies most participants agreed that the profile of future graduates of the different CCI related colleges must include
specific elements and competencies for future graduates (Neugovsen, 2009).

Initial conclusions

In general we might conclude that the transition from the Industrial Era towards the Knowledge Era constitutes a major shift in human history that has a positive impact on the perception of the value of culture, creativity, knowledge and innovation as economic and productive areas. Changes in perceptions have to be reflected in the conceptual and practical frameworks that lead the work at universities, having an impact on their teaching practices.

In the Knowledge Era it will not be possible to continue using the traditional lecture as the only teaching tool: it is necessary to change to a pedagogy that educates professionals that can deal in a proper manner with the challenges of the 21st Century. By reviewing the underlying assumptions regarding the creative and productive value of culture, knowledge, creativity and innovation, as well as updating the educational models and practices, future graduates will be ready to take a prominent place in the productive world in the Knowledge Era.

References

- Castells, M. (1996). *The Information Age: Economy, Society and Culture. Volume I: The Rise of the Network Society.* Blackwell; Oxford.
- Dos Santos Duisenberg (Ed). (2010). *Creative Economy Report 2010*, United Nations UNCTAD, Geneva.
- Drucker, P. (1969). *The Age of Discontinuity; Guidelines to Our Changing Society.* Harper and Row, New York.
- EC-European Community's Ministers of Culture, Retrieved from: http://europa.eu/rapid/pressReleases/Action. do?reference=IP/06/1564, 2006. , November 2011.
- Hamel, G. (2002); *Leading the Revolution*, Plume, New York.
- Klamer, A. (2006). *Cultural entrepreneurship*; Erasmus University and Academia Vitae; Rotterdam.
- Lev, B. (2001). *Intangibles: management, measurement, and reporting*, Brookings Institution Press, Washington, DC.
- March, J. & Simon, H. (1958): *Organizations.* New York: John Wiley and Sons .
- Neef M. M., Elizalde, A. & Hopenhayn, M. (;1991). *Human Scale Development. Conception, Application And Further Reflections*; The Apex Press; New York.
- Neugovsen, G. (2009); *Entrepreneurs and Creative Industries, Understanding the human factor. In: Creative Industries Colourful fabric in multiple dimensions*, Hagoort G. & Kooyman R. (Ed); Utrecht School of the Arts (HKU), Utrecht.
- Osterwalder, A. & Pigneur, Y. (2010): *Business Model Generation: A Handbook for Visionaries, Game Changers, and Challengers*; John Wiley and Sons; New Jersey.
- Robbins, L. (1935). *An Essay on the Nature and Significance of Economic Science*; Macmillan; London.
- Robinson K. (2006); Conference at TED Ideas Worth Spreading; retrieved from: http://www.ted.com/talks/ken_ robinson_says_schools_kill_creativity.html; 2006, November 2011.
- Timmons, J. (1989). *The Entrepreneurial Mind*; Brick House Publisher; New Hampshire.
- Weller, M. (2011). A pedagogy of abundance. In: *Spanish Journal of Pedagogy*, The Open University; London.

About the author

Gerardo Neugovsen (PN) has obtained his Master degree at the Utrecht School of Arts in the Netherlands. He has specialized in Creative Industries. He lives in Panama from where he works as researcher, consultant and university teacher at several Latin American countries. He is m ainly concern with the pedagogic aspects of developing innovative competencies at SME entrepreneurs at the Creative Industries.

gerardon@gmail.com

University Engagement with the Creative Industries

How action learning can build collaboration between a university and the creative industries

Julia Calver and Jeff Gold

Abstract

In 2010 a need for professional development targeted at chief executive or director level that would enable peer learning was identified. An action learning set would respond to a need identified by the creative sector; support learning within an appropriate peer-led framework and provide an opportunity for the university to collaborate with the sector.

Introduction

Despite the creative sector's complexity, its resistance to definition and the limitations of traditional economic measures (Potts et al., 2008; Holden et al., 2011; Universities UK, 2010), in the UK the creative industries sector has grown by an average of 5% per annum between 1997 and 2007 compared to an average of 3% for the whole of the economy, accounting for up to 6.2% of UK GVA (DCMS, 2010). It is a sector characterized by high levels of self-employment, with one in three creative graduates running their own business and/or working in a freelance capacity (Ball et al 2010). It maintains a highly flexible dynamic with micro and small enterprises, often grouping together for particular commissions and projects (Taylor, 2006; Pratt, 2005) with a tendency to operate primarily through a series of networks made up of peers (Gloor, 2006; Handke, 2004; Henry, 2007).

According to The Work Foundation, the creative industries have been identified as a key strand in the UK's economic recovery strategy, contributing to competitive advantage through to 2020 and beyond (The Work Foundation, 2011). Equally, universities have a key role to play in generating innovation, high level skills and creative thinking (Universities UK 2010). We would suggest therefore that it is imperative for universities to develop effective strategies for engagement and longer-term collaboration. The challenge is that universities are multi-faceted institutions, comprising of units and organizational structures that must adhere to long established protocols and mechanisms to preserve quality control and systems (Gibb, 2009). This organizational structure has implications for collaboration between the university and the creative sector. As a consequence, it has been difficult to attract participants from the creative sector to courses (both accredited and non-accredited) and events, especially if costs are incurred.[26] Furthermore, there is some scepticism that universities do not provide business with relevant support (Leeds City Region, 2011). However, feedback from creative professionals at an Open Space event (Owen, 2008) organized by Leeds Metropolitan University in 2010 identified a need for professional development targeted at chief executive or director level that would enable peer learning within a structured and supportive framework. An action learning set would respond to a need identified by the creative sector; support learning within an appropriate peer-led framework and provide an opportunity for the university to collaborate with the sector.

This research presents this university program, involving ten participants from the creative sector over six months at Leeds Metropolitan University in 2010/2011. We seek to answer two questions:

1 Would action learning engender better collaboration between the university and the creative sector as well as meeting their professional development needs?
2 If so, how effective is this engagement?

The project

As the funding was a one-off opportunity, it was important to build sustainability within the project. We based the program on the Six-Squared

---

[26] Taking into account the cost of the course plus the cost of the loss of a day's work.

model (Pittaway et al 2009) where participants would attend to their own needs alongside participating in and developing further understanding of action learning sets in order to establish sets with others. Two facilitators were selected based on their previous experience in the program and with a background in business development in the non-creative sector.

Ten creative practitioners were recruited from across the West Yorkshire region and included two heads of department and a director from the performing arts; a chief executive, a director and a head of department from the visual arts; two freelancers, a local authority cultural arts officer and a director from a regional arts organization. They had responded to a personal invitation and submitted a short application form.

The program involved eleven sessions of three hours led by the facilitators. At the end of session one, participants identified conflict management as an issue, so session two involved participants identifying and describing disruptive 'behaviour types' and strategies to manage behaviours. This was followed by the first action learning set, group discussions on ethics, commitment to attendance, leadership styles and the social construction of leadership (Grint, 2005). Participants completed a self-reflection questionnaire (Pedler, 2008) to review organizational readiness for action learning. Participants prepared pitches to potential recruits followed by a third action learning set and feedback from the previous action learning set, followed by discussion on the facilitation and the problem holder's reflections on the process. The final session was a review of the impact of their experience and how they would take the experience forward, followed by the fifth action learning set.

Outcomes

To address our primary question we were able to gather data throughout the programme through observations, documents and interviews. We needed to understand which factors influenced participants' decision to participate

and whether expectations had been met. Three themes emerged from the data in that participation in such a program was:

1 an opportunity to develop new skills
2 an opportunity to network and strengthen relationships
3 an opportunity to collaborate in a university program

A Developing new skills

Nine out of ten participants stated that they were participating in the program as a vehicle to develop new skills. This was evident from both their application forms and interviews. Steve for example, reflected that despite his leadership role, he had not had any specific professional development to support this. Jess recognized that working with other creative businesses could help progress her own, but acknowledged that she needed to develop skills in making this work.

The interviews revealed how they were able to reflect on their own development and implications for their working context. Penny noted how action learning enriched the dialogue, enabling 'wicked issues.'

Jane expressed how talking with others to gain different perspectives from peers was extremely useful, highlighting the trap of isolation and the tendency of becoming inward looking.

The examples above and evidence from the other participants correlated with Pittaway et al (2009) and Gibb (2009), in that business leaders of small to medium enterprises experience learning by working alongside others as part of their working day. Training and development programs therefore need to be intrinsically linked to business and entrepreneurial outcomes.

B Networking and strengthening relationships

As well as peers contributing to developing skills, five out of the ten participants valued the opportunity to network per se. As Lisa and Penny claimed, networking was key by contributing to developing their professional profile within the network. *'I never miss a chance to network with people working in my field'* Networking within the creative sector is a vital component for business; finding new contacts and professional development (Dawson & Gilmour, 2009; DCMS, 2008; Harvey 2010; Henry, 2007; The Work Foundation, 2007). Having a network of peers at the heart of the program reflected 'real' entrepreneurial business practice, thus enabling a trusted source of support to convert into potential business collaboration.

C Collaborating in a university program

Seven participants stated that the university partner brings an implicit value to the experience.

The project design included an intermediary role to bridge the relationships between the creative sector and the university evidence suggested that this impacted positively on the collaboration. Both sectors have their own language, organizational structures, systems and processes (Gibb 2002). As a result, the intermediary's role created a 'porosity' between the two cultures and transcended potential barriers or 'unknowns' that might have impacted on the group's learning experience. This was acknowledged by participants.

Conclusion

The creative industries is a transient and dynamic sector made up of micro, small and medium enterprises operating flexibly through a series of complex networks and collaborations on a project by project basis. The university sector on the other hand is multifaceted, comprising of mechanisms to preserve quality assurance, established protocols and processes. Within the context of a growing and vibrant creative industries sector and increasing pressures on universities to engage with the business community, it is essential to develop flexible, peer-led and innovative models for collaboration.

This research project was an opportunity to support collaboration and entrepreneurial activity through an action learning set drawing on university expertise and tested peer development methodologies. It responded to and reflected entrepreneurial business practice by enabling participants to experience different repertoires of talk; highlighting the role of others in resolving complex issues; developing participants' levels of confidence in particular management areas, all underpinned by opportunities to network – integral to doing business. For some participants it was an affirmation of their skills that had become intrinsic to them. Exposing this tacit knowledge, and then sharing this expertise was in itself a beneficial outcome of their involvement in the program and a contributory factor to increasing their entrepreneurial practice.

References

- Ball, L., Pollard, E. & Stanley, N. (2010). *Creative Graduates Creative Futures.* Institute of Employment Studies, University of Warwick.
- Dawson, J., & Gilmore, A.(2009). *Shared Interest : developing collaboration, partnerships and research relationships between higher education, museums, galleries and visual arts organisations in the North West;* Renaissance North West.
- DCMS. (2008). *Creative Britain: New Talents for the New Economy,* Department for Culture, Media and Sport.
- DCMS. (2010). *Creative Industries Economic Estimates* – December 2010 (Experimental Statistics) http://www.culture.gov.uk/publications/7634.aspx.
- Gibb, A. (2002). In pursuit of a new enterprise and entrepreneurship paradigm for learning: creative destruction, new values, new ways of doing things and new combinations of knowledge. In: *International Journal of Management Reviews* Volume 4, Issue 3, pages 233-269, September 2002.

- Gibb, A. (2009). Meeting the development needs of owner managed small enterprise: a discussion of the centrality of action learning . In: *Action Learning : Research and Practice*, Vol. 6: 3, p. 209-227.
- Gloor, P. A. (2006). *Swarm Creativity : Competitive Advantage Through Collaborative Innovation Networks*. Oxford University Press.
- Grint, K. (2005). Problems, problems, problems: The social construction of leadership. In: *Human Relations*, November 2005; vol. 58, 11: p. 1467-1494.
- Handke, C. W. (2004). *Defining creative Industries by comparing the creation of novelty workshop : Creative Industries – A measure for urban development?* By WIWIPOL and FOKUS Vienna, Austria, 20th March 2004.
- Harvey, T. (2010). *How public and private investment can work better together to build the creative industries in the UK*. Clore Thesis, ARHC.
- Henry, C. (2007). *Entrepreneurship in the Creative Industries : an international perspective*. Edward Elgar Publishing.
- Holden, J., Keiffer, J., Newbigin, J. & Wright, S., (2011). *The UK Creative Economy – So What Next?* Retrieved from: http://www.dhacommunications.co.uk/pdf/Ch%2009%20-%20John%20Holden.pdf , July 2011.
- Leeds City Region. (Feb 2011). *Employment and Skills - creative content industries sector roundtable summary*. Retrieved from : http://www.leedscityregion.gov.uk/uploadedFiles/Areas_of_Work/Skills/creative%20content%20sector%20summary%20with%20round%20table%20info(1).pdf , Sept 2011.
- Owen, H. (2008). *Open Space Technology*: A Users Guide (3rd ed.). Berrett-Koehler.
- Pedler, M., Burgoyne, J., & Brook, C. (2005). What has action learning learned to become? *Action Learning : Research and Practice*, Vol 2, No. 1, April 2005, p. 49-68.
- Pittway, L., Missing, C., Hudson, N. & Maragh, D., (2009). Entrepreneurial learning through action: a case study of the Six-Squared program *Action Learning : Research and Practice*, Vol 6, No. 3, Nov 2009, p. 265-28.
- Pratt, A.C. (2005). Cultural Industries and Public Policy : An Oxymoron?, In: *International Journal of Cultural Policy*, vol. 11, no.1, p. 31-44.
- Taylor, C. (2006). Beyond Advocacy : Developing an Evidence Base for Regional Creative Industry Strategies, *Cultural Trends* Vol 15(1) , No. 57, March 2006, p. 3-18.
- Townley, B. Beech, N., McKinlay, A. (2009). Managing in the Creative Industries : Managing the motley crew. *Human Relations* 2009 62 : 939 Retrieved from: http://hum.sagepub.com/content/62/7/939. July 2011.
- Universities UK. (2010). *Creating Prosperity: the role of higher education in driving the UKs creative economy*. Universities UK.
- The Work Foundation. (2011). *The Creative Industries*. Retrieved from: http://www.theworkfoundation.com/research/creativeindustries.aspx. Oct 2011 .

About the author

Julia Calver (UK) is Lecturer in Events Management at Leeds Metropolitan University and Chair of Saltaire Festival, UK

j.calver@leedsmet.ac.uk

Jeff Gold (UK) is Professor of Organization Learning at Leeds Business School and a Fellow of the Northern Leadership Academy. He is a founding member of the School's HRD and Leadership Research Unit. He is also the co-author of Leadership and Management Development, CIPD 2010, and co-editor of Human Resource Development: Theory and Practice, Palgrave, 2010

j.gold@leedsmet.ac.uk

Up for discussion: Monopolies threat cultural entrepreneurship
Creating a level playing field for diversity: no copyright, no market dominating positions
Joost Smiers

Abstract

Artists, but also their producers and commissioners, are entrepreneurs, or to put it more precisely, cultural entrepreneurs. Entrepreneurship implies taking chances, and inevitably risks. Which basic conditions need to be met to offer an average entrepreneur – in our case cultural entrepreneur – a fair chance to operate successfully? How to create a level playing field, which is at present nearly non-existent. What to do?

First we have to drive out the protective shell for huge investments of cultural monopolists called copyright. If this form of protection, which is actually a privilege, does not exist, it is not attractive any longer to invest massively in hope of blockbusters, best sellers, and stars. Second, by implementing revitalized competition, and anti trust policies, the preconditions for the production, distribution, promotion, and reception of artistic creations and productions will be normalized. There ought to be no market party that turns the access to the cultural market, and thus to audiences, into an impassable path. The result will be that many cultural entrepreneurs can offer their creations and productions to audiences without being expelled from public attention. Consequently this offers them a much better possibility to turn their work into a profit and to earn a much better income than in the present situation.

It does not make sense to speak about the blessings of cultural or creative industries if one does not start looking at market relations. The choice is for monopolistic control, or for a huge diversity of cultural entrepreneurs.

No copyright, no market dominating positions

If we profess loudly that the system of copyright – one of the intellectual property rights – must be terminated, this statement must be interpreted against a broader framework. The context involves the questioning of the concept of property, which has acquired an absolute form in our contemporary societies. This absolute character has to be put into perspective. Property must be viewed as a limited right of usage that is also associated with certain duties. The point of reference then becomes that other values can reacquire a position in the relations between people with respect to a resource, good, or service. We might think here of social aspects, the proportionality of rich versus poor in the world, ecological issues, intercultural communications, concerns about gender equality, and the sharing of knowledge.

With respect to the thematic area of this two aspects of the displacement of the absolute notion of property have to be put at the center of attention. First, upon formulating an alternative for copyright, we have to ensure that we as society maintain – or better put: regain – the control over a large stock of cultural expressions which we can use freely. A society cannot function as a democracy otherwise. Second, we have to use all resources at our disposal to create the right conditions to enable as many artists as possible – creators as well as performers – in all corners of the world to make a good living off their creative labors. In order to reach this cultural markets should be level playing fields.

Creating a level playing field

A level playing field is a situation in any kind of market in which no single party can manipulate this market to his own accord. This is an important principle which has many advantages. For aspiring entrants, entry to a position in that market is unhindered. New inventions can find their way to publics. Due to competition, prices are not driven up to ever higher levels. Products can be mutually compared in terms of quality. Markets do not by definition tend towards a neat level playing field. It is always a possibility that a certain party in the markets, due to whatever cause, will grow so strong that it becomes dominant. The purpose is, then, to re-establish a fair level playing field in which many cultural entrepreneurs – artists, producers, and commissioners – can have risk-bearing opportunities.

It is actually a misunderstanding to believe that markets and regulation are a contradiction in terms.

If we as citizens of a country desire the market to be organized in such a way that it is open to a large diversity of cultural expressions, if we as citizens insist that no party in the market dominates the production, distribution, and promotion of those expressions, and if we as citizens aspire that no one can call him- or herself the 'owner' of those cultural expressions, then we have to force our governments to commit to a cultural policy that establishes these feats. .

a First we have to drive out the protective shell for cultural monopolists called copyright. This will lead to a new situation, and will open markets in which many cultural entrepreneurs can offer their creations and productions to audiences without being expelled from public attention, which in turn offers them a much better possibility to turn their work into a profit and to earn a much better income than in the present situation.

b It is necessary to normalize the preconditions for the production, distribution, promotion, and reception of artistic creations and productions. There ought to be no market party that turns the access to the cultural market, and thus to audiences, into an impassable path. This should also prevent the growth of dominant market parties that can appropriate – after the abolition of copyright – the unprotected works of artists, producers, and commissioners.

After the copyright era

Completely new cultural markets will emerge with the proposed changes. We count several major results of our interventions.

The *first* effect we might expect from it is that, with these new conditions – no longer investment protection by copyright - the rationale is lost for cultural conglomerates to make substantial investments in blockbusters, bestsellers, and stars (actually, it is unlikely that those kind of cultural giants will still exist after the introduction of the market regulations we have proposed). After all, by making creative adaptation and transformation respectable again, and by undoing the present system of copyright, the economic incentives to produce on the present scale will diminish.

Corporations would never again reach such an exorbitant size and domination of the market as they do today. The effect is, thus, that not a single enterprise will be able to decisively manipulate the cultural playing field. At the same time, through the abolition of copyright, cultural conglomerates will lose their grip on the agglomeration of cultural products with which they determine the outlook of our cultural lives to an ever-increasing extent. They will have to give up the control over huge chunks of the cultural markets.

This has far-reaching consequences for the way publics relate to cultural productions. This is the *second* effect we might expect. Thus far, the publics' guide for making choices was what the marketing of cultural conglomerates offered them, overwhelmingly so, to ensure they did not miss the blockbuster film, the star, the best selling book. However, in the situation we propose, these conglomerates – and such huge marketing efforts - will not exist anymore, and thus, the publics' attention will not be steered in only one direction.

This is a cultural gain, much bigger than we can ever imagine. Publics will need to develop their curiosity. This will be their main compass once the marketing of cultural giants no longer exists to influence their tastes.

When copyright is abolished and when the present cultural conglomerates are substantially smaller in size – that is, are normally sized enterprises –, a level playing field is put in place in which many artistic expressions can find their way to publics, buyers, readers, users, and audiences. This is the *third* effect of our proposals. There will once again be room in cultural markets to maneuver for a variety of entrepreneurs, who are consequently no longer pushed out of the public's attention by blockbuster films, bestseller books, and music, visual arts or design stars. The plenitude of artists will be able to find audiences for their creations and performances in a normal market. If copyright were no longer to exist, works would belong to the public domain, from the moment of their creation or performance.

However, this does not mean that creators, performers and other cultural entrepreneurs would be unable to make a living from their operations and make them profitable. In order to understand this process, we should take into consideration that market relations would also fundamentally change.

The substantial gains that are to be realized, reside in the fact that the public domain of artistic creativity and knowledge will be restored. This is the *fourth* effect of the changes we propose for cultural market relations. It will no longer be possible to privately appropriate works that in actuality derive from the public domain. Public debate will then determine whether alterations are respectful, and whether the original work commands this respect. If public debate does not materialize, it is a loss for democracy. Independent and well-informed critique must once again come to play an important part. It is only by testing and dissecting works that we can sense value verses mediocrity.

Restructuring the markets

The question that makes everybody curious, of course is, what would those new markets look like, and more specifically how will more than a few cultural entrepreneurs make their money there? We should remember that included in the concept of cultural entrepreneur are artists, producers and people who provide commissions; in short, all those who are prepared to bear the risks involved in a cultural enterprise or activity. This brings us to what might be expected from the complete reshuffling of cultural markets as

we propose. The quintessence of our argument can be summarized in this question: is it likely that the work of an artist and his or her producer or commissioner will be used by others without payment or due recognition? Is it likely that another cultural entrepreneur will immediately use a work once it has come on the market?

By principle, without copyright, this would be possible. But, we should recognize as well, that there is no longer any one single enterprise that has a market dominating position. There is no longer one 'other' enterprise that might think a recently published and well received work can easily be 'stolen' (note, that if there is no copyright there is also no stealing) or used for free riding behavior. Rather, there is likely to be thirty, forty, or fifty other enterprises who all think alike. While recognizing this reality, it becomes less likely, or even unlikely, that another enterprise will make the effort and invest the money to launch an already published work on the market.

Should one fear that someone other than the original initiator and risk-bearer would run off with artistic expressions that now belong to the public domain? As stated above, we believe that it will not come to that. Investments might hopelessly go up in smoke with multiple parties trying to take a gamble; and all parties are exposed to similar hazards. The prospect that many others are almost simultaneously willing to reoffer a once published work to a range of different audiences will in most cases be enough of a disincentive to remarket a work that was marketed by another party first. In this case it is imaginable that the first marketer – the first initiator and risk-bearer – will remain the only party (or one of the few parties) that can continue to exploit the work, even if it belongs to the public domain, without being 'hindered' by competitors.

The only true risk is that another entrepreneur might possibly occupy such a strong position in the cultural market that he or she can easily distribute and promote the work without being hindered in the slightest degree by the original exploiter or creator of the work or by other market parties. Such a monopolist, or oligopolist, can reach and seduce audiences with great ease without the competition of other equally strong market players. It is therefore of essential interest, as we have said before, that cultural markets are regulated in such a fashion that *there is no single party that is above the market in such a way that it can harvest works from everywhere undisturbed and turn them into profits unrestrictedly.*

Michele Boldrin and David K. Levine describe, quite hilariously, how, for instance, the Record Industry Association of America (RIAA) constantly reminds us on their anti-piracy web site that: *'The thieves ..... go straight to the top and steal the gold.'* This would bring the record company into economic ruin. However, this argument makes no business sense, they analyze:

> *'Picking only winners means waiting until it is clear who is a winner. Well, try it: try getting somewhere by imitating the leaders only after you are certain they are the leaders. Try ruining the poor pop star by pirating her tunes only once you are certain they are big hits! Excuse us, we thought that 'being a hit' meant 'having sold millions of copies.' Try competing in a real industry by imitating winners only when they have already won and you have left them plenty of time to make huge profits, establish and consolidate their position – and probably not leaving much of market for you – the sleek imitator* (Boldrin & Levine, 2008).

If we assume that we have constructed a normal market – with no dominant party – it will matter a great deal for an artist that, for example, his or her publisher has the capability to work the market effectively. However, the proposed radical change of market relations includes the possibility that an enterprise reissues a certain work that was initially marketed with considerable effort by a pioneering cultural entrepreneur. Of course, it might happen that a well selling work is spotted by a free rider, who starts to market the work, more cheaply and without paying the original author and producer. Is this a problem? At first sight, this seems rather bitter. But is it really? This copying could take place after the artist has realized a (more than) sufficient income from his or her work. Moreover, the wider distribution of the work makes the artist more famous, which in turn contributes to her or his earning capacity from many different sources. For the general public, the distribution of such 'white' copies of the work is good news, because the price will drop.

What we have done in this text is introducing huge paradigm shifts in the structure and organization of cultural markets: the abolition of copyright. Cutting market dominating cultural, entertainment and information conglomerates in many pieces, by implementing consequent competition and anti trust policies; and halting the present huge marketing efforts by cultural conglomerates that actually falsify competition. However, we should not forget the other substantial paradigm shift: the digitization. The cultural landscape will and should change radically. This text is an invitation for further research on what will be the effects of those changes in all fields of production, distribution, promotion and reception of music, film, theatre, books, visual arts, design, and mixed forms of cultural expressions.

Reference

- Boldrin, M. & Levine, D.K. (2008). *Against Intellectual Monopoly.* Retrieved from: http://dklevine.com/general/intellectual/againstnew.htm.

About the author

Joost Smiers is Professor (em.) of political science of the arts. His books include *Arts under Pressure. Promoting Cultural Diversity in the Age of Globalisation,* with Nina Obuljen (eds); *Unesco's Convention on the Protection and Promotion of the Diversity of Cultural Expressions; Making it Work,* and with Marieke van Schijndel: *Imagine there's no copyright and no cultural conglomerates too...*
joost.smiers@wanadoo.fr

Irina Van Aalst (NL) is assistant professor Urban Geography at the Urban and Regional Research Centre of the Utrecht University. Her research and publications focus on urban nightlife and the night-time economy, the (re-)development of public spaces and the clustering of creative industries.
I.vanAalst@uu.nl

Pernille Askerud (DK) is Senior Expert for Creative industries, BDS and Entrepreneurship Development at UNIDO Private Sector Development Unit. She is International Senior Expert Strategic Planning for Development. She was lead consultant for UNESCO Bangkok's program on cultural industries in Asia-Pacific, and main editor of the Bhutanese Baseline Report on Cultural Industries (2009).
pernille@askerud.org

Oedzge Atzema (NL) works as professor in Economic Geography at the Urban and Regional Research Centre of Utrecht university. He has done research in many fields, among which evolutionary economic geography, ICT and geography of production, urban labor markets, economic restructuring of cities, regional effects of economic globalization, regional aspects of firm demography, migration and urbanization and creative economies and urban development.
o.atzema@geo.uu.nl

Esra A. Aysun (TR) is a cultural operator and a lecturer on arts management. She is the founding co-director of CUMA and is consultant for theatre DOT. She is the local Coordinator in Turkey for the Arts and Culture Program of the Open Society Foundation and a board member of IETM and the Cimetta Fund.
eaysun@c-u-m-a.org

Pieter Ballon (BE) lectures Media Economics at the Vrije Universiteit Brussel. He is the head of the Market Innovation and Sector Transitions Unit in IBBT-SMIT, Vrije Universiteit Brussel.
pieter.ballon@vub.ac.be

Serkan Bayraktaroglu (TR). Born in Sakarya, Turkey in 1982 got his undergraduate degree in 2003 in the field of Industrial Engineering. He had his graduation from Industrial Design and Manufacturing master program (2008) that is offered by a consortium of T.U. Dortmund and University of Twente. His master thesis, 'Management of communication in complex product development' was written in cooperation with Product Development Institute of T.U. Munich and AUDI A.G. He is a PhD student at Istanbul Technical University – and works as a lecturer at Kadir Has University, Turkey.
serkan.bayraktaroglu@khas.edu.tr

Christiaan De Beukelaer (UK) is a doctoral researcher at the University of Leeds Institute of Communications Studies. He previously obtained an MSc in Cultures and Development Studies, and an MA in Cultural Studies at the University of Leuven, after completing a BA in Musicology at the University of Amsterdam.
christiaandebeukelaer@gmail.com

Trine Bille (DK) is Associate Professor, Ph.D. at Copenhagen Business School (CBS), Department of Innovation and Organizational Economics, and Senior Researcher II at Telemarksforskning, Norway. She got her Ph.D. from University of Copenhagen, Department of Economics. Her main research interest is cultural economics and she has published many books and articles within this field.
tb.ino@cbs.dk

Sofie van den Borne (NL) works as researcher at Cultuur-Ondernemen. She attained her Master Arts Policy and Management in 2010 with a thesis on career development in the arts.
sofie_van_den_borne@hotmail.com

Julia Calver (UK) is Lecturer in Events Management at Leeds Metropolitan University and Chair of Saltaire Festival, UK.
j.calver@leedsmet.ac.uk

Tsen-Yao Chang (TW) is currently Assistant Professor in the Department of Industrial and Commercial Design at National Taiwan University of Science and Technology (NTUST), Taiwan. Dr. Chang recent research interests have focused on cultural and creative industries project.
changty@mail.ntust.edu.tw

Woong Jo Chang (USA) is a post-doctoral researcher in cultural policy and arts management at the Ohio State University. He holds a BA in Chinese Literature, an MA in Performing Arts from Seoul National University, and a Ph.D. from the Ohio State University. Chang was awarded the Barnett Dissertation Fellowship (2011) and the Judith Huggins Balfe Award for Emerging Young Scholars in the field of Cultural Policy (2010). His research is focused on entrepreneurial practices and the uses of IT especially in small arts organizations.
woongjo@gmail.com

Roberta Comunian (UK) is Creative Industries Research Associate at the School of Arts, University of Kent. She holds a European Doctorate in Network Economy and Knowledge Management. She is interested in the creative industries and the relationship between public and private investments in the arts. She is currently researching the role of higher education in the creative economy.
R.Comunian@kent.ac.uk

Ayşe E. Coşkun Orlandi (TR). She received her BA as Industrial Product Designer in 1997 at Marmara University (Istanbul). In 1998 received a Master in Design degree at Domus Academy, Milan, Italy. In 2003 received an MA at Marmara University (Istanbul). In 2009 she has got her PhD at Mimar Sinan Fine Arts University (Istanbul). She has been lecturing, researching, publishing in the field of industrial product design since 2000. She is currently working as Asst. Prof. at Kadir Has University, Istanbul, Turkey.
acoskunorlandi@khas.edu.tr

Paul Coyle (UK) is a Pro Vice-Chancellor for teaching and learning and Executive Dean at the UK University of Creative Arts. He holds the title of Professor of Leadership and Management and has presented papers at international conferences on the themes of creativity, culture, entrepreneurship and the connections between teaching & research.
PCoyle@ucreative.ac.uk

Karen Donders (BE) lectures European Media Policy and European Information Society at the Vrije Universiteit Brussel. She is a postdoctoral fellow with the Flemish Research Foundation (FWO) and Senior Researcher at IBBT-SMIT (Center for Studies on Media Information and Telecommunication).
karen.donders@vub.ac.be

Zeynep Enlil (TR) is professor of urban planning and teaches at Yildiz Technical University. She was one of the research directors of a major Istanbul 2010 European Capital of Culture Agency project titled 'Istanbul 2010 Cultural Heritage and Cultural Economy Mapping and Compendium Project.'
zeynepenlil@gmail.com

Yigit Evren (TR) is a senior lecturer in regional planning and urban economics at Yildiz Technical University (YTU). He is also the co-editor of Megaron, the e-journal of YTU, Faculty of Architecture. Evren holds a PhD in Urban Planning from Cardiff University and writes about regional development, industrial clusters, relational geography and cultural industries
yigitevren@gmail.com

Nancy de Freitas (NZ) is Associate Professor, Postgraduate Studies and Program Leader, Master of Arts Management, Faculty of Design and Creative Technologies works at the School of Art and Design, Auckland University of Technology (AUT) University, New Zealand. She is Editor-in-Chief of Studies in Material Thinking.
nancy.defreitas@aut.ac.nz

Jeff Gold (UK) is Professor of Organization Learning at Leeds Business School and a Fellow of the Northern Leadership Academy. He is a founding member of the School's HRD and Leadership Research Unit. He is also the co-author of Leadership and Management Development, CIPD 2010, and co-editor of Human Resource Development: Theory and Practice, Palgrave, 2010
j.gold@leedsmet.ac.uk

Alain Guiette (BE) is PhD Candidate and Teaching Assistant at the University of Antwerp at the Department of Management (Faculty of Applied Economics).
alain.guiette@ua.ac.be

Giep Hagoort (NL) is cultural entrepreneur, professor art and economics at the Utrecht University and the Utrecht School of the Arts, and dean of the Amsterdam School of Management. He is author of a collection of books on management, innovation, entrepreneurship and the cultural and creative industries. Giep Hagoort has been visiting lecturer at universities and academies in Antwerpen, Barcelona, Beograd, Berlin, Bordeaux, Coimbra, Cracow, Hanoi, Helsinki, Istanbul, Johannesburg, Kiev, Los Angeles, New York, Prague, Skopje, St. Petersburg, Shanghai, Tbilisi, Vienna, Warwick, Zagreb, among others.
giep.hagoort@central.hku.nl

Barbara Heebels (NL) is currently working on her PhD on the role of place and personal network ties in the functioning of cultural intermediaries. She is affiliated to the economic and urban geography departments of the Urban and Regional Research Centre of Utrecht University (the Netherlands). Her research interests include the geography of networks, cultural product industries, urban nightlife and the night-time economy and urban redevelopment.
b.heebels@gmail.com (corresponding author)

Joost Heinsius (NL) is a consultant and publisher on managing volunteer-professional relationships. He is Manager Knowledge & Innovation at Cultuur-Ondernemen (Culture-Entrepreneurship).
jheinsius@cultuur-ondernemen.nl

Javier J. Hernández-Acosta (PR) is a PhD student in Entrepreneurial Development at the Interamerican University of Puerto Rico. He received an MBA from the University of Puerto Rico, and is a part-time lecturer at the University of the Sacred Heart. He is also a musician and founder of Inversión Cultural, a project for cultural entrepreneurs.
javihernandez@yahoo.com

John Huige (NL) is a political economist. He researches and publishes on sustainability and works as an independent consultant. Before that he used to be director of two large Dutch NGO's and he taught economics and labor relations.
johnhuige@planet.nl

Lucie Huiskens (NL) is an independent consultant for the creative sector. She is Project Manager of KIS (Artists, Innovation & Strategy), a course for artists who want to work with business on innovation and change issues at Cultuur-Ondernemen, Amsterdam.
lhuiskens@kunstenaarsenco.nl

Sofie Jacobs (BE) is researcher Creativity & Creative Industries at Antwerp Management School.
sofie.jacobs@ams.ac.be

Frances Joseph (NZ) is co-director of CoLab, Creative Technologies Research Centre and director of the Textile and Design Laboratory at the Auckland University of Technology, New Zealand. Her current research is concerned with innovation through creative technologies, with a focus on areas of interaction design and aesthetics, e-textiles, design research methodology, creative entrepreneurship and interdisciplinary projects.
frances.joseph@aut.ac.nz

Bart Kamp (BE) is Head of the Strategy Department at ORKESTRA: the Basque Institute of Competitiveness (Spain). In addition, he is a lecturer in the strategic management of start-ups at the Université Catholique de Louvain-la-Neuve (Belgium). Kamp has written extensively on overcoming market and network imperfections in the field of entrepreneurship and innovation policies.
bart.kamp@orkestra.deusto.es

Miriam van de Kamp (BE) is a postdoctoral research fellow at the Centre for Modern Urban Studies at Leiden University. She obtained her PhD at Erasmus University in 2009. Her dissertation addressed how music and film majors in the Netherlands dealt with the Dutch market and domestic products between 1990 and 2005.
m.c.van.de.kamp@cdh.leidenuniv.nl

Adarsha Kapoor is a practicing architect (Thesis Gold medalist), and an Urban Designer with a deep interest in issues pertaining to public participation through urban spaces. He has been involved in a series of publications regarding politics, public participation and urban spaces of developing countries.
adarsha47@hotmail.com

Johan Kolsteeg (NL) held positions in contemporary and classical music as a musicologist, programmer, journalist, policy maker, advisor for funding bodies. At present he is Professor of Arts and Economics at the Utrecht School for the Arts, and conducts PhD research into strategy in creative organizations.
jkolst@xs4all.nl

Rene Kooyman (NL) graduated with a major in Urban and Regional Planning. He received a Diplôme Educations Approfondies (DEA) from the University of Geneva, Switzerland and a Master in Urban Area Development (MUAD). Recently Rene Kooyman has been Managing Editor for the EU EACEA Research Project on the Entrepreneurial dimensions of cultural and creative industries. He is Project Manager and Executive Secretary at the CURE Monitoring Board.
rkooyman@rkooyman.com

Bastian Lange (DE) is an urban and economic geographer and specialized within the creative industries, questions of governance and regional development. He has been Guest Professor at the Humboldt University in Berlin since 2011. Bastian Lange obtained his doctorate at the Johann-Wolfgang Goethe University, Frankfurt am Main, in 2006. He is a Fellow of the Georg Simmel Centre for Metropolitan Research at the Humboldt University in Berlin.
bastian.lange@geo.hu-berlin.de

Sven Lindmark (BE) holds a MSc degree in Industrial Engineering and Management (from Chalmers University of Technology in Göteborg, Sweden) and a PhD in Industrial Management and Economics (Chalmers, 2002). He is Senior Researchers at IBBT-SMIT, Vrije Universiteit Brussel.
sven.lindmark@ibbt.be

Ellen Loots (BE) is PhD Candidate at the University of Antwerp at the Department of Management (Faculty of Applied Economics).
Ellen.Loots@ua.ac.be

Gerardo Neugovsen (PN) has obtained his Master degree at the Utrecht School of Arts in the Netherlands. He has specialized in Creative Industries. He lives in Panama from where he works as researcher, consultant and university teacher at several Latin American countries. He is mainly concern with the pedagogic aspects of developing innovative competencies at SME entrepreneurs at the Creative Industries.
gerardon@gmail.com

Jacob Oostwoud Wijdenes (NL) studied psychology at the University of Amsterdam. He worked as a researcher in the field of arts education at the SCO Kohnstamm Institute. Since 2000 he works at the Utrecht School of the Arts (HKU) as Policy Advisor of Quality Assurance for Education and Research. He has published about higher arts education, e.g. on the transition from higher arts education to the labor market, on the impact of the three cycle system for arts education and on creativity.
jacob.oostwoudwijdenes@central.hku.nl

Burak Özgen (BE) works as an independent consultant in Brussels. He advises international music companies, trade organizations, NGOs and local governments on copyright, European affairs and culture related matters. He is also a member of the Fair Music standards setting expert group and a PhD researcher at the Ghent University.
burak.ozgen@eurokent.eu

Donatella De Paoli (NO) is Associate Professor, Ph.D. at BI Norwegian Business School. She got her Ph.D. from the Norwegian School of Economics (NHH) and was visiting scholar at Stanford University during her doctoral work. Her main research interest is cultural management and leadership, but also the role of aesthetics and art for business. She has published several books and articles within these fields.
donatella.d.paoli@bi.no

Maria Ptqk (ES) is a freelance curator, consultant and researcher working at the confluence of cultural policies, new media, and gender studies. Member of GenderArtNet, and moderator/initiator of the Blog: http://ptqkblogzine.blogspot.com.
mariaptqk@gmail.com

Heritiana Ranaivoson (BE) studied Economics and Management at Ecole Normale Supérieure de Cachan (ENS Cachan) and got a Master of Research in Industrial Economics at Université Paris 1, Panthéon-Sorbonne. He is Senior Researchers at IBBT-SMIT, Vrije Universiteit Brussel.
hranaivo@vub.ac.be

Annick Schramme (BE) has a PhD in Contemporary History. She is Academic Coordinator of the Master of Cultural Management (Faculty of Applied Economics of the University of Antwerp).
annick.schramme@ua.ac.be

Joost Smiers (NL) is Professor (em.) of political science of the arts. His books include Arts under Pressure. Promoting Cultural Diversity in the Age of Globalisation, with Nina Obuljen (eds.); Unesco's Convention on the Protection and Promotion of the Diversity of Cultural Expressions ; Making it Work, and with Marieke van Schijndel: Imagine there's no copyright and no cultural conglomerates too .....
joost.smiers@wanadoo.fr

Aukje Thomassen (NZ) is Associate Professor and Head of Research at the School of Art & Design, Faculty of Design & Creative Technologies at the Auckland University of Technology AUT. Her research focuses on Social Innovation (creative entrepreneurship and co-creation) through Design Research (Philosophy, Didactics and Methodologies) and thereby studying Knowledge Creation in the Creative Industries (especially in the area of Game Design/Interaction Design) within a theoretical framework of Cybernetics.
aukje.thomassen@aut.ac.nz

Fabrice Thuriot (FR) received his Doctorate in Public Law (PhD) on Cultural decentralization and territories (1998). He is a researcher and the coordinator at the Centre of Research on Territorial Decentralization at the University of Reims Champagne-Ardenne and lecturer in public law and cultural policies in France and Europe. Research fellow to the Arts, Culture & Management in Europe Chair, BEM-Bordeaux Management School (France) and to the Fernand Dumont on Culture Chair at the Urbanization, Culture and Society Centre of the National Institute of Scientific Research (INRS, Quebec).
fabrice.thuriot@univ-reims.fr

Koen Vandenbempt (BE) has a PhD in Applied Economics and Management. He is professor Strategic Management (Faculty of Applied Economics of the University of Antwerp) and also responsible for the Master of Management and the Executive MBA at Antwerp Management School.
koen.vandenbempt@ua.ac.b

Che-Ting Wen (TW) is a MA student and a research assistant of Dr. Chang in NTUST, Taiwan.
dustin_le_robot@livemail.tw